Psalm 49 and the Path to Redemption

Psalm 49 and the Path to Redemption

Janet K. Smith

RESOURCE *Publications* · Eugene, Oregon

PSALM 49 AND THE PATH TO REDEMPTION

Copyright © 2017 Janet K. Smith. All rights reserved. Except for brief quotations in critical publications or reviews, no part of this book may be reproduced in any manner without prior written permission from the publisher. Write: Permissions, Wipf and Stock Publishers, 199 W. 8th Ave., Suite 3, Eugene, OR 97401.

Resource Publications
An Imprint of Wipf and Stock Publishers
199 W. 8th Ave., Suite 3
Eugene, OR 97401

www.wipfandstock.com

PAPERBACK ISBN: 978-1-5326-0697-7
HARDCOVER ISBN: 978-1-5326-0699-1
EBOOK ISBN: 978-1-5326-0698-4

All Bible verses are taken from the Oxford NIV Scofield Study Bible, New York: Oxford University Press, 1984

Manufactured in the U.S.A.

This book is dedicated to my husband, Ted, who makes all that I do possible, and to Rev. Michael Murphy of Citrus Heights, CA.

Contents

Preface | ix
List of Abbreviations | xiii

1 In the Beginning | 1
2 Afterlife in Egypt, Mesopotamia, and Canaan | 18
3 The Davidic Revolution in Worship | 35
4 Who Were the Korahites? | 52
5 A Pilgrimage through the Korahite Psalter | 66
6 Translation and Commentary of Psalm 49 | 86
7 The Struggle for Orthodoxy | 104
8 Irrepressible Life or Certain Doom? | 118
9 Shared Semantic Fields | 133
10 Serpents, Goddesses, and Gardens | 146
11 Redemption, Resurrection, and Social Justice | 156
12 The New Paradigm of Kindness | 173
13 Afterlife Today | 183

Appendix: Brain Twisting Genealogies | 199
Sources | 203

Preface

IN THE YEARS SINCE my Ph.D. dissertation was published as *Dust or Dew: Immortality in the Ancient Near East and in Psalm 49*, I have wanted to rewrite it for the general reader. The original book was written specifically for an academic audience, and was fairly inscrutable for lay enthusiasts. Yet, there were reader-friendly segments in it that could be of interest to those pursuing a deeper knowledge of the Bible. In the present work, I have incorporated the best of the former, and have expanded on the theme of heaven, hell, and afterlife to include the New Testament and how it all could apply to us today. A great deal of academic minutia has been dropped in *The Path to Redemption*.

Dust or Dew led up to the core topic, Psalm 49, written by a Korahite Priest, perhaps in the era of King David. The Theology of Retribution in the Old Testament asserted that bad things happen to bad people here on earth. Good blessings were for the righteous. Yet, the Korahite psalmist observed, as so many of us have in life, that many unrighteous people, some rich and powerful, lived an easy life. The psalmist's only comfort was his conviction that we are justly recompensed in the afterlife according to our deeds.

Psalm 49 fits well into the broader context of afterlife in the Bible because it is the iconic and ultimate warning to those who live carelessly in this life. That is, in fact, the overall message of the entire Bible, both Old and New Testaments. It's about where we go when we die, and why. So this book is both a rewrite and an expansion.

A word about hermeneutics (rules for analytical biblical interpretation)—in his book *Cosmopolitanism* K. A. Appiah[1] shared a parable in which ultimate reality here on Earth is represented as a mirror. The mirror is accessible to us sentient and mortal humans, but it has fallen and is broken into pieces. The shards lie about, to be discovered by different groups and

1. Appiah, *Cosmopolitanism*, 8.

individuals at different times. We each have a shard or two, but we do not have enough to see the whole picture. We all tend to think that our shard is fairly representative of the whole. Because we are relatively simple beings, we must hope that the universe is sufficiently simple for us to fully grasp, even though we have the capacity to understand that it may be complex beyond our comprehension.

This parable can be aptly applied to the realm of theology and biblical studies. Any number of approaches can be employed in the academic investigation of the Hebrew Bible. No matter which approach one chooses, there will be divisions and shards and references to anatomical parts of elephants investigated by blind sages.[2] Archaeologists cannot agree on whether the Patriarchs (Abraham, Isaac, Jacob, Judah, and Job) were historical characters (most would say not), whether Israel really came out of bondage in Egypt (most would dismiss the notion), whether David was a tenth century Israelite king (some say David never existed), or who destroyed the ancient city of Megiddo. As authors and teachers, we strive to present arguments based on acceptable, credible methodology without being blinded by personal presuppositions. In this work, my goal is not to take a dogmatic stand on issues, but to attempt to interpret the intent of the author or narrator of the relevant passages. The theologian/historian cannot escape his/her assumptions, but should at least be aware of them and make the reader aware.

I make no apology for my presuppositions. The biblical tradition includes narratives in which a supreme, creator deity interacts with humans in history, imposing law codes, giving revelations, and providing miraculous interventions. This deity co-exists in a transcendent dimension with a number of other good and evil immortal and immaterial beings. If God, gods, spirits, or other such entities *do* exist, and if all analyses proceed from the perspective that such things do not exist in our universe, then our hearing of the text will be skewed. On the other hand, if trans-dimensional reality is truly non-existent and life ends abruptly at death, then believers are naïve. The biblical narrator who claims to have encountered an angel or deity is simply self-deceived or is a myth-maker, so we must discern his/her agenda, both the evident as well as the subtle or hidden goals in inventing such tales.

Analyzing the evident agenda of specific texts and discerning the historical context of a passage is certainly a legitimate function of critical thinking. On the other hand, closing one's mind to all but one interpretation of reality may not be the most productive way to understand the biblical text. I should say up front that mine is not a naturalistic reading of biblical history. I have personally experienced some of the kinds of spiritual events

---

2. John Godfrey Saxe's poem about the blind men and the elephant can be reviewed at http://www.noogenesis.com/pineapple/blind_men_elephant.html or in Linton's *Poetry of America*, 1878.

described in the Davidic and New Testament narratives, such as miracles and prophecy. Nor am I alone in what I have experienced; I dwell in a community of experiencers. Many of us have seen visions, had prophetic dreams, received promises from God that came to pass against all expectation, been healed of chronic diseases or addiction, been protected from harm, or been prophesied over. When I was forty-two years old, I myself saw my second son in a dream shortly before he was conceived and welcomed him into the family, so Israelite traditions about "houses" and establishment of family are very important to me. If there is a God who is in any way similar to that of the Bible, it should not be surprising that that deity would continue to engage humankind in similar, but progressive ways. If there is such a God, then the Hebrew Bible is not just a book of history, poetry, and epic narrative about a particular people, but a book of mysteries that reaches into all eras, ages, genders, ethnic groups, and educational levels, and which is so complex that it cannot be understood at merely one level of inquiry. I write this as a word of caution, a private reminder to the scholarly community that we may in fact live in a very complex and mysterious universe. Even my charismatic, twenty-first century, Judeo-Christian perspective may be too simplistic.

Liturgically, many churches today worship with the clapping, lifting of hands, singing, sitting, standing, and shouting described in the Psalms. I was first introduced to the idea of "Davidic worship" in the 1970s by a sermon preached in a church associated with the Latter Rain Revival. We called such liturgy The Tabernacle of David, after the passage in Amos 9:11–12:

> In that day I will restore David's fallen tent. I will repair its broken places, restore its ruins, and build it as it used to be, so that they may possess the remnant of Edom and all the nations that bear my name, declares the LORD, who will do these things.

That teaching inspired my focus in *Dust or Dew*. The sum of my life experiences helped to form my pre-understandings that the God of the whole Bible still exists and interacts with society and individuals, that he still responds positively to heartfelt worship, and that I will one day dwell in his Kingdom in a resurrected body. My experiences have sparked a long-term interest in the issues of afterlife in both Testaments. No topic on the planet could be more important, because when we die we are "over there" for a very long time. By comparison, our time here is but a blink. Since almost everyone in the ancient world believed in a God, gods, demons, angels, the power of rituals, and various superstitions, the biblical writers believed in a creator deity who was actively invested in their community. Their worldview, though perhaps different from ours today, deserves respect in the world of scholars and theologians.

Abbreviations

AKOT	John J. Owens, *Analytical Key to the Old Testament*, 4 vols. Grand Rapids: Baker, 1995.
ANE	Ancient Near East
ANET	Pritchard, James B. *Ancient Near Eastern Texts Relating to the Old Testament*. Princeton: Princeton University Press, 1969.
Ant	Josephus, *Antiquities of the Jews*
BDB	Francis Brown, editor, *The New Brown-Driver-Briggs-Gesenius Hebrew-English Lexicon with an Appendix Containing the Biblical Aramaic.* Peabody, MA: Hendrickson, 1979.
CE/BCE	Common Era (AD)/Before the Common Era (BC)
DSS	Dead Sea Scrolls
EA	Tablets from Tel el-Amarna
HB/OT	Hebrew Bible/Old Testament
JSOTSup	Journal for the Study of the Old Testament Supplements
KP	Korahite Psalter
KTU	Keilalphabetischen Texte aus Ugarit
LXX	Septuagint
MT	Masoretic Text
RS	Ras Shamra Texts

Scripture Abbreviations

Hebrew Bible/Old Testament

Gen	Genesis
Exod	Exodus
Lev	Leviticus
Num	Numbers
Deut	Deuteronomy
Josh	Joshua
Judg	Judges
Ruth	Ruth
1–2 Sam	1–2 Samuel
1–2 Kgs	1–2 Kings
1–2 Chr	1–2 Chronicles
Neh	Nehemiah
Esth	Esther
Ps	Psalms
Prov	Proverbs
Eccl (or Qoh)	Ecclesiastes (or Qohelet)
Song	Song of Solomon
Isa	Isaiah
Jer	Jeremiah
Lam	Lamentations
Ezek	Ezekiel
Dan	Daniel
Hos	Hosea
Obad	Obadiah
Mic	Micah
Nah	Nahum

Hab	Habakkuk
Zeph	Zephaniah
Hag	Haggai
Zech	Zechariah
Mal	Malachi

New Testament

Matt	Matthew
Rom	Romans
1–2 Cor	1–2 Corinthians
Gal	Galatians
Eph	Ephesians
Phil	Philippians
Col	Colossians
1–2 Thess	1–2 Thessalonians
1–2 Tim	1–2 Timothy
Phlm	Philemon
Heb	Hebrews
Jas	James
1–2 Pet	1–2 Peter
Rev	Revelations

Other Ancient Sources:

Ant	Josephus, *Antiquities*

1

In the Beginning

About the New Edition

AS STATED IN THE Preface, this is a rewrite of *Dust or Dew*, the 2010 publication of my PhD dissertation, with the hope of accessing the general audience. There are several excellent books and articles that cover some of the same material that I discuss in both books. Like the original *Dust or Dew,* they are academic works and present the information more systematically, either focusing on relevance for the Jewish nation of Israel today, or the archaeology of ancient burial practices, or the theology of death and life passages. My purpose is to follow the growth of the people of Israel and the development of their afterlife theology, as understood through the writings of scribes, prophets, and psalmists. Rather than just focus on theology, this volume focuses on the transition of the new nation's beliefs, with an emphasis on the viewpoint of the levitical writers. We work our way to Ps 49, a priest's invective against the wealthy elite who live carelessly, trusting in their own self-importance. From there we examine the development of concepts of heaven and hell for any and all as expressed through the Hebrew prophets and in the New Testament. It turns out that the entire Bible has some particular things to say to the rich and powerful.

The early descendants of Abraham naturally had fears, superstitions, and doubts about afterlife. For hundreds of years the family lived by the ancient law codes of Mesopotamia. Trusting only in Abraham's revelation of God, they lacked their own literary compass to aid them as they journeyed through this life and passed from the material world to the eternal.

They began as one family from northern Syria, then became a union of clans, then a "people," then a nation, so naturally, many of their original concepts were borrowed from the world around them. They progressed from vague descriptions of being gathered to one's ancestors, to a new hope as revealed by God to Abraham and to his monotheistic descendants.

The culmination of that transition is found in various passages that promise a release from the gloom of *Sheol*—a "taking out" of the soul by God to be wherever he exists in eternity. Psalm 49 encapsulates the desire for ultimate, eternal justice. Ethics were not entirely new to Israel. Early law codes admonished the kings of Mesopotamia and Babylon to be just and to protect vulnerable citizens like widows and orphans. Civil codes guided neighborly relationships, treatment of concubines, inheritance between the children of wives, punishments for bodily harm to others, the sale of slaves, etc. Much that is in the Torah (the Law of Moses, comprising the books of Genesis, Exodus, Numbers, Leviticus, and Deuteronomy) was drawn from cultural norms of the day. In spite of every human effort, however, justice can be elusive. The final appeal for wrongs to be righted is when the soul of the departed stands before an eternal Judge, one that knows the thoughts of every heart and who cannot be bribed.

Death in the Garden

The Hebrew Bible introduces the issue of life, death, and immortality in the earliest chapters. In the book of Genesis, two newly formed humans, Adam and Eve, were introduced to this complex topic almost immediately. In chapter 1, all is goodness. God blessed the man and woman with dominance over nature, fruitful multiplication, and unity in their relationship. Both were swept into existence ("created") in the same manner as were the stars, simply by the word of God. This is *Homo sapiens* in full maturity and glory, reflecting the image and likeness of God. They have exquisite, agile bodies and minds to invent language, math, and literature.

In chapter 2, we read that Adam was "formed" from dirt or dust. He is set in a Garden wherein lurks a strange, immortal, inter-dimensional, reptilian entity—a cunning, ready-made adversary. In verse 8 Adam is "set" or "placed" in the Garden. In verse 15, he is "settled" there. The gap between the two verses could indicate an unknown amount of time going by. The location of the Garden is described as being "in the east," probably east of Assyria, the one region mentioned in the description. Assyria was northeast of ancient Sumer, often called the Cradle of Civilization; both were located between the Tigris and Euphrates Rivers which flow into the Persian Gulf. This whole region lies in today's nation of Iraq. The author of Genesis calls the south-eastern region "Shinar" rather than Sumer (Gen 10:10; 11:2).

Whether one takes the stories of creation and the Garden literally or metaphorically, the cities and rivers of Gen 1–11 are verifiably real.

The Bible genealogies transport Adam and Eve back to the Chalcolithic Age, the Age of Copper, c. 4500–3500 BCE (Before the Common Era, which is usually called BC, Before Christ). There would be primitive pottery, domestication of animals, agriculture, fishing, mining of copper, and hunting of game. Their names wouldn't have been Adam and Eve because those are Hebrew words and there was no Hebrew at that time. In fact, there were no great Sumerian cities yet, no baked clay tablets with cuneiform letters, because writing hadn't been developed yet, so the names of a literal, historical couple would sound very strange to us today and would be lost to history without some kind of visionary revelation.

The new humans were innocent and childlike, too naïve and limited in their understanding to perpetrate great evil or conquer nature. There was no sense of the existence of death. However, without death, there can be no birth. Imagine a material planet where mosquitoes, rats, rabbits, and birds breed but don't die. The human population of the earth today would be in the tens of billions. A literal planet without death would have to be completely static and magical, with no seasons or environmental catastrophes, unlike the gritty world in which we live today. If an immortal parent did have a child, it would be difficult to teach that child to make right choices in life if the parent has no understanding of good and evil. So, the irony of the two creation stories in chapters 1 and 2 of the book of Genesis is that the peaceful naivety of the second chapter thwarts the fulfillment of chapter 1.

Some readers view the authors of Genesis as revealing literal history; others dismiss the narratives as myths and fables. I understand them to be inspired legends written to convey specific information about mankind and our relationship with God. The creation stories contained important lessons for the people of Israel in their own era who were accosted on every side with the temptation to look to foreign deities for help. For example, widely recognized Mesopotamian compositions, which we will discuss in the next chapter, described humans as having been created from the DNA of a monster. Other stories claimed that we were created to provide the labor to relieve lower gods of providing food for a higher class of deities. Listeners were told that the great Flood was brought upon mankind because humans were too boisterous. The Israelite version emphasized the wickedness and violence of humans. Their destruction in the Flood story was the result of God's justice. Humans are special but also dangerous.

The early chapters of Genesis may have been composed in the great city of Assur or Nineveh after the author had been taken there as a captive by the Assyrians in 721 BCE. Through such narratives, perfected by the holy scribes, Israelites of that era would learn about the nature and purpose of humans, their value in the sight of their Creator, the relationship between men and women, the dangers of heeding the promises of foreign deities, and the inevitability of death.

The threat of death lies at the heart of the Garden story. When Eve is confronted by the reptilian entity in chapter 3, he assures her that if she eats of the fruit of the tree, she will not die and she will become like God. One of the great puzzles of the story is what is meant by "you will die" and "you will not die" and "you will be like God, knowing good and evil?" Adam and Eve were naked primitives living in an enclosed and protected space. Their destiny according to Gen 1 was to be a reflection of God (1:26). This similarity would give them dominance over all the creatures of the earth and over nature itself. In chapter 1, there is no hint that the two are unprepared for that role. One problematic belief that could arise from reading chapter 1 alone is the idea that humans are hybrid creatures, part human, part god. Israel's foreign neighbors had already written epics with such beings as heroes. The Genesis mandate to rule and dominate the earth could be construed as permission to be despots. In chapter 2, however, the early humans are like children, only potentially immortal and subject to temptation. How then could they be the progenitors of the sentient creatures that established the first great cities, who created writing and literature, and waged wars? How could mankind live in communities without a law code, and how could they formulate law codes with no understanding of ethical behavior?

Putting the two chapters together, we see that the couple cannot fulfill Gen 1 without being disobedient, or without waiting for God himself to say, "It's time to grow up and go out into the world." To eat of the forbidden fruit of the tree without permission was disobedience. We say that Adam and Eve sinned, but a three-year-old cannot actually sin if it doesn't have the full power of choice. Surely this capacity was always their ultimate destiny, but when and how would they acquire it?

Genesis 1—2:4a and chapters 2:4b—4 are actually separate documents with different authors:

- The name of God changes from Elohim to Yahweh-Elohim. (Today's translators substitute LORD, all caps, for the four-consonant name of God. Vowels were absent in the original manuscripts. Yahweh-Elohim is usually translated "the LORD God.")
- In chapter 1, everything is "created." In chapter 2, things are "formed" or "made," never "created." Things don't just appear as God speaks. Even the beasts of the field and the birds of the air are "formed" from

the ground (2:19). They appear to have been made after man has been alone for a while. Eve is "made/built" from his side or rib.
- The order of creation is different, with humans created last in chapter 1 but first in chapter 2.
- The tone changes from carefully constructed poetry to casual prose.
- In the first document, heaven is mentioned before earth. In the second, earth is mentioned before heaven. In Gen 1, the male and female are blessed to be dominant. In Gen 2, the man and woman are punished for transgression and banished from their special status. Listening to the serpent was the real source of sin and "death."

The redactors (editors/authors) who organized Genesis 1–11 were undoubtedly aware of these discrepancies, but it apparently didn't bother them. They joined the two documents with a handshake verse, Gen 2:4a and 4b. Logic demands that since there is a clear literary discrepancy, neither chapter should be taken literally, nor need we fret that they don't reflect perfect science. However, the scribes and revelators who finalized these narratives knitted them into one for a purpose, believing that the integrity of their monotheistic religion and the future of their people depended on understanding the balanced lessons therein.

According to the story, a serpent (or reptilian entity) of friendly demeanor appeared unbidden to facilitate the advancement of the new creation by encouraging the humans to eat of the fruit and become enlightened. Paraphrasing, "Oh really? Did Elohim say that? Hmm . . . I'm here to help." Eating the fruit could be a perfect a metaphor for whatever catalyst caused humans to transform from dull, hairy cave people into self-conscious beings with higher forms of thought, but in thinking like that we are stretching way beyond the intent of the original author. The serpent's real subversion was to thwart the humans by luring them to disobey Yahweh's command, resulting in punishment, death, and disaster, not only for them but for all their descendants. Eve, never having seen any supernatural entity other than Yahweh-Elohim, stared at the serpent and at the tree, having no clue as to the implications of her choice. God said that if they ate of the fruit, they would die. The fruit was supposed to be so dangerous, they must not even touch it, she explained. The serpent assured her that they would not die but that they would be like gods, knowing good and evil. That made perfect sense to Eve, who was in charge of groceries and meal preparation. If it made them wise, what could possibly go wrong? It looked like every other tree in the Garden, and the reptilian creature seemed nice. So she bit, and handed it to her husband, who was right there beside her (Gen 3:6).

According to all prevailing conservative theology, this was The Fall. The humans fell from grace, were driven from the Garden, lost physical immortality, and dragged us all down with them. We all are now stained with original sin, separated from God until some redemptive process restores our status of life with God. According to the Apostle Paul, "death reigned from the time of Adam until the time of Moses, even over those who did not sin by breaking a command . . . " because the Law of Moses offered us animal sacrifice, a path of atonement from sin (Rom 5:14).

Genesis 3 does not say that the couple sinned or fell from grace. We infer that ourselves, but Yahweh-Elohim did promise death, a dire result, if they ate the fruit. Was physical death to be a punishment or a natural result of being dislocated from a bubble of inter-dimensionality? Sentences were passed shortly after the transgression was uncovered, but oddly, immediate physical death wasn't one of them. Nor does the story claim definitively that the *guilt* for Adam and Eve was passed on to all their descendants. We infer that from Paul's phrase "death reigned." The answer is to study how the idea of "death" is used in the rest of the Bible. The Old Testament prophets Ezekiel and Jeremiah both mentioned a proverb in Israel which said, "The fathers (ancestors) have eaten sour grapes (meaning that they have followed false beliefs) and the children's teeth are set on edge" (Jer 31:29–31; Ezk 18:1–9). The fathers sin and the descendants pay the price when the day of judgment finally comes. The Israelites undoubtedly extrapolated this proverb to pertain to individual/family sins. Both Jeremiah and Ezekiel prophesy that the parable will no longer apply. "The soul (*nephesh*, referring to each person rather than the immortal soul) who sins is the one who will die" (Ezk 18:4b). The difficulty is that one cannot verify if the prophets were referring humans dying physically in war or some other judgment or whether this is the death of the soul. If we physically die for our sins, no one would reach eighty years old.

New Testament evidence strongly suggests that the word "death" is often used as a metaphor for eternal separation from God. We have mentioned Paul's statement that death reigned from Adam to Moses. Jesus said, "For God so loved the world that he gave his one and only Son, that whoever believes in him shall not perish but have eternal life" (John 3:16). He also stated, "I am the resurrection and the life. The one who believes in me will live, even though they die" (John 11:25). He told the teacher Nicodemus that he must be born again to enter the kingdom of God. This was clearly a metaphorical reference to a renewal in his soul (John 3:3–12). Nicodemus was speaking of earthly things, but Jesus was speaking of heavenly things. If all souls are immortal, then "death" can only mean separation from God's kingdom and blessing. And that is probably why Adam lived to be almost a thousand years old. The serpent was speaking of earthly things, but God was speaking of heavenly things. Do souls actually perish? Looking at the passages above, a reference to physical death is unlikely to impossible. Souls are immortal, as we shall see in later chapters.

The other question left hanging in the Genesis narrative is whether or not Adam and Eve were created immortal or whether they needed to eat of the Tree of Life to gain that status. If they were created immortal, they wouldn't need to eat of the Tree of Life, so we should assume that mortality was their natural state. We aren't informed as whether they accessed that tree in the Garden. The intent of the author seems to be that Adam and Eve had *access* to physical immortality, but we could argue that they never acquired it. Otherwise, why bar them from access later?

The serpent was cursed first. He was reduced from a slick-talking reptilian entity to a speechless serpent slithering low on the ground, eating the dust from which Adam was formed. He is scaly, cold-blooded, and utterly lacking in empathy. The ground was then cursed, but *only for Adam's sake*. That curse of toil and sweat seemed to be lifted after the Flood (Gen 5:28–29; 9:7). Men were not doomed to hard labor forever as a punishment by God, but all were reminded that mankind was made of dirt, and to dust we will all return. By this Adam, whose name meant "Earth" or "Dirt," was assured that humans were not gods. Life would be tough for women as well. No matter how today's feminists twist and knead these passages, the author of the story is using the transgression to explain why the patriarchal culture of that era submits women to their husbands and why childbearing would be a dangerous and painful event that could not be escaped. The highly developed patriarchy described in Gen 3:16b may not have existed around 4,000 BCE and is thus, like the Hebrew names, an anachronism (an event placed out of its actual timeframe), but that didn't bother the Genesis author. He had a point to make.

According to modern science, the earth was already a violent and difficult place, both geographically and biologically. Long before Adam and Eve could have existed, our planet was birthed in rock-melting fire. Almost everything alive ate other living things. Among the common artifacts found by paleontologists today are jaws full of fearsome, pointy teeth. There were already volcanoes, floods, forest fires, droughts, crashing meteorites, earthquakes, steamy heat, and stunning cold. If science is right, the world was a tough place for anything to survive and didn't need Eve and the apple to make it be that way. The world wasn't broken or fallen. Death and pain were built into the system.

In the story, Adam and Eve lost their status as innocent, childlike creatures who could acquire immortality. But humans also gained the freedom to reach all of the potential residing in exquisite bodies and fertile minds. Humans were creatures with free will and an intellect to explore, invent, and question. That requires the maturity to choose between one action or another, or to choose whom to believe or whom to follow. Perhaps, in spite of the apparent intention of the Genesis author, the narrative is describing the maturation of mankind from a simple creature living naked in a place that required no great inventiveness to survive, to *Homo-sapiens*, a creature that would be challenged every day in the mortal world. Perhaps God's reluctance to permit that advancement was the angst of a loving parent who says to the darling toddler, "Don't get any older. You're so cute and innocent just the way you are now, and I'm totally in control of you. It's such a dangerous world out there. When you're a teenager, all kinds of mischief will be available to you. Some of it will hurt you and some of it you will commit." Even God acknowledged that once they had eaten the fruit of the tree and their eyes were opened, they became like Him, knowing good and evil (Gen 3:22).

So what of the serpent's plan? He was right that Adam and Eve were enlightened. He was correct in that they didn't physically drop dead, and he nailed it that they became "like one of us." So being created in the image and likeness of God requires an understanding of good and evil. Once that status is acquired, humans will be held accountable for the choices they make. There are consequences for their actions. There is always a price to pay in growing up. In declaring that the way back was barred, the author banishes the possibility of pursuing rituals, potions, sacrifices, or magic promising to extend physical life. It is inconceivable that the Creator would consider it a sin for humans to rise to the condition for which He blessed them in chapter 1. It again begs the question, is physical death a sign of growth?

Another interesting principal was established in the story. When God takes you from one place to another, one status to another, one revelation or understanding to another, you aren't supposed to go back. You are not even to pine for the old situation. You must totally commit to the new place God has brought you, understanding that in important ways, it is a better situation than what existed before. Painful though it may be, this is growth.

Of course, the serpent did not literally become a common snake, but his character is unveiled and his end is foreshadowed. He wanted to ruin the new creation, but all he did was set them up to become all they were destined to be. As for the naïve little woman that he tempted, yes, she would be thwarted and oppressed by patriarchal men who would happily keep her in check, but she would grow and learn and rise to become the serpent's worst enemy. We see the serpent and woman at odds in Gen 3 and then again in Rev 12. In the last book of the Bible, a great red dragon faces off with a sun-clothed woman with a garland of twelve stars and the moon at her feet. Both dragon and woman have become cosmically powerful. The dragon has one greater enemy, the One prophesied in Gen 3:15 who would crush his head.

Cain and Abel

God continued to relate to Adam and Eve with no mention of ritual or sacrifice to atone for their transgression, so if death reigned after that, perhaps grace and mercy did as well. After expulsion from the garden, Eve "acquired" a man-child from Yahweh and was greatly comforted. She had a second son named Abel, who became the family favorite. Out of jealousy, Cain killed Abel. As he was contemplating this heinous act, God spoke to Cain and said, "Why are you angry? And why is your face downcast? If you do right, will you not be accepted? But if you don't do what is right, sin is crouching at your door; it desires to have you, but you must master it" (Gen 4:6–7). Most modern versions translate verse 7c as if sin, crouching like a demon, desires to rule Cain, and he must master sin.

However, verse 7c is exactly the same wording as Gen 3:16c: "Your desire will be for your husband, and he will rule over you." Only the pronouns change.

These verses have been greatly misunderstood. The word "desire" in both passages is *teshuka*. Its meaning is uncertain and is translated according to the context rather than how it is used in the Bible because it only appears three times. The root *suggests* "turning," but what does that tell us? An ancient tablet which dates from the Mosaic era was found in Egypt (Amarna EA 267).[1] A high official in Canaan is writing to Pharaoh in the humblest terms possible. He says, "I turn my eyes to you . . . " meaning that he is waiting for any command from his beloved protector. He is saying, "I am your servant." The King James Version comes closest to getting Gen 3:16 and 4:7c right, "And unto thee shall be his *teshuka*, [submission], and thou shall rule over him." The terminology is referring to the patriarchal family structure in which the man rules (yes, *rules*) the wife and the first-born son rules over his younger brothers and everyone else except his father and older uncles. It's about inheritance, hierarchy, and blessing. I would argue that the Hebrew is telling Cain that if he does what is right, he will inherit the status of patriarch, and Abel will have to submit to him.

Cain had one challenge from Yahweh. "Do what is right." He chose to do what he wanted. As a result, he was barred from any future success

---

1. Moran, *Amarna*, 315.

as a farmer and was cut off from his people, never to see his family again. He was not murdered as he feared by the foreigners he would encounter, and he didn't become a vagabond as Yahweh originally said he would (Gen 4:10–16). Once again, grace and redemption trumped judgment and loss. Settling down, he married a foreign wife, had children, and built a city. He became one of history's earliest developers. For Cain, the wrong choice did not cause him to fall down dead. "Death" for his wrong choice was loss . . . loss of inheritance, loss of family fellowship, loss of ethnic identity, and loss of intimacy with Yahweh. We are not told what the eternal consequences of his actions were.

The narrative of chapters 1–4 makes perfect sense if we take the time to study the world in which the *author* lived. Notice in Gen 4:4, Abel brings the fat portion of the first-born of his flock as a sacrifice to Yahweh. This is a sacrifice from a law code that had not been written in the days in which this family lived (see Lev 7:25). Like the Hebrew names, the sacrifice is an anachronism that alerts us that the story could possibly be a theological construct rather than an accurate presentation of history. The serpent represented the gods and goddesses of the author's era, but he can also embody anything in any era that separates humans from their Creator. The Genesis author is warning his people: their promises sound good, and they seem to offer life, help, promotion, healing, and protection, but their fruit is poison. Foreign deities are not our friends, cautions the author. It was God who taught Adam and Eve to dress themselves and God who ushered them into the outer world. God granted Eve conception (4:1) and continued to watch over their children. God used anointed servants like Moses and the prophets to put a barrier between what the serpent represents and His beloved humans. Only the God of life can offer life, whether physical or spiritual. Throughout the Hebrew Bible, this message will be preached in every era of Israel's history. Yahweh-Elohim would continue to wrestle with His glorious mud creature down here on this material planet full of joy and pain. The Adam would die physically and sink into the dust, but if God's beloved people make the right choices in life, they will be like trees planted by the waters, both in this life and in "the judgment," and all that they do will prosper (Ps 1:3). Gen 2 and 3 are not about mankind literally losing immortality. It's not about dying, but about choosing. In the choosing, we find redemption and eternal life . . . or spiritual death. The author of the book of Deuteronomy presented the same challenge:

> See, I have set before you today life and prosperity, death and destruction. For I command you today to love the Lord your God, to walk in his ways, and to keep His commands, decrees,

and laws; then you will live and increase, and the Lord your God will bless you in the land you are entering to possess. But if your heart turns away and you are not obedient, and if you are drawn away to bow down before other gods and worship them, I declare to you this day that you will certainly be destroyed. You will not live long in the land you are crossing the Jordan to enter and possess. This day I call heaven and earth as witnesses against you that I have set before you life and death, blessing and curses. Now choose life, so that you and your children may live and that you may love the LORD your God, listen to his voice, and hold fast to him, For the LORD is your life, and he will give you many years in the land he swore to give to your fathers, Abraham, Isaac and Jacob. (Deut 30:15–20)

The Quest for Longevity

There is no age or culture in which apprehension about death and what comes after is lacking. Even in our modern era, TV shows such as Paranormal State and Ghostly Hunters prove that an interest in afterlife will always be a current topic. The problem with ghosts, however, is that they do not adhere to orthodox belief patterns. There is just no official accountability in ghostly culture. The shades tend to not cooperate with scientific experiments, nor do they show up in laboratory test tubes. They cannot be caught in a net or sucked into a container as in the movie Ghostbusters.

In the Hebrew Bible, particularly in the book of Psalms, the book of Job, and the Prophets, there are many references to *Sheol*, the residence of all ghosts. Rather than offering a timeless, theological, systematic understanding of the afterlife, which is what we would expect if God had dictated those passages, references appear to be contradictory. Does everyone go there or just the wicked? Is there a final glorious resurrection for the righteous or is the dust of *Sheol* the resting place for all for eternity? Who rules in *Sheol*, Yahweh or some foreign Lord of Death? Are the references to *Sheol* a reflection of cultural beliefs, or were they dictated by God? Does the soul sleep there? In the Ancient Near East, including the Hebrew Bible, there are few explicit references to a blissful afterlife in heaven where the righteous spend eternity with loved ones and their deity. Those Hebrew Bible passages that hint at immortality are balanced by others suggesting that a grim and dusty existence in *Sheol* is the final fate for man and beast alike. The two biblical characters who were purported to have escaped death, Enoch and Elijah, did not linger in the earthly environs to describe or explain their new plane of existence.

Genesis 6:1–3 tells the story of a time when humans began to multiply on the earth, and violence erupted everywhere they went. God hated the wickedness and violence, so he altered the biological clock that increases or diminishes longevity, bringing the human lifespan down to a mere one hundred twenty years. Today, many of us would be delighted to live so long. With modern advances in medical science and nutrition, that desire is not so elusive, since there are people alive in the world today who are 115 years old or older.[2] Some of these centenarians live simple, rural lives with a healthy diet and plenty of exercise. Several people in Scripture are said to have lived a similar span of life: Moses died at 120; his brother Aaron was 123 at death; their sister Miriam was older than both. Other biblical claims from what we would designate as the Late Bronze Age era include Levi, 137; Kohath, 133; and Amram, 137 (Exod 6:16, 18, 20). Later claims include Jehoiada, 130 (2 Chr 24:15); Job, 140 (Job 42:16); Tobit, 112 (Tob 14:2); Tobias, 117 (Tob 14:14); and a reference to some life spans being 100 years (Sir 18:9). The writer of Ps 90 is not so optimistic, however, and offers seventy to eighty years as the outer range of human longevity (verse 10). He encourages people to count their years carefully and gain a heart of wisdom (verse 12) since all humans ultimately return to dust. "You sweep men away in the sleep of death; they are like the new grass in the morning—" the psalmist writes. "Though in the morning it springs up new, by evening it is dry and withered" (90:5–6). The author of Ps 90 has little to offer the seeker of answers about the afterlife and eternity. Discouraged and pummeled by life, his plea to the Almighty is modest, "May the favor of the Lord our God rest upon us—establish the work of our hands for us—yes, establish the work of our hands" (Ps 90:17).

Of course, the long-lived Bible characters are mentioned for the very reason that they were the remarkable exception to the rule. They lived in a world unpolluted by auto and factory emissions, and that purity of atmosphere may have supported a healthier ozone layer. During times of prosperity, their daily existence included exercise, whole grain emmer wheat and barley, olive oil, figs, honey, eggs, roast duck and goose, and vegetables stewed in savory spices, all grown in soil that was not as depleted of

---

2. In 2003 a report was published about a Chechnyan woman named Zabani Khakimova who was 124. She had seven great-great grandchildren, and was still living a mobile life in her home at the time of her death. See http://news.bbc.co.uk/2/hi/europe/3110525.stm, July 30, 2003, accessed January 14, 2008. Her death left three other women in the world who were 115. The Sacramento Bee reported on November 30, 2008 that one of those women, Edna Parker, recently died. Today's oldest person, Emma Morano, is 117. An Indonesian man is claiming to be 145 and apparently has ID and relatives to prove it. http://www.snopes.com/2016/08/30/145-year-old-man/.

resources as our soil is today.³ Their belief in the protection and blessing of God would reduce the stress of the possibility of immanent disaster. If they somehow avoided the depredations of famine, war, disease, wild animals, injury, and murder, they had the ideal conditions in their environment to gather in a great harvest of years.

Nevertheless, the grim reaper had a full complement of methods to dispatch the mortal whose fate was more prosaic. Fields could be burned by enemies, villages could be raided by marauders, and towns could be overrun by a foreign host. Men could be lanced, women raped, and babies thrown against the wall. The Israelite spies in Num 13:32 complained of a land with fortified cities and tall inhabitants, a land that "devours its inhabitants." The life expectancy in Egypt was thirty to thirty-five years as bodies were ravaged by arthritis, bone tumors, viral trachoma, parasitic tapeworms, hookworm, roundworm, and blood flukes. Psalm 91 lists a host of dreaded fates that all humans feared: the snare of the fowler (a destructive trap, deception, or ambush), pestilence, plague, terror by night, the arrow that flies by day, and the destruction that wastes at noonday. Men were eaten by lions, women died in childbirth, children were bitten by snakes, and travelers were brutalized by brigands.

When times were good and food plentiful, the wealthy could anticipate a comfortable life. One could take enough bribes and foreclose on enough properties to dine and sleep in luxury. Bones could wax fat and cheeks could bloom with health. Money loaned at high interest could pay for teak furniture with ivory inlay or servants to pour endless cups of wine. Sheets could be soft, imported clothing and jewelry exquisite, and music could soothe the soul. A wealthy person might come to think he or she could buy their way out of anything, forgetting that *Sheol* cannot be bribed or forestalled in any way. In fact, the only real certainty in life was the tomb. Such were the issues of life and death about which the psalmist ruminated as he laid fingers to the lyre and sang to the Korahite choir leader the riddle that we designate as Ps 49. The wealthy lived in denial that they would die and leave their worldly possessions behind. Conversely, the poor felt that eternity was their only hope of relief. The authors of the book of Psalms remind all men and women everywhere that death is inevitable and that all pride turns to ashes and worms. Estates are left behind. Death feeds on the corpse. What

---

3. Num 13:23–25 describes the return of the spies sent out by Moses. It took two of them to carry a single cluster of Canaanite grapes, some figs, and some pomegranates. The name of the town of Eshcol was a memorial to that remarkable cluster of grapes. This wilderness moment, added to the phrase "flowing with milk and honey," depicts a fruitful land.

happens to the soul is the real thrust of the author's production and the theme of this present exploration.

Female Psalm Writers

Could any of the authors in the book of Psalms be women? It is unlikely, but certainly possible. Female songwriters were not unknown in either ancient Israel or the broader Near East. Deborah's song comprises all of Judg 5, and Hannah's psalm is recorded in 1 Sam 2. One of the oldest songs ever recorded was written by a priestess from Ur named Enheduanna. She edited a collection of hymns and wrote a hymn of her own in the twenty-third century BCE. Her hymn to Inanna was reminiscent of David's pleas for help and vindication. She was history's first female author.[4]

Female singers were also a regular feature of Mesopotamian temple practice. Ezra 2:65, Ps 68:25, and 1 Sam 18:7 describe women participating in festal and temple worship services or creating songs that celebrate contemporaneous events. Ezra 2:65 records two hundred male and female singers who returned from Babylon with the Judean captives. Lastly, the story of Judith ends with a psalm, allegedly written by the Second Temple heroine. If the psalmist was a woman, however, her work might go unacknowledged, be partially suppressed, or be ascribed to a male author. In Exod 15:1–18 Moses is said to have sung the Song of the Sea, but 15:19–21 reads,

> When Pharaoh's horses, chariots and horsemen went into the sea, the LORD brought the waters of the sea back over them, but the Israelites walked through the sea on dry ground. Then Miriam the prophetess, Aaron's sister, took a tambourine in her hand, and all the women followed her with tambourines and dancing. And Miriam sang to them: "Sing to the Lord, for he is highly exalted. The horse and its rider he has hurled into the sea."

Verse 21 has suggested to some scholars that Miriam was the true author of the Song of the Sea.[5] When victories were celebrated in ancient Israel, it was the women who danced with their tambourines and sang the praises of the conquering general (1 Sam 18:6–9).[6] Although female authorship of the Psalms is a possibility, for the sake of simplicity the remainder

---

4. Leick, *Mesopotamia*, 26, 120–22.

5. For an exposition on Miriam's contribution to the Song of the Sea see Trible, "Miriam," 14–25, 34.

6. For a discussion of terracotta figures of women playing hand drums in Iron Age Israel and the ANE, see Meyers, "Drums and Damsels," 16–27; see also Wright, "Music and Dance," 217.

of the present work will utilize male personal pronouns in referring to the authors.

Additional Background Information

These days, biblical scholars have many manuscripts with which to study both the Hebrew Bible/Old Testament. One set of manuscripts is called the Masoretic Text (MT) because a family of Jewish scholars in the Middle Ages devoted themselves to copying the texts as exactly as humanly possible. They put notes on the margins called *masora*. Another family of manuscripts is called The Septuagint (LXX, around the first or second century BCE). This Greek translation of the Hebrew was the Bible of the disciples of Jesus. The translation does not exactly match the original Hebrew texts, but it is very close and sometimes helps to solve difficulties in translation of obscure MT Hebrew. A final set of manuscripts is called the Dead Sea Scrolls (DSS), which were lost to history shortly after they were created. They were found again in 1947, parchment scrolls rolled up and secured in large jars which were hidden away in several caves. Thanks to the dry weather in Israel, they survived and were a priceless addition to biblical scholarship.

Among all these copies of the MT, the LXX, and the DSS, there are thousands of variants. That means that mistakes were made in the copy process, that explanatory phrases were added, others dropped or changed, and that it is sometimes impossible to deduce which was the original autograph (writing). However, skeptics who say we can't possibly have a correct transmission of what the biblical authors wanted to convey are mistaken. Jesus certainly had no doubts that the message of God was clear enough and that every "jot and tittle" that was critical in the writing process was sufficiently preserved (Matt 5:18).

In 1998, Peter Flint wrote an excellent article concerning the transmission of the Psalms literature.[7] It is a compilation of little-known facts about the scrolls, some of which are reviewed below:

- The Dead Sea Scrolls include forty Psalm scrolls or manuscripts that incorporate psalms. Thirty-seven were found in eight locations at Qumran. Two were found at Masada and one at Nahal Hever.
- Of one hundred fifty psalms in the MT, twenty-four are missing from the DSS, probably due to deterioration. Of Psalms 1–89, nineteen are missing. Of Psalms 90–150, five are gone.

---

7. Flint, "Book of Psalms," 453–72.

- There are many variants in the phrasing and the organization.
- A chart of variances between DSS and MT shows that Books I–III, comprising Pss 1–89, were much more stable than 90–150, both in arrangement and in text. Book III was the most stable. Flint sees two distinct phases of book development, with 1–89 (the books that contain the entire Korahite Psalter and Elohistic Psalter) being the earlier works and 90–150 comprising the later works.
- The original Dead Sea editors believed that David wrote close to four thousand psalms for a variety of liturgical purposes, four hundred songs, and four songs for making music over those who need healing, and that they were all given by prophecy.
- Superscriptions have been in place from the earliest manuscripts onwards.

The latest psalms, some dating from the second century BCE, are found in the last third of the Psalter.[8] The final editing of the Psalter is the work of sages who have released the psalms from the historical moorings in order to infuse them with timeless application and power.

Modern psalms studies further indicate that the Psalms are deliberately and highly organized; that common sense and restraint will result in more understanding than a great body of wild speculation; and that the Dead Sea Scrolls have much to offer in a greater understanding of the biblical Psalms.

Conclusion

The academic trend today in biblical studies is to avoid theological issues that deal with a belief in miracles. Academic restraints almost require a neutral or negative approach to dealing with or explaining miraculous events in the Bible.[9] Although biblical characters were not perfect and had the capacity to commit horrendous acts in the name of their God, they still believed in a world where invisible powers roamed the skies with the potential to aid humans or do them great damage. Out of fear and superstition, they worshiped wood, rocks, and rivers. Talismans, little objects held in one's hand, had power to bless or burn, because statues were infused with the spirit of one deity or another. Spirits could be capricious; they needed constant appeasement. One trend today is to dismiss any genuine spiritual

---

8. Wilson, "Shape, 132, Also, Hurvitz, "Linguistic Criteria," 74–79.

9. Marsden, *Outrageous Idea*, 84, calls this trend "methodological atheism," citing a discussion in Berger, *The Sacred Canopy*, 179–85.

sensitivity on the part of biblical characters and to substitute ambitious motivations seen in the marketplace today. Our linear, modern thinking makes it difficult to really understand why they acted in the ways that they did. It also is important to recognize that their theology sometimes changed and coalesced over time. There is a danger of pulling passages out of context as if one statement represents what all believed in all eras. If the message of Ps 49 is so important, why was it written as a riddle with its significance controversial and opaque? Parables, proverbs, and metaphors grab our attention and provoke analysis. Even in the ancient world, wisdom literature was extremely popular. In the New Testament, Jesus Christ loved to preach in parables. Sometimes it was to obscure information but more often to make the lesson more unforgettable. Perhaps if we could mount a time machine and step off into the author's era, we would encounter as much controversy and diversity then as we have now.

2

Afterlife in Egypt, Mesopotamia, and Canaan

How *Sheol* Got its Name

SHEOL—DEATH, GRAVE—THE VERY IDEA sends shivers through most of us, but if we think we dread the thought today, in ancient times this unavoidable fate had negative implications that we can hardly imagine in our modern world. For many religious people today, heaven is always a pleasant option. For many of the ancients, there was no heaven, no redemption, no relief from the fear of death.

The study of how *Sheol* got its name has a long and contentious history. Eminent names are cited in modern articles as having made important contributions to the debate, yet in 1946 Ludwig Köhler surveyed the literature on the subject and found no really satisfactory answer to the question. Gesenius offered *shaal*, "ask, demand" as the source, and his proposal is often cited. *Sheol* is thus viewed as a "place of inquiry" into the life and deeds of the deceased. Suggestions included the same Hebrew root in its sense of "attack, burst in, or penetrate something." Deep penetration suggested to that scholar the "abyss" or the "underworld." Another rejected possibility is the concept of a "huge, underground hole."[1] In 1886 F. Delitzsch proposed an Assyrian derivation from a root meaning "underworld." Others looked to Arabic and Akkadian candidates that suggested "limp, weak, slack, or dull."

Ludwig Köhler proposed a combination of words that are consistently associated with "tumult, rage, rubble, ruin, heap, roar, uproar."[2] meanings that fit a conception of *Sheol* as a place of grim torment. The problem with this proposal is that *Sheol* is often described as a place of silence where souls

---

1. Köhler, "Alttestamentliche Wortforschung," 71.
2. Like Jer 17:12–13; 48:45; Isa. 5:14; 6:11; 17:13; 37:26, 29; Ps 40:3; Amos 2:2.

lie on beds and need to be aroused. Köhler's suggestion therefore runs counter to the nature of *Sheol*.

In the same year Walter Baumgartner answered Köhler's article.[3] He appealed to an obscure 1926 article by W. F. Albright that proposed the Babylonian word *schuara*, the abode of the vegetation god Tammuz.[4] Drawing from other ancient Middle Eastern sources, he connects the word with the underworld. In Akkadian, the consonants *r* and *l* are often exchanged. A consonantal shift in this case would give us *shaalu*, a construction similar to *Sheol*.

More attempts were to follow. Philip Johnston favors the solution *shu-wa-la*, an underworld deity named in a text from Emar which other scholars translate as *Sheol*. Such a possibility adds rich meaning to those texts that seem to personalize *Sheol*.[5] In a paper presented at the 2007 conference of the Society of Biblical Literature in San Diego, E. J. Pentiuc developed the same theme, adding that the name may be the short form of *Shuwaliyat(ti)*, "The Pure Brother of the Storm God." Songs were sung to him and to Nergal, god of the Nether World, and sheep were offered to both.[6] Pentiuc proposes the following development: *shuwala* > *shu'al* > *shu'ol* > *Sheol*.

Although the origins of the word *Sheol*, the assumed final stop of all mankind, will probably never be resolved, one common ingredient in all of these explanations is the negative connotation of every possibility. The Israelite name for the place of afterlife was unique, but the concept of a dark, gloomy place, especially in early biblical texts, was similar, but not identical, to the Syrian model. The fact that the soul actively goes down to the nether world rather than being laid or placed there implies that *Sheol* is more than just the earthly grave.

Fear and Hope in Egypt

Egypt shared many beliefs about the afterlife with neighbors and nations to the north. Although the concept of a soul living on after death was pervasive, uncertainty arose as to the characteristics of that eternal life. In Egypt, three things were necessary to enjoy a blissful afterlife in the Field of Reeds or the Field of Offerings: a proper burial with correct mummification and

   3. Baumgartner, "Zur Etymologie," 233–35.
   4. This deity, equated with the Sumerian vegetation god Dumuzi, was believed to die and resurrect each season and was still being ritually mourned in Ezekiel's day (Ezk 8:14).
   5. Johnston, *Shades of Sheol*, 77–78.
   6. Emar 328:2; 385:23; 388:6; 388:57.

magic rituals, a good and ethical life, and descendants to bring offerings of food, water, and beer to keep the soul content and vigorous.

The idea of a sympathetic connection between corpse and soul was also widespread in the ancient Near East. The inhabitants of the ANE believed that an object could be inhabited by a spirit or that somehow a spirit could access some aspect of a material object and use it in the non-material world, so food was left in the grave for the spirit of the deceased. They knew the corpse wouldn't use it, but somehow the spirit of the dead would be hungry without it. The Egyptians mummified the body and left identifying inscriptions so the soul could recognize its own corpse. The tomb was designed to be an apartment equipped with all that the deceased would use in the afterlife. Great treasures and practical goods were heaped into the darkness with the hope that a magical relationship would allow the deceased to benefit from their use. Terrible curses were written on the lintels to ward off grave robbers or those who would erase an inscription on a tomb or stela.

Before the Old Kingdom, afterlife was mainly beneficial for the Pharaoh. The king would join Re (the sun god) in his bark across the sky and become a star. Even Queen Hatshepsut harbored such aspirations:

> As Re rests in the evening bark,
> As he prevails in the morning bark,
> As he joins his two mothers in the god's ship,
> As sky endures, as his creation lasts,
> As I shall be eternal like an undying star,
> As I shall rest in life like Atum . . .[7]

The queen is clearly counting on an eternal life the equal of any Pharaoh. In the Pyramid Texts of Pharaoh Unas, the king is described as becoming a star that looks down on Osiris in the nether world. He has grown glorious falcon wings, described as "Plumes of the holy hawk" (Utterance 245).[8] Unas appears to be quite a rascal in the afterlife. He is lusty and grabs the wife of any man he wishes, which is probably a way of portraying his king-like power in the nether world (Utterance 317). Even worse, he becomes a demon who devours men and gods alike. He has monstrous helpers (like Horn-grasper, Serpent Raised-head, and Khons, slayer of lords) to capture, butcher, and prepare the victims (Utterance 273–274). As he devours the lords and gods, he absorbs their power. He is also said to climb a ladder, much like that of Jacob, to get to heaven. A god and goddess await him. The incantation helps him pass, so he is welcomed into the Field of Offerings because of his purity.

7. Lichtheim, *Ancient Egyptian Literature*, 2:28.
8. Ibid., 1:33.

In Utterance 373 and 374 King Teti arises from death and comes to the gate beyond which commoners may not go. The gatekeeper welcomes him. The star-spirits worship him and abundant food is prepared for him. He apparently will be treated in the afterlife as the monarch that he was on earth. He wanders the field of offerings and follows the deity in the daily circuit of day and night.

Later in the Old Kingdom, immortality began to be democratized. Anyone could live forever if they could afford the right scrolls and receive the proper burial. Mummification and scrolls of the Book of the Dead were common internment requirements. The Opening of the Mouth caused the corpse and soul to feel and hear and breathe (chapter 23). Other utterances helped the deceased keep his or her head (chapters 43, 77, 105).[9]

The righteous life was not discounted in Egyptian belief, but magic was a way to hedge one's bets. Chapter 125 of the Book of the Dead contains a long list of sins that the soul must profess not to have committed. These declarations must be made to forty-two gods who are mostly minor demons.[10] The soul is interrogated. If it passes every test, and no soul from its earthly life stands up to testify against it, and the good deeds outweigh the bad, the soul will survive the dangerous journey to a blissful afterlife. In the Instructions of Amenemope we have practical and ethical guides that the compiler of Prov 22:17—24:22 considered worthy of borrowing.[11] Amenemope was one who felt that cheaters would wind up in the abyss.

Finally, the offering of sacrifices of food for the dead was imperative, because the deceased chieftain or official hoped to eat bread with the god. Thus in one inscription the deceased official Paheri is made to say from beyond the grave,

> The dead is father to him who acts for him,
> He forgets not him who libates for him,
> It is good for you to listen.[12]

Paheri's instructions suggest that great blessing comes to those who offer much bread and beer to Osiris and the other gods. In time, however, generations would pass or war would interrupt the daily routines and the offerings would dry up, leaving the dead to languish. Beginning in the Old Kingdom, statues of servants and craftsmen were left in the tombs. They were enlivened by the Opening of the Mouth ritual so that the deceased

---

9. Ibid., 2:120–23. See also Brandon for a review of these concepts in "Life after Death–IV," 217–20.

10. Lichtheim, *Ancient Egyptian Literature*, 2:132.

11. Ibid., 2.135–63.

12. Lichtheim, *Ancient Egyptian Literature*, 2:15–21.

could benefit from their service in the afterlife. Infused with magic, they could sow, reap, bake, and provide sustenance forever. In the First Intermediate Period the idea developed that all the deceased, regardless of rank, would do menial labor in the Field of Reeds. Thus many wealthy tombs included hundreds of *shabti* or *ushabti* servants to do this manual labor. The *shabti* were kept in line by overseers.[13] Each figure was inscribed with the owner's name. It seems that Paheri was left to do his own work:

> Your heart rejoices as you plow
> In your plot in the Field of Reeds
> You are rewarded with what you have grown,
> You gather a harvest rich in grain.[14]

The scribe, Any, who worked in the Palace of Queen Nefertari (1200s BCE), wrote an instructional dialogue between a father and a son. One of his instructions mentions the importance of libations (ritual pouring of fluid) for the dead,

> Libate for your father and mother,
> Who are resting in the valley;
> When the gods witness your action
> they will say: "Accepted."
> Do not forget the one outside,
> Your son will act for you likewise.[15]

Egypt had hundreds of gods and goddesses, most of them depicted as part of the natural world, usually animals that Egyptians saw every day. Divine imagery includes humans, falcons, crocodiles, jackals, serpents, cows, frogs, and various other living creatures. The most intimidating were usually reptilian. Wadjet was the cobra goddess of the *uraeus* which was affixed to the crown of Pharaoh. She was a protectress who breathed fire against the king's enemies, thus empowering him. Apophis was the most devilish deity because he battled Re every day to impede the progress of his bark as it crossed the sky. He was associated with storms, earthquakes, and anything else that suggested chaos in the cosmos. The dread of him was muted by the frequent depiction of him as defeated. Wepset was also a serpent goddess whose name means "she who burns." The average Egyptian would have understood her to be a protectress of the king. Weret-Hekau's name means "great of magic," but her magic did not threaten the citizens of Egypt. Ammut was a goddess whose name means "female devourer." She

---

13. David, *Handbook to Life in Ancient Egypt*, 154–55.
14. Lichtheim, *Ancient Egyptian Literature*, 2:18.
15. Ibid., 2:137.

devoured the dead who were unworthy to enter the afterlife.[16] Thus, it seems that only the unworthy or wicked Egyptian might have cause to fear the gods and demons of the nether world. One who could not honestly disclaim the list of sins at the judgment would need to employ some serious magic to overcome the threatened punishment there.

The soldier who died on a foreign battlefield, the slave, or the official who was buried far from home might also be plagued with uncertainty as to what awaited him or her. The question might arise as to whether charms could overcome a profligate life or whether a good person who was too poor for mummification would suffer eternally because of it. What would happen if the line of descendants ended, or if civil upheaval or drought dried up the bread and beer offerings? It is hard to know how confident Egyptians, whether king or slave, could be when faced with their mortality, but they at least had the hope of immortality. The way there was a dangerous and uncertain journey, but the Field of Reeds lay in the West awaiting the fortunate ones who found favor with the gods.[17]

Afterlife in Mesopotamia

When it came to envisioning a nether world full of monsters and gloom, Mesopotamia and Syria were unmatched. Each city state in Sumer had its own patron gods, goddesses, and temples. Some people had a personal deity who guided, protected, and benefitted the individual.[18] The personal god was expected to act as intercessor or representative in the assembly of the gods. This understanding may be echoed in the book of Job:

> Even now, in fact, my witness is in heaven,
> and he that vouches for me is on high.
> My friends scorn me;
> my eye pours out tears to God,
> that he would maintain the right of a mortal with God,
> as one does for a neighbor. (Job 16:19–21)

Job is not looking for a personal god to worship in a temple, but he does sense that there is some kind of heavenly, immortal intercessor that can vouch for him. He senses that this entity is there, but has not been activated as such. The alternative is the dust, forgetfulness, and gloom of *Sheol*.

---

16. Wilkinson, *Gods and Goddesses*, 218–28.

17. Also see Johnston, *Shades of Sheol*, 230–32.

18. Kramer, *Sumerians*, 126. This practice continued into the era of Babylonian dominance. Oates, *Babylon*, 176.

King Gudea (2141–22 BCE)[19] of the Sumerian city of Lagash revered a personal serpent god named Ningizzida. He built temples all over Sumer to promote the cult of this deity. Ningizzida's cult declined after the third dynasty of Ur, but did not disappear for many years. Tammuz's sister was Ningizzida's bride. His name meant "Lord of the Tree of Truth."[20] He was associated with magic rites, divination, music, and healing. When depicted on a seal or ceramic, he is shown with a horned and crowned serpent head emanating from each shoulder. He stands upon a monster with a head and forked tongue like a horned serpent. His body is scaly, his front legs are like a lion's, his back legs are like a bird's, and he has a long tail. This serpent-dragon was called the lion-bird.[21]

The Akkadians had a tradition of an intercessor in the assembly of the gods. An Akkadian document called "A Vision of the Nether World" portrays the frightful experience of a palace scribe named Kummu who had been taking bribes.[22] He had followed his father in the post, and both had become corrupt. One night Kummu had a dream in which he confronted Namtar, the vizier of the nether world, and fifteen other demonic deities. Namtar, whose head was that of a serpent-dragon, grabbed Kummu by the hair with one hand; he was holding a sword in the other. One of the demons was treading on a crocodile with one foot. Another had the head of a lion. One was just a normal lion standing on two legs. The Upholder-of-Evil had the head and wings of a bird, but human hands. Remove-Hastily, the boatman of the nether world, had the head of a Zu-bird. Nedu, the gatekeeper of the nether world, had the head of a lion, human hands, and the feet of a bird. All-That-is-Evil had two heads. One had a body that was black as pitch. He was wearing a red cloak, his face was like that of Zu, he was carrying weapons in his hand, and he trod on a serpent with his left foot.

That terrifying image was just the beginning. Kummu then noticed Nergal himself, the prince of the underworld. All the terrified Anunnaki (a sub-class of deities) were paying him homage. He had a scepter like a viper. He shrieked at Kummu like a storm and was about to kill him. It was then that "Ishum, Kummu's counselor, the intercessor who spares life, who loves truth, and so forth, spoke up; 'Put not the fellow to death, thou *doughty* ruler of the nether world! Let the subjects of all the land ever hear [. . .] of thy fame!'" So instead of being killed, Kummu was given a severe rebuke and a curse. He awoke from the dream and cried out in lamentation and

19. Bertman, *Handbook*, 86.
20. Van Buren, "The God Ningizzida," 62.
21. Ibid., 71.
22. Pritchard, *ANET*, 109–10.

woe, throwing dirt from the market into his mouth. To show his intent to reform, he told the story to the people of the palace.[23]

Sumer offered scant answer to those who inquired about the fate of the upright soul after death. "... the problem of death and nether world was beset with enigmas, paradoxes, and dilemmas, and it is no wonder that the Sumerian ideas pertaining to them were neither precise nor consistent..."[24] An obscure document that may contain a part of "The Death of Gilgamesh" suggests that when Gilgamesh died and was buried, he entered the nether world with his personal retinue, who may have been buried with him. Gilgamesh made sacrifices for all of them—his wife, son, concubine, and a host of servants of various kinds. This kind of burial was attested archaeologically when Leonard Woolley actually uncovered a huge grave filled with people, animals, chariots, gold, and the king of the same era as Gilgamesh.[25]

Sacrifice and gift-giving did not end in the nether world. Ur-Nammu (2112–2095 BCE), who founded the Third Dynasty of Ur, also had to placate the seven gods when he arrived. The gods were the prince Nergal, god of pestilence[26] with his serpent scepter; Gilgamesh of the epic; Ereshkigal the Queen of the Dead; Dumuzi the companion of the serpent god Ningizzida; Namtar the vizier of nether world who could also release his sixty plagues against earthlings;[27] and Ningizzida himself. Gilgamesh, former King of Ur, greets Ur-Nammu, introduces him to the rules, and helps him find the place allotted to him. In the world above, Ur begins to languish and slide into decline.[28]

Scholars often point to *The Epic of Gilgamesh* as a representation of the dark, thirsty world where souls become birds and most of them eat dust. But while those scholars are usually looking for a depiction of the underworld itself, they overlook the fearsome nature of the deities there. In the vignette "The Death of Gilgamesh," Gilgamesh's dear companion Enkidu is dying. In a dream, he sees the fate that awaits him in the nether world. He is met by:

> ... an awful being, the somber-faced man-bird; he had directed on me his purpose. His was a vampire face, his foot was a lion's foot, his hand was an eagle's talon. He fell on me and his claws were in my hair, he held me fast and I smothered; then he transformed me so that my arms became wings covered with feathers. He turned his stare towards me, and he led me away to

23. Ibid.
24. Kramer, *The Sumerians*, 129.
25. Ibid., 129–30.
26. Oates, *Babylon*, 174.
27. Ibid.
28. Kramer, *Sumerians*, 131.

the palace of Irkalla, the Queen of Darkness, to the house from which none who enters ever returns, down the road from which there is no coming back. There is the house whose people sit in darkness; dust is their food and clay their meat.[29]

In the "house of dust" kings were servants. One who was said to have ridden an eagle to heaven was now imprisoned in the gloom of the nether world. Gods were there as well. Ereshkigal, the Queen of the Underworld, presided over the Book of Death. Upon seeing her, Enkidu was "like one whom the bailiff has seized and his heart pounds with terror." Perhaps the man-bird was the "king of terrors" to whom the wicked are marched away in Job 18:14. Israel would later produce literature incorporating a Book of Life, in contrast to the Book of Death here. Enkidu has died in more ways than one. There was no Field of Reeds for him. No beer offerings would slake his thirst in the house of dust. In Tablet XII of the *Epic*, Enkidu is allowed to come up through a hole in nether world to tell Gilgamesh what it was like down there. He prepares his old friend by telling him to sit down and prepare to weep. He said his body was eaten by vermin and was full of dust. Both men grovel and lament in the earthly dust together. Gilgamesh asks Enkidu if he has seen this one or that. The text is partly destroyed, but the preserved fragments are telling:

> "Him whose corpse was cast out on the steppe, hast thou seen?"
> "I have seen: his spirit finds no rest in the nether world."
> "Him whose spirit has no one to tend (it), hast thou seen?"
> "Lees of the pot, crumbs of bread, offals of the street he eats."[30]

In the tale "The Descent of Ishtar to the Nether World" Ishtar decides to visit her sister:

> Yea, the daughter of Sin (the moon god) set [her] mind
> To the dark house, the abode of Irkal[la],
> To the house which none leave who have entered it,
> To the house wherein the entrants are bereft of li[ght],
> Where dust is their fare, and clay their food,
> (Where) they see no light, residing in darkness,
> (Where) they are clothed like birds, with wings for garments,
> (And where) over door and bolt is spread dust.[31]

Ishtar's visit does not go well. She is stripped of garments and jewelry at each of seven gates. Her sweet sister Ereshkigal flies at her with curses of

---

29. Sandars, *Gilgamesh*, 92–93. Note the similarity of phrasing and the contrast of restorative content in Isa 9:2, "The people who walked in darkness have seen a great light; those who lived in a land of deep darkness—on them light has shined."

30. Pritchard, *Ancient Near Eastern Texts*, 99.

31. Ibid., 107.

miseries and has the vizier lock her up in the palace. In the streets of the world above, all mating of beasts and of humans ceases. The wise Ea sends a eunuch to save Ishtar with the water of life. He is successful in his mission, but is cursed by Ereshkigal. Ishtar is redeemed from her miseries by the water of life and by the fact that her lover Tammuz takes her place there.

The Babylonian world and cosmos ruled by Marduk was no cheerier than that of Sumer. Marduk arose out of the Sumerian cosmological system, but he soon replaced Enlil as the father of the gods. He was the son of Ea, the one god who was consistently well-disposed toward humans. Ea was the son of Apsu, who fathered several rambunctious godlings whose exploits kept him awake. So Apsu began to plot with his vizier Mummu to slay his children. Ea murdered Apsu in his sleep, bound Mummu, and took the crown of authority. He and his wife then brought forth their darling son Marduk, with four faces, four eyes that see all four directions at once, four large ears, and lips that breathe fire when they move. His iconography would be a horned serpent head, a lion's body, talons for feet, and a scorpion's long tail. He was the delight of his father and grandfather.

Strife arose again, and this time Tiamat was aroused to battle against the gods. Let us make monsters, she decided.

> Mother Hubur, who can form everything,
> Added countless invincible weapons, gave birth to monster serpents,
> Pointed of fang, with merciless incisors,
> She filled their bodies with venom for blood.
> Fierce dragons she clad with glories,
> Causing them to bear auras like gods, (saying)
> Whoever sees them shall collapse from weakness!...
> She deployed serpents, dragons, and hairy hero-men,
> Lion monsters, lion men, and scorpion men,
> Mighty demons, fish men, bull men,
> Bearing unsparing arms, fearing no battle.[32]

One of the warriors became their leader and Tiamat's consort. Not to be outdone, Marduk armed himself with weapons and with seven winds that included cyclones, whirlwinds:

> He mounted the terrible chariot, the unopposable Storm Demon,
> He hitched to it the four-steed team, he tied them at his side:
> "Slaughterer," "Merciless," "Overwhelmer," "Soaring."
> Their lips are curled back, their teeth bear venom,
> They know not fatigue, they are trained to trample down.[33]

---

32. Hallo, *Context of Scripture*, 1:392.
33. Ibid., 1:397.

Marduk lured Tiamat into a one-on-one duel in which he blew her up like a balloon with his "ill wind," then shot an arrow into her. With the pieces of her carcass he created the world.

There are several classic descriptions of the nether world in the above tales. All of them are reflected in later Hebrew literature minus the gods and monsters. The place is dark, devoid of light, and dusty. Worms continue to feed on the soul. In dealing with the afterlife, scholars have neglected the statement of Enkidu that his corpse is full of vermin. The apocalyptic vision of Isa 66:24 may reflect a later affirmation that the infidel will inherit a similar fate in death.[34] The only available food is clay. The seven gates have bars and bolts and are guarded by gatekeepers (cf, Jonah 2:7). People turn into birds. The overseers are demons and deities who sometimes plot, connive, and thwart, and try to kill one another. The names of doomed souls are written into Ereshkigal's Book of Death. Even eminent souls must placate the gods there (one of which is a serpent-dragon) with gifts and sacrifices. In one narrative, kings become servants. Servants are servants still. There is no sense of redemption, no hope. The intercessor Ishum may delay the day of death with his soothing words, but die one must. No one gets out of the nether world, including Enkidu and Gilgamesh. The Egyptians had the hope that some Pharaohs would mount Re's bark at dawn and at least see the light of day. For those in the Sumerian nether world, there was no light and no reprieve. Gilgamesh's great sorrow was that nothing he could do, pay, or offer could ward off the fate that Enkidu described to him.[35]

The Demons of Canaan

In the West, concepts of mourning and afterlife were similar to those of Mesopotamia. Stelae (standing memorial stones with writing inscribed on them) helped the memory of a king remain current, which in turn invigorated the deceased. To be forgotten was another kind of death. One of the oldest Aramaic mortuary inscriptions highlights the importance of stelae as memorials before gods and men:

---

34. "And they shall go out and look at the dead bodies of the people who have rebelled against me; for their worm shall not die, their fire shall not be quenched, and they shall be an abhorrence to all flesh." The bodies depicted are those fallen in battle who would not be properly buried, mourned, or libated. According to the lore, these would find no rest in the nether world. See also Isa 34:3 and Mark 9:48 wherein Jesus Christ is describing Hades. Here undying fire is added to the torment of the nether world.

35. For further discussion as to the location of the nether world, see Kramer, "Death and the Nether World."

To the great god, his lord, Hadad-yith'i, king of Guzan, son of Sas-nuri, king of Guzan, set up and gave (the statue) to him, so that his soul may live, and his days be long, and to increase his years, and so that his house may flourish, and his descendants may flourish, and his people may flourish, and to remove illness from him, and for making his prayer heard, and for accepting the words of his mouth.[36]

There follows a lengthy curse on the house, farm, servants, and descendants of anyone removing the stela. Its presence in the temple before the deity was understood to have personal, generational, and national consequences. Its removal would mean a loss of blessing. Thus the Kulamuwa Inscription,[37] which tells of the heroic exploits of a North-Phoenician-Aramaic king, also pronounces a curse on any son who would remove the inscription from the temple. Another inscription, dedicated to the Phoenician high official Azatiwada of the Danunians, appears on the gate of a city and curses anyone who would remove the gate.[38]

The injunctions of these stelae were obeyed, frequently with satisfying results. Panamuwa, king of Y´dy, erected his stela in his "eternal abode" [his tomb]. First he tells of all his great deeds, and then he blesses the son who remembers eternally his spirit and who sits on his throne and says, "May the dead spirit of Panamuwa eat with you, [i.e. Hadad, the Syrian/Aramaen deity also known as Baal], and may the dead spirit of Panamuwa drink with you."[39] Naturally, curses are heaped on the head of any son of his who takes the throne without ritually reciting and blessing the name of his father. Panamuwa was nearly killed by Tiglath-Pileser III (mid-700s BCE), but he made peace with the Assyrian king and was required to join him in the imperial campaigns against other countries. Panamuwa's dutiful son, Bar-Rakib, continued the policy of loyalty to the king of Assyria. He "ran at the wheel of his lord," as did his father. When Panamuwa died, Bar-Rakib set up a statue for him and intoned the required blessing over his father. He became so rich and powerful that other kings envied him. He built a palace that surpassed any residence of the former kings of Sam'al.[40]

Citation of all the mortuary inscriptions would require too much space, but suffice to say that curses written upon the lintels were common.

---

36. Hallo, *Context of Scripture*, 2:154 (Alan Millard, "Hadad-yith`i").
37. Ibid., 2:147 (K. Lawson Younger Jr., "The Kulamuwa Inscription").
38. Ibid., 2:150 (K. Lawson Younger Jr., "The Azatiwada Inscription").
39. Ibid., 2:157 (K. Lawson Younger Jr., "The Hadad Inscription").
40. Ibid., 2:160–61. (K. Lawson Younger Jr., "The Panamuwa Inscription" and "The Bar-Rakib Inscription").

On occasion, an inscription would state that no silver or gold resided in the tomb, so that grave robbers and agents of vengeful enemies would leave the bones in peace.

The taunt of Isaiah against the pride of the king of Babylon in Isa 14 plays on Near Eastern anxieties concerning the afterlife. On earth, the king thought he was a god. He thought he would be like the pharaohs and ancient kings who rose from their tombs to become a star. This king, however, had grander ambitions than that. He would rise above the stars and join Baal and the assembly of the gods on the heights of Mt. Zaphon. He would be like God himself. But instead of going up, the prophet declares, the king will descend to the depths of *Sheol*. Instead of being welcomed by the assembly of the gods on Zaphon, he will be ridiculed by all the kings of the earth who have died before him. These are not the mighty *rephaim* of Ugaritic myth, but are merely shades, weak even while they sit on their thrones. They must be aroused from their slumber in order to greet the newcomer. But that is not the worst of it. Instead of attendants to play music and entertain him, as was hoped for by the kings of Sumer, this king will have a bed of maggots and a covering of worms. These worms will never die. Kings who may have kissed his feet in life, who may have gone to an early grave because of him, will stare at him disrespectfully in wonder. Although this king undoubtedly prepared a grand tomb for himself, and expected it to be full of treasures that he would use in the afterlife, the prophet Isaiah proclaims that he would be cast out of his tomb, probably by an invading army, to rot on a battle field. He would join those who fell in battle to be carrion for birds and animals. Foreign soldiers would come through the field looting the corpses of anything of worth. Then the corpses would all be tossed into a pit, their king with them. His dynasty would end; no loyal son would call his name during the New Year festival or raise a stela for his glory. The last pride of all kings is the monumental building projects that they leave behind for future generations to wonder at—the temples, the palaces, the grand gates and walls—but these would all be buried in the blowing sands of time.

> "I will rise up against them," declares the Lord Almighty. "I will cut off from Babylon her name and survivors, her offspring and descendants," declares the Lord. "I will turn her into a place for owls and into swampland; I will sweep her with the broom of destruction," declares the Lord Almighty. (Isa 14:22–23)

The *Rp'u* (hereafter, *Rephaim*) of Ugarit (a Bronze Age Proto-Canaanite city located on the Syrian coast of the Mediterranean and destroyed in the late thirteenth century BCE), are known to us due to several fragmentary clay tablets that describe the rituals in which they were invoked.

There may be no more complete and detailed analysis of these documents than Klaas Spronk's 1986 book *Beatific Afterlife* (which unfortunately is not widely available).⁴¹ The present author has no intention of second-guessing his conclusions. The theme of this study is the fear of death and afterlife. According to Spronk, one can find a host of reasons to fear the *Rephaim*. There is some debate as to whether the *Rephaim* of the Ugaritic documents are deceased kings, minor underworld deities, demons, or heroes of the past.

A few years after Spronk's work, Brian Schmidt suggested that some of the *rephaim* mentioned in the tablets were living warrior-nobility who were invited to the feast. He understood the role of the deceased *rephaim* of ancient times to be limited to welcoming the newly deceased king to the afterlife, and asserted that they never leave the nether world.⁴² Schmidt bases his conclusions on one tablet (RS 34.126), but all documents considered together tend to support Spronk's belief that all the *rephaim* texts describe dead heroes or divinized kings.

The traditional Syrian understanding of the *Rephaim* was that, as divinized heroes and kings, they had special power to bless or harm.⁴³ They were summoned forth at the New Year's Festival or at the coronation of the new monarch. KTU 1.161/RS 34.126 appears to commemorate the death of king Niqmad and the installation of Ammurapi (not to be confused with Hammurabi). The *Rephaim* of the earth are invoked, some by name. The dead in general, from the mighty to those who are weak and have no one to tend to them, are also invoked. The throne and footstool of Niqmad are induced to weep and mourn for him. Later the throne would be lowered into the tomb for Niqmad to sit on in the nether world. The sun goddess Shapash is petitioned to bring warmth to the affair. Seven sacrifices are offered (perhaps because demons are noted to act in groups of seven).⁴⁴ At the end of the ritual, blessings are invoked upon Ugarit.

In other texts wherein the dead are invoked, they are invited by the priest Dan-el) to flutter like birds to the holy place (KTU 1.20:I). They harness their horses and climb into their chariots. They fly around the temple, the threshing floors, and the orchards for three days. On the third day of the festival, Baal arises and comes to (temporarily) call up the un-dead:⁴⁵

41. Spronk, *Beatific Afterlife*, 219.

42. Schmidt, "Afterlife Beliefs," 236–39.

43. Levine and Michel de Tarragon, "Dead Kings," 649–59.

44. Spronk, *Beatific Afterlife*, 166, n. 5, notes that even the New Testament speaks of seven demons coming into a "house" or being cast out of someone (Mark 16:9 and Luke 11:26).

45. In 1986 this interpretation of souls as birds was challenged by Mark Smith and Elizabeth Bloch-Smith (see below), but considering that the harvest threshing floor

> Then Daniel should say:
> Come into the house of my Marzeah,
> go into my house for the *rp'um*.
> I invite you into my house,
> I call [you into] my [pa]lace.
> May the *rp'um* ghosts flutter to the holy place,
> may the ghosts flutter to the holy place,
> may they come into the house of my Marzeah.
> Then he will heal you,
> the Shepherd will give you life again.
> Now I will go, one day and a second,
> on the third day I will arrive at the house,
> I will come in to my place.[46]

Daniel then finishes his psalm by re-invoking the *Rephaim* with repetitions of the invitation. One can only imagine what such imagery might have stirred in the imaginations of the superstitious Ugaritians—every bird call on the threshing floor would have had them looking for the undead. A misplaced hoe might have been stolen by the dead; a sudden illness might mean that they were displeased;[47] any blessing, such as a healing, would be attributed to them. Their chariots would haunt the orchards at night. Horsemen, perhaps armed with weapons, would ride the clouds with Baal and cross the harvest moon.

The semantic similarity of this document to the declarations in Hos 6 is striking. The biblical prophet Hosea proclaims:

> Come, let us return to the Lord,
> for he has torn us to pieces, but he will heal us;
> he has injured us, but he will bind up our wounds.
> After two days he will revive us;
> on the third day he will restore us,
> that we may live in his presence.
> Let us acknowledge the Lord;
> let us press on to acknowledge him.
> As surely as the sun rises, he will appear;
> he will come to us like the winter rains,
> like the spring rains that water the earth. (Hos 6:1–3)

---

and the ripened orchards in the fall would be a major gathering place of hungry birds, Spronk's assessment is not far-fetched.

46. Ibid., 169.
47. Pitard, "Ugaritic Funerary Text," 65–75.

So, instead of the undead shades and ghoulish birds, the Israelites get sunshine and spiritual dew. These inspiring words are presumed by modern Jews to refer to the restoration of the people of Israel. Christians view them as prophetically referring to the resurrection of Jesus Christ on the third day. The life-giving rain and sunrise are metaphorical and occur in other prophetic and poetic writings as symbols of God's healing presence and grace. It is possible that the prophet is using recognizable Baal and Shapash (the sun goddess) iconography and deliberately transferring it to Yahweh in a poetic context to show the great contrast between the two religions.

Several documents indicate that souls are seen as birds. This conforms with the imagery in "The Death of Gilgamesh," in which Enkidu describes himself as turning into a bird-like entity. KTU 1.20:I describes *Rephaim* and ghosts being summoned to eat and drink at a sacrifice "on the day of summer fruit." The god of the nut tree arrives and a goddess sits on a twig. We have already seen that in KTU 1.21–22 Dan'el summons the *Rephaim* to flutter to the holy place. Spronk cites KTU 1.20:II; 1.21:II.3–4.12; 1.21:II.5–6.10–11.20–21 among others as depicting souls fluttering or being startled like birds.[48] KTU 1.22.I, another Dan'el text, not only mentions souls as birds but portrays El (the chief Canaanite god, depicted as a bull) as being the one who uses the religious festival to revivify the dead. Baal is the first of the *Rephaim* to arise. After him,

> There rustled the host of the filth,
> the highness, the king, the unrelated,
> as when Anat chases the game,
> causes to fly up the birds of heaven.

The *rephaim* eat and drink for six days.[49] On the seventh Baal arrives. According to Spronk, the *rephaim* can only be revived by being part of Baal's retinue of warriors.[50] In KTU 1.108, when Baal and the ghosts arrive, the king is encouraged to ask Baal for blessings.[51] In Spronk's presentation, there is no evidence that the blessings brought by the *rephaim* directly benefit anyone besides the king and his officials.

Although Israel's early concepts of the grave and afterlife were vague and contradictory, the Mesopotamian and Canaanite views were unrelentingly gloomy. Spronk points out that the difference between the

48. Spronk, *Beatific Afterlife*, 167.

49. In Pitard's rendition of KTU 1.161/RS 34.126, the *rephaim* arrive sad and starving. They eat and are revived. In other translations, it is the throne and footstool that weep.

50. Spronk, *Beatific Afterlife*, 173–74.

51. Ibid., 179.

Mesopotamian and Ugaritic understanding of the afterlife is that at Ugarit, the elite dead could look forward to a temporary, yearly reprieve from the gloom of the nether world. That, of course, is not the same as a "beatific afterlife." "There are many things to be feared there," he writes, "Darkness, coldness, hunger, thirst, and the god of the dead who devours his victims. But that does not mean that the people of Ugarit did not also have expectations for a bearable afterlife or even more than that." Here, Spronk is merely speculating. There is really only the slightest hint of anything bearable about the afterlife at Ugarit. One such hint is that the soul may eat and drink with the deity if (and only if) the son or relative blesses the deceased and invokes the presence of both soul and deity at a sacrifice which includes offerings of bread, beer, water, and other tasty morsels.[52] It might even be argued that the satirical "rousing/stirring" of the denizens of *Sheol* to greet the king of Babylon in Isa 14 was the result of the invocation of the living mourners at the Babylonian king's funeral.

Akkadian myths suggest that there are different locations in the nether world, and hopefully a noble soul such as a king will have a more bearable corner than the soldier who dies in battle or the commoner with no one to care for them. But the point is that there is no certainty, no confidence other than bravado. The worst case scenario is laid out in the epic of Gilgamesh: being grabbed by the claw of the fierce god of death, eating dust and clay food forever, sleeping on a bed of worms, and consorting with demons in the dark—a fate that had Enkidu and Gilgamesh wailing in the dust together.

---

52. Levine and de Tarragon, "Dead Kings," 657.

3

The Davidic Revolution in Worship

The Ark, the Heart of Redemption

WHEN THE ISRAELITES CROSSED the Red Sea (or perhaps the wet, reedy, marsh lakes on the border of the Egyptian delta and the Sinai wilderness), they had no law code, no tabernacle, no statue of their god, and no governmental hierarchy. Having sojourned in Egypt for 215 years,[1] they were slowly losing their language and their cultural identity as a people from the north (Syrians, Canaanites, Israelites). In time, the memory of their patriarchs, Abraham, Isaac, Jacob, Joseph, and the elders of the twelve tribes, would have faded, and we would have no Hebrew Bible at all. With the prophet Moses in the lead, Elohim brought them to the holy mountain, Mt. Horeb, also known as Mt. Sinai, possibly located just beyond the eastern finger of the Red Sea, in what is today Saudi Arabia. They stayed there for just over a year. They received the Ten Commandments there by the audible voice of God as He spoke to the people from the mountain, and on stone tablets.

Before the Israelites had a portable tabernacle, Moses set up a tent outside the camp called the Tent of Meeting. He and Joshua would inquire of the LORD there. When Moses and Joshua left the camp to go into the tent, the people would watch from their own tent doors. A pillar of cloud would come down and linger at the entrance, while inside God spoke to Moses "face to face, as a man speaks with his friend" (Exod 33:7–11).

After Moses came down from the mountain with the two tablets, he was commanded to build an ark or chest in which to carry them. The two

---

1. The LXX, Gal 3:17, and other sources indicate that the Israelites were in Canaan and in Egypt for 430 years.

tablets were called "the Testimony," and the ark that held them was designated "the ark of the Testimony." It was made of wood and covered over inside and out with gold. It had a solid gold cover with two beaten gold cherubim that faced each other. Their wings stretched upward and over the cover. Cherubim were winged animals that were known throughout the Middle East as guardians of tabernacles and thrones of kings. The cover had an interesting designation in Hebrew. It is often translated as "mercy seat" or "atonement cover." The Hebrew root comes from a word meaning "cover over," but the grammatical pointing turns it into "cover over or make atonement for sin." This golden lid is associated with atonement because once a year, the high priest of Israel would enter into the Holy of Holies of the tabernacle and sprinkle blood onto the ark. In this manner, atonement was made for the sins of all of the people of Israel. It was also the place where God would meet with his people and speak to them (Exod 25:10–22). The sacred cover had a triple purpose. It protected the Testimony in the chest, it was God's "throne" where he met with His people, and it was a conduit of God's mercy and covenant grace.

The ark was housed in a tabernacle into which only the new Aaronic priesthood could enter and which only males from the tribe of Levi could break down and carry. The concept that only the High Priest could approach the ark may have been an artifact of a much later time, because as we shall later see, it was carried into war for many years. The place where the ark rested was called the Holy of Holies. It was pitch dark in there because a curtain separated the Holy of Holies and the Holy Place where a golden lamp stand with seven lamps gave off light. The lamplight glistened off a golden table and an incense burner. In the desert heat, it would have been hot and stuffy as well as smoky in the tabernacle. It was covered with animal hides and there were no windows. At the beginning of the second year in the wilderness, while they still lingered at the foot of Mt. Horeb, they put the tabernacle together. The name "tent of meeting" or "tabernacle of meeting" transferred to the new tabernacle (Exod 40:1). It was also called "the tabernacle." When all was finally crafted and assembled there at the foot of Mt. Sinai, a glory cloud appeared that was so powerful that Moses, who had so recently spent eighty days immersed in God's glory cloud on the mountain, could not enter.

> Then the cloud covered the Tent of Meeting, and the glory of the Lord filled the tabernacle. Moses could not enter the Tent of Meeting because the cloud had settled upon it, and the glory of the Lord filled the tabernacle. In all the travels of the Israelites,

whenever the cloud lifted from above the tabernacle, they would set out; but if the cloud did not lift, they did not set out—until the day it lifted. So the cloud of the LORD was over the tabernacle by day, and fire was in the cloud by night, in the sight of all the house of Israel during all their travels. (Exod 40:34–37)

According to the book of Leviticus, God still called Moses to the Tent of Meeting to speak with him. The same term is used for the place of sacrifice (Lev 1:1, 3). Since Aaron was his brother and Moses was not a priest, let alone the High Priest, it is possible that the ark's extreme isolation was locked in at a much later time.

In addition to the tabernacle, there were various animal sacrifices required at Sinai. The Israelites did not invent animal sacrifice. Early Mesopotamian and Canaanite literature describes this practice as a means to appease the gods and sustain their strength. Without humans to sacrifice the animals and ritually pour out water and wine, the gods grew hungry and thirsty. They would gather around the sweet aroma of the holocaust with relief and contentment. The Torah/Pentateuch echoes this thinking with the phrase that the Hebrew sacrifices would be a "pleasing aroma" to Yahweh.[2] The Hebrew of Exod 29:25 is sparse and needs help to be understandable. It's also controversial, making us a little uncomfortable, so translations vary. The literal Hebrew indicates that the priest will receive the gifts of the people and burn them as a food offering to Yahweh, making a gift of a pleasing aroma. Some translators change "food" to "smoke" or "burnt offering." The LXX just dropped the word "food." Leviticus 3:15, KJV, reads: "And the priest shall burn them upon the altar; it is the food of the offering made by fire for a sweet savor: all the fat is the LORD's." The language of food and pleasing aroma being associated with the sacrifices is dropped in later writings. Future prophets would totally repudiate the idea that Yahweh requires food or, for that matter, animal sacrifices.

The Israelites were also given civil law codes at Mt. Sinai. Many of those laws reflect the codes of earlier kings and emperors in Mesopotamia and Babylon. An eye for an eye, repeated three times in the Torah, is found in the law code of Hammurabi, which was contemporary with Abraham. The commandments for dealing with inheritance, multiple wives, concubines, children, servants, and possessions are similar to the law codes of Eshnunna and Lipit-Ishtar of Sumer. Other commandments were common sense or the general practice of Asiatics.

The ritual purity laws may have been unique to the Israelites. They had some hygienic value and served to keep the Israelites separate from

---

2. Exod 29:18, 25; Lev 1:9, 13, 17; 2:2.

their neighbors, but the root understanding of the people was that certain foods or health issues, imperfections, sores, or things that people touched made them unclean. It had nothing to do with hygiene or morals or heart attitude toward God. Only prescribed rituals could restore the status of being clean. The unclean had to avoid touching people or approaching God in the tabernacle.

Also in this world view, men were the holy gender. Women were their supports and mothers of their children. A woman had to do something truly extraordinary to be mentioned in the records. Men were patriarchs and lords of the family, including over their grown sons and their children. The first-born son was favored over the younger brothers, and he was understood to be the future patriarch of the family.

The purpose of the discussion above is to help us understand that the Israelites were still half-Canaanite in the wilderness. They lived in a world where the living and the dead were not yet entirely separated; they still needed one another for well-being. It was a world full of superstitions. Ritual created reality, and spirits interfaced with the living through rituals, incantations, and through solid items like rocks and statues. The monotheistic prophets would cry out against these ancient ideas for hundreds of years to come. There were two fates awaiting the ones who broke covenant; they could be stoned to death or they could be "cut off from their people." Whether being cut off meant physical execution, exile as in the case of Cain, or eternal separation in *Sheol* is anyone's guess.

At this point, it's time to ask if the Israelites had developed any new concepts of afterlife or resurrection. We can point to the book of Deuteronomy, but with a caveat. Today, scholars suggest that the fifth book of the Torah was actually written in the sixth century BCE, shortly before Babylon invaded Jerusalem for the last time and took the nation captive. They say that it was a needed upgrade in old theology, the purpose being to prepare the Israelites for days of crisis to come when their temple would be destroyed and their ark would disappear forever (Jer 3:16–17). It would be a time when Israel would ask, has God abandoned us? Are we dead as a nation? Are our sins forgiven? Hilkiah the High Priest declared that as the priests picked through the rubble of the Temple of Solomon, they found a scroll purporting to be a scribal record of Moses's last speech on the Plains of Moab, at the encampment before the people crossed over into the territory west of the Jordan River.

The scholars may well be right; I could make some strong arguments in favor of that idea myself, but rather than argue that point in this study, there is value in just looking at the book as it was intended to be read by whichever set of scribal authors wrote it. Embedded in the intent is the message, and the message is what lasts. In this scroll, the scribes of Moses's day (or the priests of Hilkiah's day) wrote,

> The Lord will judge His people
> and have compassion on His servants,
> When he sees their strength is gone,
> and no one is left, slave or free.
> He will say: "Now where are their gods,
> the rock they took refuge in?
> the gods who ate the fat of their sacrifices,
> and drank the wine of their drink offerings?
> Let them rise up to help you!
> Let them give you shelter.
> See now that I myself am He!
> There is no god besides me.
> I put to death and I bring to life,
> I have wounded and I will heal,
> And no one can deliver out of my hand. (Deut 32:36–39)

Yahweh is claiming to be the true God of deliverance, blessing, and life. It's important to note that in verse 39b, Yahweh kills and makes alive. Is there a message in the fact that "kills" speaks of death and "makes alive" suggests resurrection? The verse could be metaphoric, but considering the miraculous claims of the Torah (and the rest of the Hebrew Bible) on behalf of God's people, there is cause to reach deep into this verse and find hope of deliverance from *Sheol*.

There is also the hope that when God judges his people in times of apostasy, there is the hope of forgiveness and relief from the terrible consequences of turning to foreign gods. Judgment was communal in those ancient times. Whole families could be stoned for the sins of the patriarch. Whole communities feared God's wrath if one person, known or unknown, committed a major transgression like murder. The nation could be banished from the land if the leaders turn to abominable practices. The focus in those days did not seem to be what occurred after death, but how the redeemed community could maintain God's favor and protection while alive. A person could be stoned for breaking Sabbath restrictions. Obedience brought fertile wives, abundant harvests, and victory in war. The reward, as scholar Dr. Jon Levenson aptly explained, was inheritance, prosperity, and the longevity of the whole community. But we will discuss that in depth later.

The Ark in Canaan

Once the tabernacle was constructed, the Israelites came to the southern border of Canaan, where they prepared to enter *en masse*, armed with goods and weapons given them by average Egyptians who desperately wanted them to go away. In the wilderness, Moses sent out twelve spies, ten of whom returned with a negative report. Because of that lack of faith, the Israelites spent thirty-nine more years in the desert, surrounded by hostile neighbors. The first generation of soldiers died there, but the second generation followed a prophet named Joshua into the land of Canaan, the land promised to the descendants of Abraham, Isaac, and Jacob.

As the Levites hoisted the ark on their shoulders and approached the Jordan River, it once again demonstrated its sacred power. They stepped into the water, and the river separated as an earthquake occurred upstream, temporarily damming the stream. Water downstream flowed away, leaving a way for all of the Israelites to cross in a single day. When the last child, lamb, and donkey had crossed over, the priests left the river bed. Upstream, the river broke its dam and sent a wall of water rushing along its customary path.

Once Israel was established in Canaan, they built a tabernacle in central Israel, in territory claimed by the tribe of Ephraim. People brought their tithes and sacrifices to Shiloh in accordance with the Mosaic Law. Government during this three-hundred-year period comprised priests, Levites, and appointed officials as judges. In times of crisis, God raised up special leaders called Judges. When Israel repented of their relapse to foreign gods and practices, the Judge of the day would lead them in battle and deliver them from foreign oppression. When they turned back to foreign gods and ignored the Law, oppression returned. The book of Judges opens with the poignant story of a barren woman named Hannah, who was loved by her husband but persecuted by his other wife. Hannah was a woman of faith. She was at the tabernacle deep in prayer when the High Priest Eli found her. He thought she was drunk, but she assured him she was just agonizing in prayer due to her desire to have a child, so he prayed for her and she soon conceived. When baby Samuel was weaned, she brought him to the tabernacle and dedicated him for service. She then wrote a beautiful Psalm laden with theological principals, one of them being the concept of reversals:

> The bows of the warriors are broken,
> but those who stumbled are armed with strength.
> Those who were full hire themselves out for food,
> but those who were hungry hunger no more.
> She who was barren has born seven children,

but she who has had many sons pines away.
The LORD brings death and makes alive;
He brings down to the grave and raises up.
The LORD brings poverty and wealth;
He humbles and he exalts.
He raises the poor from the dust
and lifts the needy from the ash heap;
he seats them with princes
And has them inherit a throne of honor.
For the foundations of the earth are the Lord's;
Upon them he has set the world. (1 Sam 2:4–8)

In verse 6, Hannah revisits the idea of the grave not being so final. Or perhaps, if the scholars are correct that Deuteronomy was written in Jeremiah's era, she was the first to suggest it. In both Hebrew and Mesopotamian literature the grave is described as a place from which no one returns. But Hannah's womb, like that of Sarah, was dead. God brought life to bodies that were closer to the grave than to fertility. But why be surprised? The ancient narratives recorded that God brought water from a dry rock and manna from the skies where there was no bread. He turned a family of Asiatic slaves into a people with a unique relationship with their God.

Hannah notes that God resists the proud. Foreign kings had many exalted titles. Letters addressed to Pharaoh in the Amarna age are written by men who cravenly called themselves the "dust under your feet." Royal hubris in the Ancient Near East was boundless. Hannah's psalm sets a new challenge for her people. She then went on to prophesy that Israel would someday have a monarch: "He will give strength to His king, and exalt the horn of His anointed."

Although many in Israel were faithful to their Law, many were hedging their bets by mixing religious traditions. It was a tumultuous era when the Israelites often battled the neighboring Philistines, a people who lived along the southwest coast of the Mediterranean Sea. In one of those fights, the ninety-eight-year-old priest Eli sat on a chair beside the Shiloh gate, awaiting news of the battle. He had been Israel's leader for forty years. He was now quite heavy and mostly blind. How could they lose? The embattled Israelites shouted with joy when the holy ark arrived in the camp. Yet, God's new prophet, Samuel, had affirmed a dire prophecy given years ago about the house of Eli and the fate of Israel. Alas, word came that the battle was lost. Eli's wicked sons were dead, and the ark was captured by the Philistines. In Ps 78:58–74 we also learn that the Shiloh tabernacle was destroyed and that many priests and soldiers died in the battle. Heartbroken, Eli fell of his chair and died on the spot.

The Philistines soon learned that harboring Israel's golden talisman was not the same as looting an idol. A dread disease which sounds a bit like black plague spread throughout the cities of Philistia. The statue of Dagon, their god, was found flat on the temple floor with hands and head cut off. After seven months, the Philistines packed the ark onto a new cart which would be pulled by two cows that had never been yoked. Inside the ark was an offering of golden tumors, one for each major Philistine city. What is more, the cows had recently calved. Their calves were penned up, yet the mothers took the cart back to Israelite territory with no resistance and no guide. The farmers of Beth Shemesh were harvesting wheat when they heard the lowing of the cows. Their hearts leaped at the sight. They called for Levites to take the ark off the cart and put it on a large rock. They chopped up the cart to make a fire so they could sacrifice the cows. The Philistines watched all of this from afar, affirming that the ark had indeed been the source of their plague.

Being an Israelite didn't make one immune to Yahweh's dislike of being disrespected. Some Israelites opened the ark and were infected with something as deadly as what hit the Philistines. Joy turned to fear, so the ark was moved to Baalah (it was Kireath Jearim when the story was written down), a town about twenty miles northeast of Beth Shemesh. It sat there for about twenty years in the house of Abinadab and his son Eleazar, apparently without incident, while the people mourned and fretted about the loss of their way of worship. Finally Samuel arose and called for a revival meeting at another town in the high country of central Israel called Mizpah. He told the people to give up their Baals and Ashtoreths, which they did. There in the field, with no ark or tabernacle, they poured out libations of water, fasted, and confessed their sins, and wept. And while they were turning back to Yahweh with their whole hearts, the Philistines attacked. As everyone cried out to God, Samuel quickly offered a lamb as a burnt offering. As if to show that obedience is better than tabernacle sacrifice, a fierce thunderstorm panicked the Philistines and encouraged the Israelites to chase them away.

Throughout Samuel's life, he was the chief leader of Israel, but his sons were corrupt judges who inflamed the people with their perversion of justice. The leaders demanded a king. Against Samuel's better judgment, he obeyed Yahweh and anointed Saul, a Benjamite. King Saul ruled all the people for about forty years, but he was not a whole-hearted monotheistic devotee of Yahweh, so Samuel anointed another handsome young man who took the Law seriously. David, the seventh son of an old man named Jesse, grew up watching his father's sheep. During that time, he became skilled on a stringed musical instrument and gained a true sense of God's presence and protection. He saw God's creative power in the white dusting of stars that flowed from horizon to horizon at night. He became a fit, confident young man who looked great on a horse. David and the jealous Saul played cat and mouse until a final battle when Saul and his two sons, the crown princes of Israel, were killed in battle with the Philistines.

An important event occurred during the tension between Saul and David that is pertinent to our theme of afterlife. Shortly before Saul's last battle, in which he and his two sons would lose their lives, Saul consulted the medium of En-Dor (1 Sam 28). She probably wasn't a full-blown witch. She conducted séances, which were forbidden by the Torah, and could call up the dead. Whether mediums are calling up actual deceased persons, are tricking people, or are being deceived by demons is a question for another study. Because the Law of Moses forbids consulting the dead, Saul had banished all spiritists from the land, so this woman, who treated Saul with great hospitality, feared for her life. At Saul's insistence, she called up the spirit of Samuel. The author of the narrative isn't interested in the issue of demons versus spirits. The spirit is Samuel. The literal Hebrew reads, "Elohim I saw, ascending out of the earth." The author did not mean God here. Elohim is translated various ways to blend with the context, so we see "gods," "a god," "spirits," "a spirit," "a ghostly figure," "a divine being," etc. Elohim is a word with several uses, but usually its intent is singular in spite of its plural construction.

The point in the story is that Samuel ascended out of the earth, out of *Sheol*, which is where everyone at the time, including the author, would expect him to be. He was not in the foreign nether world, the dusty hell where humans turn into demon bats. Furthermore, Samuel did not say, "Why did you wake me up?" We don't learn much about what *Sheol* was like in the story, but it wasn't our concept of "heaven." The other aspect of Samuel is that he appeared to be an old man and wore the cloak of a monk or holy man. Today when people see the ghost of loved ones, especially if that deceased person winds up in a blissful place, they appear young again, as if they were in the prime of their lives. Rather than pulling some inerrant doctrine out of this narrative, perhaps we should understand that the author is using the beliefs of the day to paint a vivid, creepy scenario.

David moved to Hebron in Judahite-Calebite territory. There he was crowned king of all Judah, ruling there for seven years. The rest of Israel was ruled by a son of King Saul named Ish-Bosheth. After more tension between the tribes, intrigue, murders, finger-pointing, and tragedy, David won the hearts of all Israel. The era of the United Monarchy continued with a strong, spiritual leader.

And the ark? It was still parked in the house of Abinadab, except after all these years, it would be Eleazar's house or even his son's house because many decades had passed. All that time there was no mention of the ark, nor any attempt to build another tabernacle. People brought their sacrifices to the ancient high places and their tithes to the designated levitical cities where there were storehouses to keep them all for distribution.

During the era of the Judges, when the people sought their Lord, he sent them deliverers to break the chains of foreign oppression. The lack of Mosaic tabernacle worship did not prevent Yahweh from hearing the hearts of his people. But now Israel had become an actual state with an army and a king. There would need to be taxes, a palace, court officials, a national budget, archives, ambassadors, perfumers, bakers, vine tenders, horse trainers, cattle keepers, shepherds, farmers, architects, and stone cutters to support the court, as well as the children and wives of the king. One group that had little to do was the priesthood.

King David settled into his brand new palace in the fortress of Zion, which he called the City of David. He had wives and children, all the goods that he could desire, and all the food and wine that he could consume. Neighboring kings came to congratulate him and draft treaties. But something really important was missing. No self-respecting nation could exist without a state religion.

The Ark Comes to Jerusalem

Once King David consolidated his rule over the twelve tribes and built his palace, his thoughts turned to the ark. When he announced the idea of bringing the ark to Jerusalem to his counselors, officials, military leaders, and clerics, enthusiasm rumbled through the assembly. Drawing from 2 Sam 6 and 1 Chr 13, I've added a few details from my own imagination and speculation to bring out the drama of the situation.

First of all, King David prepared an enclosed tent within the walls of the City of David. Then the administration invited "all Israel," from the border of Egypt to Lebo-Hamath, north of Damascus in Syria. There doesn't seem to have been restrictions as to who was allowed to attend. There were soldiers, scribes, mayors of cities, troubadours, historians, slave girls, farmers, felons and sinners, prostitutes, and various ethnic groups. It added up to tens of thousands of people, lining the roadway from Baalah to the gates of Jerusalem. Musicians brought every kind of instrument, so the procession marching outside the City of David toward Baalah was diverse and noisy. Pilgrims from far away crowded the region. Have you ever watched the Tour de France? The roads are line with screaming, shouting fans who blow horns and wave flags. I can imagine the smell of food preparation everywhere and the bleating of animals. People came to see history being made. They probably brought their children on their shoulders so they could tell their children about the day the ark came to Jerusalem.

Baalah/Kireath-Jearim is over ten miles from Jerusalem, so it probably took a good portion of the day to arrive at the house of Abinadab. Did they sojourn there for the night and start again the next day? Did thousands of people create ad hoc camps and fires for cooking, sleeping in any field they could find that wasn't planted with crops? Did they sing, play instruments, curse the crying children, shiver in the cold?

The next morning, it was time to place the ark on a small, brand new cart. The ark wasn't very big, only 4' x 2 ½' x 2 ½', so it fit easily in the little conveyance. After all, that is how it came from Philistia to Beth-Shemesh and then to Baalah. It was exposed, so all could see it. It was top-heavy, because the solid gold lid with its two cherubim was quite a bit heavier than the wooden chest overlaid with a gold leaf. The cattle were hitched up. The parade lined up, with different groups noisily jockeying for position. The road ahead was of course not paved as roads are today. There would be rocks and pot holes, so Ahio and Uzzah, the sons (grandsons?) of Abinadab accompanied the ark itself. Ahio walked in front and guided the cattle pulling the cart, while Uzzah walked beside the ark. David took the lead, and I assume that the musicians were behind him. Then I can imagine a large group of scribes following with their arms laden with scrolls. In those scrolls were the ancient records and writings that would later become the Torah, and the books of Joshua, Judges, and 1 Samuel. These records must have survived the holocaust at Shiloh when the Philistines burned the tabernacle there. Marching in the throng were priests, Levites, important officials, soldiers to protect the proceedings, then just anyone who could manage to tag along.

The noise must have been deafening. Not only David, but many paraders danced with all their might along the way. There were songs, harps, lyres, tambourines, cymbals, and trumpets. The Israelites hadn't danced like that since they cavorted around the golden calf in the wilderness, hundreds of years previous.

When they got to the threshing floor of Nacon, the oxen stumbled and the cart lurched, causing the ark to rock unsteadily. Uzzah reached out to steady it, but as soon as he did, he collapsed and died. The stunned procession came to a stop. I've read naturalistic explanations as to how this happened—mainly that Uzzah was electrocuted by natural physics. There is no need to seek a natural cause. There are several possibilities:

- Remember that in the Law, only Levites from the clan of Kohath may actually touch the ark. It was carried into battle on poles, and only the non-priestly Levites may bear up the poles (Num 7:9; 3:29–31).

- The religious leaders must have scooped up all the records of the past, including the four or five books of the Law, but they hadn't read them, so they were unaware of how to proceed.

- Those were severe times regarding religious rituals and procedures. In the wilderness, after the Israelites had bound themselves to the Law by covenant, a man was stoned for picking up sticks to make a fire.

- The ark had shown a spectacular talismanic power when a cloud of glory infused the tabernacle when it was first dedicated at Sinai. Not even Moses could touch it. It was Yahweh's throne. It's where His Name was called and where He spoke with the High Priest. It caused the parting of the waters when the Israelites needed to cross the Jordan and enter the Promised Land. It also knocked Dagan off his pillar and sent plague throughout Philistia. The men of Israel who lifted the lid and looked inside were also struck with plague. In order to maintain a proper continuity between past and future, The Law of Moses had to be taken seriously, and there had to be a dire consequence for an unqualified Israelite touching the ark.

- It's also possible that Uzzah walked beside the ark with wrong motives, wanting attention and fame. We can't say for sure. We can't fully explain it except that it happened and David had to deal with it.

Does God hate to be touched? At Mt. Sinai, Moses told the people that not even a donkey could touch the holy mountain or it would die. God's Presence was accompanied by thunder, wind, fire, and trumpets. However, in the New Testament, Jesus Christ, who claimed to be the very image of God the Father, did not mind at all that the disciple John leaned on his breast at meals. Once when Jesus was pushing his way through a crowd, a woman with an issue of blood, which made her unclean and untouchable, dove for the hem of his garment. He felt power go out of Him, but instead of killing her, the power healed her chronic condition. But Jesus came to usher in the era of Grace, bring to a close the era of the Law.

David was horrified. The music stopped. The priests and soldiers told everyone to go home. The ark was diverted to the home of a man named Obed-Edom for three months. During that time a whole new approach was organized. The scrolls were studied, revealing the requirement that the priests and specific families of the Levites play the prominent role in the new procession. This time, all was highly organized as to who did what, who carried the ark, who played instruments, who sang, and who offered the sacrifice as they got started on their way. David was dressed similarly to the priests and wore a linen ephod to emphasize the holiness of the process. In his wild dancing, he may have exposed some body parts that usually don't get seen, because his wife Michal made a sarcastic remark when he got home that seems to have affected her future in a negative way. She never produced a child.

The ark was settled into a tent that David had prepared before the first attempt to bring it into the city. It was protected by an enclosure with gates. This was not a formal temple, and it was not the Tabernacle of Moses. David had already learned the power of worship, prophecy, and music from his own life experiences, most of which had little to do with animal sacrifice. Saul's demons were suppressed somewhat by David's music as he strummed his lyre. Since he was anointed as a young man by a prophet, he was sustained throughout his dealings with Saul by his careful walk in obedience to God. Through it all he consistently turned to God in prayer and worship. However, the disaster of the first procession taught him that the ark and the Law of Moses are bound together like conjoined twins. David instituted animal sacrifices before the ark, and a contingent of Levites "to commemorate, to thank, and to praise the LORD God of Israel" (1 Chr 16:4).

The New Order of Worship

The rest of this narrative must be drawn from 1 Chronicles, because that is where the authors describe in great detail the new worship set up by David and his priestly court. In the old tabernacle of Moses, as well as in the temple at Shiloh, atonement depended solely on the rituals of sacrifice performed by the priests and Levites. The ark sat in a dark room, visited only once a year on the Day of Atonement. Animal blood was sprinkled on it by the High Priest. Although it was God's throne where he would meet with his people, if a prophetic word was needed, the enquirer went to the High Priest, who donned an ephod with a breastplate laden with twelve precious stones, each representing a tribe of Israel. On each shoulder was another stone. This was the Urim and Thummim by which God could be consulted by the king or some official. Somehow the answer would come through the ephod and not through a theophany involving the ark. Occasionally the ark was taken into battle, where its mere presence was seen as a guarantee of victory. It was not as if anyone who viewed it other than the High Priest would drop dead. Even in the days of King David, the ark was taken into battle.

At this point important new characters are introduced in the narrative—priests, musicians, song writers, and poets. They helped King David write the book of Psalms. Asaph, the chief over the Levites who ministered before the ark in the City of David, is credited with Psalms 73–79 and 81–83. The name Heman is found in relationship with Ps 88. Levites were appointed as prophets, petitioners, and gatekeepers. They were commanded to prophesy and give thanks (1 Chr 16:37–43).

While the ark remained in the City of David, Heman and Jeduthun (another whose name is found in the Psalm headings) ministered before a tabernacle on the high place at Gibeon. This is possibly the remains of the tabernacle that Moses built in the wilderness; on the other hand, those remains and all the furniture associated with it may have been burned or captured when the Philistines destroyed the Shiloh Temple. Most likely, David is co-opting a tabernacle that had been in this high place for many years. Zadok the priest, Heman, and Jeduthun supervised animal sacrifices day and night according to the Law of Moses. They all answered directly to David. Their relatives were musicians, gatekeepers, treasury guards, and judges (1 Chr 25:1–8; chapter 26).

There is no record of glory fire falling on either of the two facilities, but considering that the atonement sacrifices are separated from the ark, one should note that no fireballs of judgment fell, either. In fact, until David's egregious sin of murder and adultery with Bathsheba, David's reign was a time of revelation and blessing. Whether for blessing or for accusation, the prophets were ready with a vision or word from God. For instance, when David wanted to build a house for God (a temple), Nathan the prophet came with a word that God would build David a house (a royal dynasty). David would have a son who would build the future temple. Nathan uncovered David's sin with Bathsheba and prophesied the misery and rebellion that would follow.

David used to sit before the ark and pray. In the old Mosaic system, that would not have been possible. "Yet you are enthroned as the Holy One, you are the praise of Israel" (Ps 22:3). David, like the Apostle Paul, was able to make the transition from the outer ritual and material reality to the true essence of inner piety in Yahwistic monotheism. He learned this important lesson from his mentor Samuel:

> Does the LORD delight in burnt offerings and sacrifices
> as much as in obeying the voice of the LORD?
> To obey is better than sacrifice,
> and to heed is better than the fat of rams.
> For rebellion is like the sin of divination,
> and arrogance like the evil of idolatry. (1 Sam 15:22–23)

David understood that the future of his own dynasty depended on him internalizing that message, applying it to every associated attitude and action. His reign would usher in an array of miracles and revelations, not only through David, but through his circle of prophets and priests. The devotion and correct understanding of Yahweh's true intentions opened a portal of revelation regarding sacrifice, afterlife, and a Messianic Person who would appear in the future.

Redemption in the Davidic Era

The most remarkable theological innovation formulated by King David and his court of priests, prophets, and musicians was that ritual atonement involving animal sacrifice was subordinated to a loving relationship toward God and genuine inner virtue. This must have been a constant offense to conservative priests who could not make that leap in understanding.

The book of Leviticus describes the Mosaic sin and guilt offerings. All of the fat had to be burnt in offering to God, and the animal's blood had to be sprinkled on all sides of the altar. The officiating priest kept the meat and animal hide to provide for his family. This meat was considered to be especially holy, so it could only be eaten by the Aaronid priests or their immediate families, and that only in a holy place. If the priest didn't perform the ritual exactly, he could die. If he failed in some manner to be ritually clean, he could be executed for approaching God's holiness in a defiled state. Repentance was assumed, but not required. Most sacrificers would believe that the ritual itself covered any lapses on their part.

Any Israelite who ate the grain offering or the fat of cattle, sheep, or goats being offered to Yahweh would be "cut off from his people." What that cutting off implied is unclear. Since the wording didn't specify stoning or physical death, my best guess is that it referred to physical banishment.

An absolute requirement of the new Davidic outlook was gratitude for what God had already done for the Israelites. The "sacrifice" that God desired was represented in the thank offering of Lev 7. The thank offering came under the general category of fellowship offering. Along with the chosen animal were cakes with yeast and without, both of which would be given to the officiating priest. All of the fat must be burnt, and part of the animal is given to the officiator. The rest must be eaten by the one bringing the sacrifice that day or the next, so it was customary to gather friends and family and to use the opportunity to testify to God's goodness in the person's life. This is the offering promoted by the Davidic prophets:

> I have no need of a bull from your stall
> or of goats from your pens,
> for every animal of the forest is mine,
> and the cattle on a thousand hills.
> I know every bird in the mountains,
> and the creatures of the field are mine.
> If I were hungry I would not tell you,
> for the world is mine, and all that is in it.
> Do I eat the flesh of bulls
> or drink the blood of goats?
> Sacrifice thank offerings to God,
> fulfill your vows to the Most High,
> and call upon me in the day of trouble;
> I will deliver you, and you will honor me.
> . . . Consider this, you who forget God,
> or I will tear you to pieces, with none to rescue:
> he who sacrifices thank offerings honors me,
> and he prepares the way
> so that I may show him the salvation of God. (Ps 50:9–15; 22–23)

The Davidic way also demanded confession and repentance for sin, without which no animal sacrifice was sufficient. In fact, if all animal sacrifices were halted by circumstance, a proper attitude toward God, a humble walk, and goodness toward one's fellow man would result in perfect redemption and forgiveness. And what exactly did redemption entail? Blessing here on earth, safety, peace, and prosperity. But that was not all. Redemption included release from *Sheol* in the judgment. There would be no worms or dust for the redeemed! They would dwell in God's presence forever.

But David was not perfect. When he grew older and jaded with wealth and power, he committed an egregious transgression involving adultery and murder. The little babe, the fruit of his tryst with Bathsheba, grew ill and died, throwing David into a state of intercession and mourning. He fasted when the child was sick, and washed his face and ate after it died . . . the very opposite of tradition. David explained to his servants that the fasting was intercession rather than mourning. He was calling on God's mercy. But when the finality came, the intercession ended and the real mourning began. He said, "I will go to him, but he will not return to me." (2 Sam 12:23). There is no indication in the narrative of exactly where the child is, but David fully expects to join his child. There is no reincarnation in the tale, and no annihilation of the soul. Nor does David expect to go to a house of darkness and dust. David wrote one of his most compelling psalms of repentance as a result:

> Create in me a pure heart, O God,
> and renew a steadfast spirit within me.
> Do not cast me from your presence
> or take your Holy Spirit from me.
> Restore to me the joy of your salvation
> and grant me a willing spirit, to sustain me.
> ... You do not delight in sacrifice, or I would bring it;
> you do not take pleasure in burnt offerings.
> The sacrifices of God are a broken spirit;
> a broken and contrite heart, O God, you will not despise.
> (Ps 51:10–12; 16–17)

Nathan prophesied that because of David's sincere repentance, his sins were forgiven, but there would be earthly loss to pay for his transgression. So asleep or awake, the child is in a good place. It will not be left in *Sheol*, and neither will his father. As we shall see later, they shall both be "taken."

Psalm 40:6–10 also rejects Mosaic sacrifices and calls instead for public acknowledgment of one's love for God along with testimonial of his faithfulness and righteousness. Psalm 22, a powerful Messianic psalm that Christians believe look toward Christ's death on the cross (22:12–18; John 19:24), promotes a combination of thanksgiving, praise, feasting, and public testimonial (Ps 22:22, 25–26). Later prophets in Israel's history would repeat these sentiments: Isa 1:10–17; 66:1–3 (requiring righteousness and social justice); Amos 5:21–24 (calling for justice rather than sacrifice); Micah 6:6–8 (a call for humility, relationship with God, justice, and mercy). These prophetic statements could not be expressed in stronger terms. Yet, the lure of ritual was very powerful, and these subjective concepts never gained a lot of traction in Israel.

4

Who Were the Korahites?

The Patriarch Korah

UNDERSTANDING THE HISTORICAL CONTEXT will help to track the developing theology of immortality in Israel and to locate Ps 49 within a possible timeframe. This chapter is not meant to argue for or against the veracity of the history of the Korahite clan. The narrative itself is important because it contributes to the development of later theology and is woven into the understanding of life, death, redemption, and worship by the authors and editors of the Hebrew Bible. It also enriches the life of those who take it seriously enough to probe it for life lessons. It is a consistent story that spans the Hebrew Bible from the wilderness wanderings to the exilic Second Temple Reform, shaping their concept of God as well as liturgy

Both the ancestry of Korah and the location of his clan in Palestine are subject to dispute (nothing goes uncontested in theology), so it will help to step back a bit in Israel's history. In Gen 13 (1800s BCE), God promised the land of Canaan to Abraham's descendants. At the time, Abraham was a Syrian (also called Aramean) and came from a polytheistic family living "beyond the River," close to what is southern Turkey today (Deut 26:5; Josh 24:14). The Lord told him that they will be in Canaan and in Egypt 430 years,[1] and would be in Egypt for four generations (it works out to 215 years), but in the fourth generation, they would be led out. Abraham sired Isaac, Isaac sired Jacob, and Jacob had twelve sons, among whom are Levi, Joseph, Benjamin, and Judah. Jacob's name was changed to Israel, meaning "He Rules with God." Each of Jacob's sons became a clan or tribe. The family of seventy moved to Egypt during a famine, so the twelve sons were

---

1. According to the MT they were in Egypt 430 years, but according to the LXX, Gal 3:17, the Samaritan Pentateuch, Josephus (*Ant* 2.15.2), and Hippolytus, *Refutation*, 10.25, it was 215 years.

generation one of the promise. One of the sons, Joseph, was a vizier in Egypt at the time, and as long as Joseph was alive, the family prospered in the fertile region of the Nile Delta. During the 1400s BCE, the Asiatic slaves (the Hebrews, plus captives from Canaan, Phoenicia, and Syria) became so numerous that the Egyptians began to fear and persecute them. Then Moses led the Israelites and a restless multitude of other polytheistic Canaanites (Exod 12:38), along with much livestock and goods given to them by the Egyptian populace, into what today is called the Sinai Peninsula. Exodus 6:16–25 is where we first meet Korah, the ancestor of the psalmists.

Korah was the son of Izhar, the son of Kohath, the son of Levi, who is one of Jacob's twelve sons. Korah and those of his era were the key fourth generation from Abraham who were prophesied to be rescued from Egypt by Yahweh (Gen 15:16). According to the narrative, these Levitical Korahites (descendants of Levi) later settled all over Canaan. When Canaan became the nation of Israel under Kings Saul and David, Korahites could be found in the hill country of Ephraim, the northern reaches of Dan, the allotment to Judah, and the territory of the half tribe of Manasseh, which was their inheritance given by lot in the days of Joshua (Josh 21:5). They were not Judeans, and they did not inherit any part of Judah, because Levites became the priestly class and didn't inherit large portions of the country. Rather, they were settled in strategic cities. Portions of the Hebron region south of Jerusalem were set aside for any descendants of Levi who were priests (Josh 21:13).

The rebellion began peacefully and democratically in Num 16 when two hundred fifty men, all appointed by their various tribes to be a committee, came to the established leadership to request a change in procedure. They were angry that Moses had appointed only the tribe of Levi to act as priests and tabernacle attendants and only the descendants of his brother Aaron to be priests. They felt that corrupt nepotism was keeping their own children from having these sacred appointments and that a theological error was being propagated that would affect Israel's future. The accusations began to escalate. Moses charged the group with basely coveting the priesthood (Num 16:10) and of falsely accusing Aaron of the same ambition, when in fact it was Yahweh Himself who had set up the hierarchy. The plaintiffs in turn blamed Moses for their suffering and privation in the harsh wilderness. All of the miracles that rescued them from Egypt were disregarded. In their view, it was Moses who brought them out to the wilderness to die hungry, thirsty, and landless. Korah's accusation that Moses exalted himself and his own brother's family could have caused a civil disturbance that would change Israel's future. At this point, the narrator is clarifying that the motives of the assembly were purely vain and political and had nothing to do with the will of Yahweh.

Korah was a man who should have been content with his lot. He was respected, wealthy, and came from an important clan. He clearly had the capacity to muster a large assembly of leaders behind his cause, nor was he afraid to confront difficult issues. However, it is God who knows the true motive of hearts, and it is God alone who exalts and demotes (1 Chr 28:9). The fearless Korah, accompanied by his Reubenite companions, Dathan and Abiram, forgot to fear Yahweh, and thus used God's name and authority to support his own argument—an approach which never ends well in the HB. Moses summoned Dathan and Abiram, but they refused to come, repudiating Moses's leadership and committing the ultimate blasphemy of preferring Egypt as the real land "flowing with milk and honey." Anger and pride had trumped reason. The rebels expressed the same doubts as the twelve spies, accusing Moses of making a false promise to lead them to Canaan.

Moses challenged the men to meet him before the tabernacle the following morning for a trial by fire. All two hundred fifty arrived carrying censers (metal vessels filled with incense and flame). The leaders of the three clans and their supporters gathered beside their tents, as everyone else stepped away. Moses declared, "This is how you will know that the LORD has sent me to do all these things and that it was not my idea." The earth trembled and cracked open, swallowing tents, belongings, and people. The rest caught fire and burned up. Although not explicitly stated, the inference of the passage may be that the fire of the censers leaped out and consumed those who were not swallowed alive by the earth.

Moses declared that all the censers were holy, since they had been dedicated to Yahweh. The descendants of Aaron picked them up, and Moses had them beaten down into gold plating with which to cover the altar as a sign to the Israelites. The narrator has left an important message in the text—only the Aaronids (Aaron's descendants) may be priests. This was Yahweh's doing and not any man's idea. So Korah died that day, but apparently many of his children and kin had stepped aside.

New circumstances needed credible justification. Carefully recorded genealogies and an archive of strategic prophecies were critical for establishing a natural order of change with a minimum of conflict and jealousy.

Moses must have rolled over in his grave when one of his own grandsons, Jonathan, moved to the city of Dan early in the era of the Judges. He and his descendants, although not Aaronids, performed priestly duties there in the presence of two graven images until Israel was scattered by Assyria in 721 BCE (Judg 17–18). The author of the book of Judges crafts his account of the establishment of the city of Dan in such a way that the pious reader automatically disapproves of all aspects of the city: the illicit priesthood, the graven images, the brutish character of the Danites themselves, and the slaughter of the unsuspecting Canaanites living there when it was called Laish.[2]

As we have already seen, King David brought the Ark of the Covenant to Jerusalem. He set the ark in a tent in an enclosure with gates, guards, and some kind of altar. Although there are many references to the tent that David set up, it was also called a "house" on occasion. David set up three singing guilds, with representatives from the clans of the three sons of Levi. Heman represented the Kohathites, Asaph the clan of Gershonites, and Ethan the clan of Merari (1 Chr 6:31–47). As a very large company of these Levites prayed, sang, and played musical instruments, David offered one of his own compositions to launch the new era of offering—the offering of praise and thanksgiving before the Lord (1 Chr 16:4–36). The Spirit of God is said to have inspired the singers (1 Chr 25:1–3), and the leaders were considered to be prophets and seers.

Heman and Job

There is a particularly personal note regarding the Korahite worship leader Heman. Psalm 88 is a relentlessly dark, personal lament (although the author may be considered a representative of all Israel). Using a generous application of *Sheol* imagery, Heman complains of sufferings that seem to extend from his youth (verse 15). He is at death's door (verses 3–7). As with Job, his friends have all abandoned him (verses 8, 18), and he wonders if God has not done the same. Yahweh's terrors and wrath sweep over him, much like the waves and torrents of anguish washing over the author of Ps 42 (verses 7, 15–17), resulting in sharp questions about death and afterlife

---

2. For M. D. Goulder's extensive analysis of that narrative, see "Chapter 3: Priesthood." He dismisses the negative moral and spiritual assessment of the Judges narrative as Korahite propaganda. He also believes, with several other scholars, that Zadok was really a Jebusite and that his genealogy, like those of so many others, including King David, is pious fiction. See Rowley, "Zadok and Nehushtan," 113–41, especially 117 for a statement that in the older sources, Zadok seems to be without antecedents. Actually, Zadok's genealogy is located in several different passages. The confusion lies in the fact that there is evidently more than one Ahitub, one related to Eli and the other to Eleazar. Roy A. Rosenberg follows Rowley in "The God Sedeq," (1965). Confusion as to the proper identification of Ahitub begins on page 1 of Rowley's article and leads to bold assertions of error about the record throughout the article. Saul Olyan answers Rowley with "Zadok's Origins," 177–93, in which he places Zadok firmly in the Aaronid line. However, at the very end of his article, he, too, stumbles over the identity of the patriarch Korah (p 193, n 68).

that are also asked in the book of Job. The redemption passage in Job is antithetical to the death imagery in Ps 88:

> I know that my Redeemer lives,
> and that in the end, he will stand upon the earth.
> And after my skin has been destroyed,
> yet in my flesh I will see God;
> I myself will see him
> with my own eyes—I, and not another.
> How my heart yearns within me! (Job 19:25–27)

Although Heman is cast down, he is not defeated. As with Job, his time of trouble passes, and the Lord exalts him (Heb: "exalts his horn"). The horn is a linguistic term found in Hannah's song, 1 Sam 2:1, 10 and in several Davidic psalms. In the case of both good and evil, the horn signifies strength, endurance, and influence. Heman is given fourteen sons and three daughters (1 Chr 25:4–5), which is also reminiscent of Job, who began with seven sons and three daughters. All of Job's children were feasting in the house of the oldest brother when a wind storm blew in from the desert and collapsed the house. The *naarim,* the young men, were all killed, but at the end of the epic, the Lord restored to Job seven more sons and three more daughters, fourteen sons in all. The friends were required to sacrifice fourteen animals in reparation. If the book of Job were based on the life of any individual, no better candidate could be found than Heman. Some gifted and enlightened individual, who may have been an associate of Heman and David, wrote at least the first draft of the book to demonstrate in high literature that good people suffer and that a higher value should be placed on revelation and relationship with Yahweh than on ritual and sacrifice. Job's ritual sacrifices were not especially effective because they were not enlightening, but his repentance and acknowledgement of God's wisdom in the end put Job in a position to make priestly intercession for his friends. The theology of the author's era promoted the idea that only sinners suffer, whereas the pious are delivered from death and sickness, prosper financially, and are blessed with many descendants, (e.g., Deut 28). The note on Ps 88 in *The New Oxford Analytical Bible* makes an important connection between Ps 88, Job 19, and Psalms 42 and 43, and it's easy to see why. Heman is a good candidate for the author of Psalms 42 and 43. His illness and the reproach of his former friends, now accusing him of being a sinner, could account for the forced separation from the tabernacle and for the waves and torrents of trouble lamented in Ps 42.

Another famous Korahite pair was Heman's great-grandparents, Elkanah ben Jeroham (1 Sam 1:1; 1 Chr 6:33–34) and his wife Hannah. They were of the Levitical clan of Zuph, which was located in Ephraim since the time of the Judges. Any claims that they were of the tribe of Ephraim is a misunderstanding of the terminology.[3] Hannah lived toward the end of the era of the Judges. Her son Samuel was the last generation of that era. The temple at Shiloh housed many essential archives relating to Israel's history. The two tablets were still in the ark. The scrolls of the Torah were there, as well as the record of all the Judges. The serpent on a pole survived the destruction of the war with the Philistines and was still in the tabernacle. By then, Rahab, Hannah, and Ruth (characters from the books of Joshua, Judges, and Ruth) had joined Sarah, Leah, and Rachel (characters from the book of Genesis) as matriarchs of powerful generational houses. Hannah's connection to the Korahites may have helped her particular writing be included into the final rendition of the book of Samuel. Those records were also critical to preserving the genealogies of the guilds of singers and musicians.

Mitchell makes the interesting point that the Korahite Psalter is laden with *Sheol* imagery and language. This preoccupation may stem from the family tradition that their patriarch either was swallowed by the earth, in which case he and others fell alive into *Sheol,* or was burned alive with the remainder of the rebels. Korah's sons, however, did not follow their father or stand with him in the rebellion (Num 26:11). Their exaltation later in Israel's history is akin to being redeemed from *Sheol,* making redemption a family theme and a theological theme of the Korahite Psalter.[4]

The guilds of the singers and musicians were restored after the exile in Babylon. It is very clear that both men and women sang in the choirs and most likely marched and sang in the sacred processions (Judg 21:19–21; Ezra 3:65; Ps 68:11, 24–26).[5] The slender mention of women is likely an indication of male resistance to the acknowledgement of female contributions to anything sacred.[6]

---

3. In agreement with Mitchell, "God Will Redeem," 370, notes 17 and 19.

4. Ibid., 369.

5. The word "company" in verse 68:11 is in feminine form and is considered to be a company of women who often sang local history and tradition with songs and dances.

6. Some New Testament examples: in Heb 11, Barak is mentioned, but not Deborah; only John, writing the last Gospel, identifies the woman with the alabaster jar as Mary the sister of Lazarus (Matt 26:6–13; Mk 14:3–9; John 12:1–8). Paul, in 1 Tim 2, wishes all men to pray for kings and authorities, but wants women to dress modestly and not teach. In 1 Cor 11:5 the fact that a woman may pray and prophesy is contradicted by the command that a woman be silent in the church (14:34).

Structure of the Korahite Psalter

The group to which Ps 49 is connected is the collection of psalms having the Hebrew superscription "For the sons of Korah," called by scholars the Korahite Psalter (KP). The KP, in turn, is placed in the setting of Books II and III of the book of Psalms, which contains another overlapping grouping called the Elohistic Psalter (EP). Noting which section of the Psalms a particular work is in and the characteristics of the section helps the reader to be oriented to the mindset of the author. Thus each psalm may be compared to a room in a house. The house belongs in a neighborhood. If the room lacks definition, a study of the house and neighborhood may be enlightening, adding an additional dimension to our understanding.

Scholars have for some years recognized these macro and micro structures in the book of Psalms.[7] Psalms is divided into five smaller books: Book I, Psalms 1–41; Book II, Psalms 42–72; Book III, Psalms 73–89; Book IV, Psalms 90–106; Book V, Psalms 107–150. Doxologies, genre labels, wisdom topics, headings that refer to biblical characters, and declarations of thanks and praise help to frame the various books.[8] The final shape of the Psalter has a strong wisdom influence and was reshaped from the original writing to release the songs from their "historical moorings" and the "confines of the cult" so that they might speak to people living under very different circumstances.[9]

At another level, the largest collection within the Book of Psalms is the Elohistic Psalter (Psalms 42–83). The name Elohim is used predominantly to designate the deity in this set of psalms whereas the name Yahweh is used most often in all the others. Laura Joffe charts the use of the names of God in the EP and finds that this collection not only uses the name Elohim more times than the rest of the Psalter, but that the EP uses all varieties of the name of God to a greater extent that the remaining psalms.[10] In the several cases of parallel passages in both collections of psalms, Joffe concludes that

---

7. There are a number of psalms that never made it into the actual book of Psalms, but which were archived in other Psalters such as "The Book of the Wars of the Lord" or "The Book of Jasher." The Song of the Sea (Exod 15), Deborah's Song (Judg 5), Hannah's theological thanksgiving song (1 Sam 2), and the Oracles of Balaam (Num 23–24) are examples. Craigie, *Psalms, 1–50*, Ps 19:25–27.

8. Wilson, "Shape," 129–42. For an excellent literary history of such psalms studies, see Howard Jr., "Editorial Activity," 274–85. Several of the reviewed authors recommend that the final shape of the Psalter was more liturgical and was for a different context than the original work, and that we should be flexible in our designations of the purpose of the original psalm and of the editor's agenda.

9. Wilson, "Shape," 138.

10. Joffe, "Elohistic Psalter," 147, 150.

the Yahwistic version was the norm and the highly nuanced Elohim editing came after.[11]

Addressing the motive for the editing, Joffe sees a magic triangle between the number 42, the name of God, and disaster, blessing, or cursing.[12] The EP contains 42 psalms, beginning with Ps 42. The name of Yahweh is used 42 times in the EP. She cites an ancient practice of connecting the number 42 to the name or names of gods.[13] Besides various biblical samples of a link between the number 42 and disaster (such as the 42 children killed by a bear in 2 Kgs 2:24), Joffe makes reference to a Talmudic tradition of the 42-lettered name of God. The number was important in Jewish magic and Kabbalah. Joffe sees the purpose of combining the 42 psalms with the name of God as a way to turn the curse of the number into a blessing.[14] Joel Burnett adds references from Egyptian and Mesopotamian literature to 42 deities of judgment.[15]

Going down another level, there are the smaller collections of David, Asaph, Songs of Ascent, Hallelujah Psalms, and the Korahite collection. Most of the Korahite Psalter lies within the Elohistic Psalter. However, since Joffe considers Psalms 84–89 to be "the tail of the Elohistic Psalter," one could say that the entire KP lies within the EP. David Mitchell points out that "although the collection, including Psalms 86 and 89, is less than ten percent of the Psalter, it contains more than a third of the Psalms references to *Sheol*." The KP also has more than its share of references to the location of afterlife: grave, pit, *abaddon*, depths, and *rephaim* (shades).[16]

It was Michael Goulder who first realized the connection between the first set of Korah Psalms (42–49) and the second set (84–88, including 89, which is not listed as a KP psalm) in what he calls a close "tissue of relationships." Psalms 42 and 43 correlate to 84; 44 to 85; 46–48 to 87.[17] Psalms 42/43 are pilgrim songs expressing a desire to be in the presence of God as experienced in his tabernacles and courts. Psalms 44 and 85 are national laments. Both appeal for a release from wrath, but neither admits to any guilt. Yahweh is not accused of capriciousness, but he is appealed to as if he were a Canaanite god who had inexplicably broken out in wrath against his people and needed to be appeased by ritual practices

---

11. Ibid., 162, 165.
12. Joffe, "Answer," 223–35; and Burnett, "Forty-two Songs," 81–101.
13. Joffe, "Answer," 224.
14. Ibid., 229–30.
15. Burnett, "Forty-two Songs," 96.
16. Mitchell, "God Will Redeem," 376.
17. Goulder, *Psalms*, 10–12.

and priestly ministrations. Psalms 48 and 87 are Songs of Zion. In neither psalm is Jerusalem mentioned. Psalms 88 and 49 are filled with references to *Sheol,* but Ps 88 knows no relief from *Sheol's* grip, whereas Ps 49 has no lapse of confidence in redemption from *Sheol.* Goulder contends that one set is likely earlier than the other and that an attempt had been made to rework the original set, indicating the important cultic purpose of the final form of these psalms. Goulder made an important observation, that the correspondence between these two groups is unmistakable, and his interpretation as to cultic use well founded.

The crucial point of Peter Flint's article on the structure of the collections as evidenced by the Dead Sea Scrolls is that the first three books of the Psalter (Psalms 1–89) were canonized earlier and were much more stable over time than the last two books.[18] James Sanders proposed the "Qumran Psalms Hypothesis," arguing that Psalms 1–89 were in a fixed form when the Essenes left Jerusalem. The order of Psalms 90–150 was stabilized later.[19]

The above research, produced by scholars who focus on patterns and structures, demonstrates that the final redactors (editors) used books, titles, topics, and superscriptions to organize and locate the psalms in a meaningful way. A study of the patterns and relationships enriches our understanding of the purpose of the psalms and the historical and liturgical context for which they were written.

The Power of Inspired Worship

Ancient and modern historians agree that music seems to have developed at the dawn of civilization. Genesis mentions that Jubal is the father of all those who play the lyre and pipe (Gen 4:21); there is evidence of music and musicians as far back as 3000 BCE.[20] Music is well attested in Bronze Age Canaan and Ugarit. Depictions of musicians and musical instruments are found in ancient Near Eastern literature on pots and jugs, and painted on walls. Musicians were always found in the royal courts, and were sometimes listed as part of captured national treasures being transported from a conquered nation to that of the victor.[21]

In Israel, music had an additional function. It was often associated with a miraculous manifestation of divine presence, deliverance, or prophecy. When the waters closed over the Egyptian army in the

---

18. Flint, "Book of Psalms," 453–72.
19. Ibid., 459.
20. King and Stager, *Life in Biblical Israel,* 285; Braun, *Music.*
21. King and Stager, *Life in Biblical Israel,* 285.

wilderness, the women sang the Song of the Sea (Exod 15), "Horse and rider He has thrown into the sea." As they neared Canaan, the people were desperately thirsty, and the LORD commanded Moses to gather the people so he could give them water. The princes and nobles dug the well with the precious symbols of their authority (their scepters). Then Israel began to sing, "Spring up. O well!—sing to it!—the well that the leaders sank, that the nobles of the people dug with the scepter, with the staff," (Num 21:17–18). The passage does not draw a clear causative connection between the singing of the song and the bubbling up of the water, but such a connection seems justified. At the very least, there is a chronological connection between the two events and a suggestion that the people may have sung their way from Egypt to Canaan.

Second Chronicles 5–7 illustrates how important the connection was between the sacred song and the manifested presence of the LORD in Solomon's Temple. Kenneth Spawn contrasts the Chronicler's version of the story with that found in 1 Kings 8, in which music and singing by the priests, Levites, and congregation are not mentioned at all (2 Chr 5:11—13; 7:3, 6). The Chronicler has also added a second manifestation of the divine glory cloud and fire (7:1–3).[22] Asaph, Heman, and Jeduthun/Ethan led the Levitical singing. The narrative relates that when the music and the song of praise and thanksgiving to the Lord were raised, the glory cloud filled the house and the priests were not able to minister.

The connection between song and miracle arises in another of the Chronicler's narratives in 2 Chr 17–22, the story of the Judean king Jehoshaphat. Drawing on records from the Annals of Jehu son of Hanani (2 Chr 20:34),[23] the Chronicler paints a vivid picture of the reign of King Jehoshaphat of Judah and his restoration of Mosaic and Davidic worship. In chapter 20 we read that Judah was attacked by neighboring Moabites, Ammonites, and Edomites. Jehoshaphat prayed while the Kohathites and Korahites rose up to praise. The next morning the army marched forth with *singers* (not necessarily all Korahite nor all male) in the lead. "As they began to sing and praise, the Lord set ambushes against the men of Ammon, and Moab and Mount Seir (Edomites) who were invading Judah, and they were defeated" (verse 22).[24] One would have to be a very devout and confident singer to have the whole army at your back and the enemy in your face! The Israelites did not have to fight that day. The Chronicler describes the

---

22. Spawn, "Sacred Song."

23. As stated in 2 Chr 20:34, this is the same source used in 1 Kgs 22, a duplicate record of 2 Chr 22.

24. Goulder calls this Korahite propaganda.

thanksgiving celebration in the Valley of Beracah ("blessing") and in Jerusalem, in which the musicians, and undoubtedly the singers, participated. The very fact of placing a band of civilian singers in harm's way would support the contention that the "as" in verse 22 indicates a causative connection between the ambush set by the Lord and the singing. The Chronicler also describes the act of singing as "the splendor of his holiness" (2 Chr 20:21), infusing the performance with the might of the presence of God.

David's harp calmed the evil spirits tormenting Saul as well as the sheep he cared for. Music was also associated with prophetic ecstasy.[25] Davidic Israel took music to a new level. It would seem that the narratives present the singers and musicians as a significant factor in encouraging the manifest presence of Yahweh. Their contribution equaled that of the priests who offered the atoning sacrifices. This would make the clan of the Korahites not only influential, but mystical. Thus when the author of Ps 49 writes about being taken from *Sheol*, we may take his words literally rather than as a metaphor for a more mundane event. This was a community that believed in miracles. That is not to say that all biblical meaning is always literal, but the transcendent nature of the historical and ceremonial traditions of sacred music should remove modern narrowness in our own understanding.

Liturgical Use Versus Personal Lament

The form-critical scholarship of Hermann Gunkel (1862–1932) was the great divide in Psalm studies. He believed that all of the psalms were written for personal reasons but were adapted to, and connected to, the Temple ceremonies. This methodology is called "cult-functional" by his pupil, Sigmund Mowinckel (1884–1965), who went a step further in proposing that most psalms were composed for the ceremonies and were tied to an autumn harvest festival celebrating the new year, the return of the rainy season, and the yearly enthronement of Yahweh as king over the universe. References to Yahweh "coming" meant arriving anew (borne by Levites in the festal procession), and had little to do with end time issues. Psalms with a more personal outlook were associated with ritual appeals for healing from sickness.[26] Mowinckel also contended that, as in Canaanite and Mesopotamian rites, the king played a central part in the cultic ceremony.[27]

---

25. King and Stager, *Life in Biblical Israel*, 287. Also see their description of twelve- and ten-stringed harps as well as other musical instruments. For a detailed discussion of dance in worship in the Davidic narrative, see Wright, "Music and Dance," 201–25.

26. Mowinckel, *The Psalms*, 1.121; 2.1–15.

27. See also, "Psalm Criticism," 15, 17.

Mowinckel, like Goulder, writes with abundant detail concerning this yearly enthronement festival (the Feast of Tabernacles), but both scholars push their speculative theories into areas in which there is no substantiation. In 1974, Erhard Gerstenberger wrote a balanced analysis of the history of Psalms scholarship that was a corrective to some of the more speculative theories. He felt that more knowledge of Israel's feasts was needed before we could be certain of the exact nature of the relationship between psalm and ceremony. He called for a consideration of "empirical details" rather than hypotheses based on generalizations from known facts.[28] Gerstenberger used the term "ceremonialists" for those who insisted that all psalms were written for ceremonial purposes. Rather, he noted a "wandering of texts" much like what we find in hymnbooks today. Many hymns were written to express an individual's personal experience and faith, but they became expressions of the collective community because of the beauty of expression.[29]

It appears probable, then, that the KP was based on psalms written in the throes of crisis or celebration but were adapted for ceremonial use and were arranged as a ceremonial progression from distress to redemption. These psalms are rife with the language of pilgrimage. Although they may have been written by northerners, they advocate loyalty to Jerusalem. The one or two psalms that seem deeply personal may not actually belong to the KP. The personal hope expressed in Ps 49 was composed as an inspiration for all of Israel, north and south.

Relationship of the KP to King David and Mt. Zion in the Tenth Century

There are several references to Mt. Zion in Jerusalem in the KP and associated psalms (48:2, 12; 84:5, 7; 87:2, 5; 89). It was King David who captured Jerusalem from the Jebusites and who set aside Mt. Zion as the location of Solomon's Temple. At that time the mountain, which was not impressive as far as height, trees, or gushing water are concerned, joined a host of other sacred mountains that were believed to be the special abode of one god or another.

Some modern scholars doubt the historical accuracy of the narratives concerning King David. They suspect that his kingdom was smaller than is described in the Hebrew Bible. A few scholars today deny that David and Solomon existed at all. A full treatment of that controversy is beyond the scope of the present work. Nevertheless, one simple argument may be

28. Gerstenberger, "Chapter V: Psalms," 218.
29. Ibid., 199, 206.

offered in favor of their existence. No one denies that the First and Second Temples were a genuine part of the heart of Israel's history. The First Temple was built by a Judean king, but which one? Ancient Middle Eastern kings all wanted essentially the same things in life: to crush their enemies; to have a strong army with an abundance of chariots and the finest horses; to boast of a large harem full of princesses from foreign neighbors as a hedge against political betrayal; treasure rooms full of gold and silver, booty from war, or tribute from their neighboring kingdoms; a long, comfortable life; a male heir: a legacy of great buildings, tombs, and monumental public works by which to be remembered and admired; and to build a great temple to some deity. A temple on the scale of Solomon's could well have been the work of two kings—one to lay up the materials and the other to finish the construction. The king who built such a temple would be honored for centuries by his people and allegedly by his deity. It is doubtful that a ninth- or eighth-century BCE king would build the Temple in Jerusalem and allow his recorders and scribes to attribute his difficult and expensive project to a fictional pair of kings.[30] If David and Solomon were a late fiction, it is unlikely that such a dreaded sin as David's tryst with Bathsheba and the even more heinous murder of her husband would be a central part of the story. Nor would the clever writers have the wise and wealthy Solomon end his reign as a king who over-taxed his people, abused the slave labor, squandered the national treasury on a thousand women, and burned his children in the fire to abominable gods. The literature of the ancients reveals that they genuinely feared to lose the favor and presence of their patron deity. In their worldview, such neglect could lead to drought, war, famine, pestilence, poverty, and infertility of humans and animals. Why then, write so many moving psalms in praise of the deity, describing the life and sorrows of a fictional king? If the priests were afraid to offer a blemished lamb or goat upon the altar, what would the deity think of phony hymns written for political control and manipulation of the populace? The space and energy devoted to the existence of the united monarchy, the listing of the prophets and scribes who wrote the original records (e.g., 1 Chr 24:6), the mention of the name of the record (1 Chr 27:24; 29:26–30), and the inclusion of the minutiae of everyday facts and conversations all support the conclusion that the biblical record of this period generally finds its basis in reality.

David was a skilled musician who was dubbed the "sweet psalmist of Israel" (2 Sam 23:1). He arose from the shepherds' fields to be king of Israel. Given his background, he must have been a talented and charismatic

---

30. Sparks, *Ancient Texts*, 155–57 for literature from Mesopotamia regarding kings and temple buildings; see also Keel, *Symbolism*, 269–80 for king and temple building from the Egyptian perspective.

individual in order to win Israel's loyalty. Hannah's song of the divine overturning of circumstances in 1 Sam 2 was probably as much about Israel's and David's humble beginnings as it is about Hannah and her problems with her rival. His affinity for music would certainly be a motivation for him to organize music guilds and incorporate them into the national worship, especially since singers and dancers had always been a part of Mesopotamian, Egyptian, and Canaanite worship.

    David's exuberance and the passion of the priests and Levites that wrote the psalms should be a worthy model for our churches today. We would do well to emulate their joy, gratitude, sharing, ecstatic worship, and total trust in God. Those Levites were not rule-bound, judgmental bureaucrats. They were humans like us, with doubts and fears, illnesses, and debts, but in all of it, they were sustained by a new vision of eternity and their relationship to it.

5

A Pilgrimage through the Korahite Psalter

> "Oh, how small a portion of earth will hold us when we are dead, who ambitiously seek after the whole world while we are living!" Philip II of Macedon, king, father of Alexander the Great (382–336 BCE)[1]

SINCE PS 49 IS the focus of this study, it might seem that an attempt to place the entire Korahite Psalter in a historical and liturgical context would be unnecessary. Yet in the sense that Ps 49 is a part of an organic whole, understanding the historic and literary context will help us evaluate the mindset of the Korahite authors and perhaps locate them geographically. We can better appreciate their profound zeal for Zion, the Jerusalem Temple complex, and the joy and comfort they felt in their mediations. Many of us love our churches in exactly the same way, illustrating that although we are greatly separated in time, we are similar in spiritual practice.

Even before the monarchy split north and south after the reign of Solomon, there were idols in the northernmost city of Dan. When Solomon's son, Rehoboam, gathered counselors around him to decide how he would rule, the young men advised him to be harsh. The chief manager of Solomon's workmen warned him to be fair to the people and correct the abuses. Rehoboam listened to the rash young men, which sparked a rebellion that split the Israelites into two nations. The new northern nation, with its populist king, is called Israel, but is referred to as Jacob, Joseph, or Ephraim. The southern nation, where Solomon's Temple was situated, is referred to as Zion or Judah. The capital was Jerusalem, where Solomon's descendants carried on his dynasty.

---

1. http://www.cybernation.com/victory/quotations/subjects/quotes_deathanddying.html.

Psalm 42/43

Psalms 42 and 43 belong together. Shared language, topics, refrains, and the lack of a title in Ps 43 imply that originally the two psalms were one. The Septuagint title mentioning David suggests that post-Babylonian captivity Temple editors (sixth and fifth century BCE) associated the Korahite Psalter with the Davidic era.

Another key feature is the lament of the psalmist, who is describing a crisis in which a national enemy has caused so much upheaval that his usual ability to lead the processional and festal worship (verse 4) is temporarily interrupted.

> These things I remember as I pour out my soul:
> How I used to go with the multitude,
> with shouts of joy and thanksgiving
> among the festive throng. (Ps 42:4)

Psalm 42/43 cannot refer to the post-exilic situation or to the eighth century Assyrian invasion because the author believes that the current crisis will pass and normal life will once again prevail (42:11; 43:4). The psalmist may be the king,[2] a heretical Danite priest, or, more likely, a Korahite Levite, one of the Temple musicians (43:4), living somewhere in northern Israelite territory and longing for Zion in Jerusalem. The psalm reflects the custom in Exodus and Deuteronomy in which three times a year Israelite males were to make a pilgrimage to "appear before the face of God" with sacrificial offerings and tithes (Exod 23:17; Deut 31:11; Isa 1:12).

In the pre-monarchial era (reflected in the book of Judges), the pilgrimage would have been to Shiloh. During the united monarchy under Saul, David, and Solomon, with Shiloh having been destroyed, all Israel would stream towards Jerusalem (with the possible exception of those attached to Baal and Asherah in Dan and in other local sanctuaries still extant in the land). In the divided monarchy, people of the south would journey to Jerusalem or Bethel, and many in the north would make their way to Dan. One must realistically expect a plurality of practice in Palestine, so that no simple formula would perfectly describe all loyalties and beliefs. The monotheists (not all Yahwists were monotheists) of both north and south, however, and those loyal to Judah, the house of David, and the Jerusalem Temple, would have shunned the golden bulls of Bethel and Dan.

As with other Ancient Near Eastern feasts, Israel's festivals were associated with the seasonal progress of sowing and harvesting. Rather than being an inconvenience, these gatherings were a time of profound rejoicing,

---

2. Eaton, *Kingship*, 70; and *The Psalms*, 181.

reunion, story-telling, music, morning prayers, sacrificial offerings, confessions, reflection, songs in the night, dances, campfires, and intense worship. Marshmallows would have been so welcome.

For all three of the music guilds of the tenth century and later, the festal music, repentance, public thanksgiving, public testimonial of God's faithfulness, corporate confession, and ritual lamentation were the shortest path to drawing near to a living God. Whatever reward awaited the God-fearer here on earth and in the afterlife, this was in addition to the Mosaic path. Although one could pray or praise anywhere, the relational approach to holiness was pursued most vigorously on the sacred feast days.

For the priests, whether the Aaronid priests of Jerusalem (descendants of Moses's brother, Aaron), or the unorthodox Mosaic descendants ministering in Dan, sacrifice and purity rituals were the way to perfection and cleansing. However, even Ps 66, which promotes animal sacrifice (verses 13–15), includes a rehearsal of God's goodness to the singer individually and to Israel, with a public proclamation of joy and praise.

In Psalms 42/43 there is clear reference to northern topography. Many scholars have suggested that the entire KP is a northern work,

> Why are you cast down, O my soul?
> Why so disturbed within me?
> Put your hope in God, for I shall yet praise Him,
> my Savior and my God.
> My soul is cast down within me;
> therefore I will remember you
> from the land of Jordan, the heights of Hermon
> from Mount Mizar.
> Deep calls to deep in the roar of your waterfalls;
> all your waves and your breakers
> have swept over me. (Ps 42:5–7)

Mt. Hermon and the land of Jordan are just outside the northern border of Israel. Mt. Hermon is a little northeast of the city of Dan. One could say that the present day ruins of Dan are snagged on Hermon's hem. The streams that come rushing down its slopes water the city and feed the Sea of Galilee and the Jordan River.[3] The location of Mizar is unknown, but it may be the hill upon which the city of Dan stood.

Granted that the waters rushing off Mt. Hermon are referred to (verse 7), Michael Goulder is likely correct that the use of the term for "deep" (*tehom*) seems to refer to the fountains of the deep from which come the

---

3. As ably described by Goulder, Mitchell, and Rendsburg, *Linguistic Evidence*, 52.

earthly springs rather than the dangerous deeps of chaos.[4] The context is that the psalmist is comforting himself in his misery. The remembrance of the waves and billows may refer to an ecstatic experience as well as to troubles as in Ps 88:7 and 17. These are the waters that will nurture the land and fill the rivers and the Sea of Galilee, but they can also be dangerous in a time of flood. Similarly, being chosen by God can be an unmitigated blessing if Israel is obedient or a danger if God's wrath is provoked. To whom much is given, much is required. Taking that metaphor into the narrative of King David, we read that he was attacked by the Philistines as soon as he was anointed king over all Israel. He defeated them soundly, naming the place of victory Baal-Perazim because "As waters break out, the LORD has broken out against my enemies before me" (2 Sam 5:20). Yet later, that bursting forth worked against David when he tried to bring the ark into Jerusalem.

There are several layers of meaning juxtaposed in this verse. One level is suggestive of what the land needs in time of harvest, in the Fall when the rains begin and the wheat is being harvested and the rivers are at flood stage.[5] The abundance of waters may give the psalmist hope that God's blessing will endure and the land will see his goodness. At another level, the author may be referring to the metaphysical springs that emanate from the throne of God. The thirst is not literal since it is the *soul* that is thirsty for God's presence. That thirst is clearly related to *seeing* God (or the ark of his presence) in Zion, and is not something that is sated with a quick prayer at home. This author *thirsts* for God's presence at his tabernacle with a thirst that seems to threaten his very existence. Thus the priestly psalmist goes about mourning rather than rejoicing.

The case for a northern setting of the Korahite psalms does not rest solely on the topographical references. Expert linguist Gary Rendsburg has argued convincingly that there are constructions in several of these Korahite psalms that display northern characteristics which he calls Israelian Hebrew (IH).[6] He classifies the book of Job as northern, which fits well with the similarity between Ps 88 and Job. All of the KP is northern as well.

4. Goulder, *Psalms*, 28.

5. Israel first crossed the Jordan when Jericho's harvest was ripe for harvest and the river was swollen from rain (Josh 3:15). As soon as the Israelites began to appropriate the harvested grain of the land, the manna stopped.

6. Rendsburg, *Linguistic Evidence*, 54. One of his methodological approaches is to look for word parallels in Phoenician, Ugaritic, Syrian, and Moabite, as well as Amarna usage, since Israel shared borders and relationships with these nations or their heritage. He also looks for nouns with feminine plural endings where the context is clearly singular, 3msg verbs with a *t*-preformative, the *bal* negative particle, and the phrase for "mountains of." In the KP, the word for "tabernacle" is often in the plural, although it is translated as singular (Psalms 43:3; 49:12; 84:2; 87:2).

Goulder puts the authors in Samaria at the head of a procession going north. He believes that the Danite priesthood (descended from Moses or from just anyone who wanted to be a priest) was maligned in the Hebrew Bible by jealous Korahites, that the images set up by King Jeroboam I were not idols but were cherubim like in the Temple of Solomon, and that Dan was really the focus of all pilgrimage until the Assyrians destroyed it. There are three basic problems with that scenario:

1. The Chronicler's displeasure with everything associated with Dan suggests that the images depicted Baal or other Canaanite gods. It is unnecessary to assert that the narrative is twisted and that rival priesthoods are at stake rather than rival sanctuaries.

2. The Hebrew prophets railed against Dan and all the other towns that hosted sanctuaries in the First Temple era (i.e., Bethel, Shechem, Arad, Beersheba, and Gilgal), not only for their idols but for their arrogant, luxurious, and exploitative lifestyle.

3. The psalmist seems to already be in the north, which is *far* from where he wants to be. That his patrimony and diction are northern does not warrant major revision of the Psalter or suggest that his loyalty was to Dan rather than Zion. Levites lived all over Israel and Judah. The northern locale is another reason to suppose that the author is a Korahite rather than a king, such as David, because a Judahite king would be in Jerusalem and an Omride king would be south of Galilee in Samaria or Tirzah.

Psalm 43:4 speaks of the psalmist going "to the altar of God" with his harp to sing praises. This altar resided on a sacred hill or mountain on which stood a holy sanctuary. There were two altars in the Jerusalem Temple; the first was in the courtyard where animals were offered. That would be a smoky, foul-smelling, fly-ridden, bloody place to meditate upon God's faithfulness with a harp. The incense altar would have been unavailable to a Korahite because it was closest to the ark of the covenant in the holy of holies. Thus the psalmist may have lived in the Davidic era when the ark was available to a broader spectrum of worshippers. David's altar was available to king and musician alike (2 Sam 7:18). It was a late king, Josiah (640–609 BCE), who retired the ark permanently to the holy of holies (2 Chr 35:2–3). Until then, the Levites carried it in the presence of the people. Another possibility is that the author referred to the entire temple complex as God's altar, which would explain how the sparrow could find a place to build her nest there (Ps 84:3). To whichever court or enclave the Korahite had access in his era, being there with his harp was his greatest joy in life.

Psalm 44

Psalm 44 seems to reflect a similar theme, but the lament is now national. An enemy has attacked the people of God, killing many and selling others into slavery. The attackers may be a neighboring tribe or nation (verse 13); or the neighboring gentiles are taking advantage of a foreign attack and are buying the prisoners of war as slaves. These foes are not monotheists. The psalmist lays out his complaint before God:

> All this has happened to us,
> though we had not forgotten you
> or been false to your covenant.
> Our hearts had not turned back;
> our feet had not strayed from your path.
> But you crushed us and made us a haunt for jackals
> and covered us over with deep darkness.
> If we had forgotten the name of our God
> or spread out our hands to a foreign god,
> would not God have discovered it,
> since he knows the secrets of the heart?
> Yet for your sake we face death all day long;
> we are considered as sheep to be slaughtered. (Ps 44:17–22)

The psalmist does not describe an army broken beyond repair. He simply wants to understand why his people are defeated when God was formerly so strong on their behalf. His people have been "boasting" in God continually (verses 7–8), so this defeat is a stunning surprise. It may have been one of the first disastrous engagements of Judah's armies. Groups of men were executed like sheep in a pen waiting to be slaughtered. Others were sold into slavery for a cheap price (verses 11–12). As a result, the enemy, which is finally triumphant, mocks Israel and its God.

There are some linguistic connections between Psalms 42/43 and 44. In Ps 43:3 the singer wants "light" and "truth," two metaphoric graces, like guiding angels, to lead him to God's altar. The author of Ps 44 develops a play on the concepts of light/darkness, sleep/death, and arousal/redemption themes that will be echoed throughout the KP and in Ps 49.

> But you crushed us and made us a haunt for jackals
> and covered us over with *deep darkness*.
> . . . *Awake*, O Lord! Why do you *sleep*?
> *Rouse* yourself! Do not reject us forever,
> Why do you hide your face
> and forget the misery of our oppression?
> We are brought *down* to the dust;

our bodies cling to the ground.
Rise up and help us;
Redeem us because of your unfailing love. (Ps 44:19, 23–26)

In both psalms, light serves as a metaphor for God's favor, his presence, and redemption. There is no purpose in seeking his face through pilgrimage if his face is turned away. The result is metaphysical darkness and death. But God will not slumber forever. The defeat is a pause, a test of some sort. The psalmist is confident that God will show himself mighty once again.

Psalm 45

The next four psalms in the Korahite Psalter relate to a time when the psalmists could celebrate good times—a popular king, a secure city, and a strong sense of God's protection and control. The author of Ps 45, considering himself both skilled and inspired (verse 1), writes a wedding song which is addressed to the king. Rendsburg naturally points out several linguistic idiosyncrasies which peg the song as a northern sonnet, including Aramaisms and Phoenician grammatical constructions. The identity of the king is unknown.

The mention of Tyre (a northern coastal city in what is today Lebanon) is not much of a clue because David, Solomon, and later Judean kings had treaties with Tyre, but most Christian readers assume that the psalm refers to King Solomon, and may even intimate a Messianic figure. John Eaton believes that the psalm is Davidic. Goulder would say it flatters a northern Israelite king, perhaps even Ahab and Jezebel.[7] Others say it is an idealized king, too perfect to be real. Of course, on such a festive occasion, the scribe would undoubtedly paint an ideal picture to please any king, whoever he was, or he might find his head in a basket. The king is described as a graceful speech maker, handsome, majestic in his military gear, parading on his horse, just in all his judgments, and victorious in his battles, and therefore blessed by God (verses 2–5). His dynasty will endure a long time. Because of his righteous and just nature, God adds to the anointing oil poured upon him from the priest, which is meant to imbue him with God's authority. God anoints him with gladness above the usual joy of other kings and officials.

The people cheer and admire the king of Ps 45 as he processes through the city. Like King David and every other ANE monarch, this king has

---

7. Goulder, *Psalms*, 130. He makes the interesting point that it seemed important that both Adonijah and Solomon were anointed beside a stream (p 128). That may have implications in Ps 110:7 where the king drinks of the brook by the way and therefore lifts up the head.

several royal foreign wives who are but pawns in the treaty-making process of the ancient world. The new bride seems to come from Tyre, because once she is anointed and wed, she will be in a position to petition the king for favors for the wealthy citizens of Tyre. She may not be excessively important to the king, but she will now be a political player among the wealthy denizens of her home city.

Only three verses are addressed to the princess. Bowing to her new husband as her lord, she must forget her people and her father's house (but not necessarily her gods) and accept her new position in the royal household. She will live a privileged life and wear the best garments. She will receive lavish gifts from her petitioners.

She smiles at the people, foreign to her, as her procession of servants, soldiers, handmaids, musicians, and priests move through the streets to the king's palace. She is gloriously attired and coifed. She passes ivory houses with the music of lyres wafting into the concourse. There is undoubtedly feasting and rejoicing amongst her well-wishers. At that point in the psalm, the scribe crafts a blessing for the king's dynasty as a prophecy from the Lord. Instead of ancestors, he will have sons, and they will be princes in the earth. God will cause the king to be renowned and praised throughout all generations.

Depending upon the circumstances, such effusive flattery of a monarch can have a dark side. If the psalm is read as eschatological (referring to end times) or messianic (or just a blessing), it can be spiritually moving. There is enough temporal detail in the psalm, however, to make a messianic application problematic. Ironically, particularly if the psalm is written for a real northern king, all of whom were considered to be sinners by the Bible authors, the people described in the psalm are those that the author of Ps 49 and the prophets inveighed against (Amos 3:15). They would be those who trust in idols, who live carelessly and luxuriously, and who exploit the poor.

On the other hand, the king described may be an ideal. The psalm may have been written and sung as a challenge for the monarch to live up to. Or perhaps it described a young Judahite king who was genuinely admired like David, Solomon, or Asa—handsome, intelligent, still idealistic, spiritual, and on good terms with priest, scribe, and *Elohim*.

Psalm 46

A perfect king needs a secure city, and Ps 46 provides such a scenario. The city is unnamed, but it could be none other than Jerusalem, the holy city where God dwells. The progression from Ps 45 to Ps 46 strongly intimates that a Judean king is referred to in Ps 45:

> God is our refuge and strength,
> an ever-present help in trouble.
> Therefore we will not fear, though
> the earth give way and the mountains
> fall into the heart of the sea,
> though its waters roar and foam and
> the mountains quake with their surging. *Selah.* (Ps 46:1–3)

The whole land is in distress. A huge earthquake has the waves of the sea foaming and the islands skipping; mountains are trembling and sliding, rocks are falling, and all is changing. Zion, however, is serene with a secure water supply that nurtures rather than destroys:

> There is a river whose streams make glad the city of God:
> the holy place where the Most High dwells.
> [Heb: the Holy Place of the tabernacles of Elyon]
> God [Elohim] is within her, she will not fall;
> God will help her at the break of day. (Ps 46:4–5)

Those in favor of a northern usage of the psalm point to the abundance of water at Dan and the paucity of it in Zion, but the mystic author is not imagining real water (or, if he is doing so, it is only at a lower level of meaning). The phrase "when the morning dawns" alerts the reader that this metaphysical city is calm and unshakable only because God is enthroned in the midst and from his throne issue waters that quench spiritual thirst. Dawn is symbolic of Elohim rousing himself to deliver his beloved.

Closely related to Ps 46 is Ps 78, a historic review of the rejection of the house of Joseph and the sanctuary at Shiloh. God has transferred his glory and presence to Zion and to David of the house of Judah.

> He abandoned the tabernacle of Shiloh,
> the tent he had set up among men.
> He sent the ark of his might into captivity,
> his splendor into the hands of the enemy.
> ... Then he rejected the tents of Joseph,
> he did not choose the tribe of Ephraim;
> but he chose the tribe of Judah,
> Mount Zion, which he loved.
> He built his sanctuary like the heights,
> like the earth that he established forever. (Ps 78:60–61; 67–69)

Zion then becomes a microcosm of the cosmos, and in that sense more beautiful and exalted than any earthly mountain because it is the source of redemption for the wounded planet and for fallen mankind. In that sense one could cast it as a contrast to the Garden of Eden, because Zion is the way back to inheritance, tranquility, and safety.

In Ps 46:6–7, the nations are all in the same turmoil as the physical earth. Kingdoms totter and reel, while God is a refuge for Jacob.[8] The earth is a burnt out waste, but the wars have ceased because Yahweh has put an end to them, burning the shields and breaking the bows and arrows. Through it all, Israel is tranquil:

> Be still, and know that I am God;
> I will be exalted among the nations,
> I will be exalted in the earth. (Ps 46:10)

Psalm 47

The safe and tranquil city needs a holy and mighty God enthroned in its midst. The festive celebrations described in Ps 47 are as usual noisy and raucous. God's name is Elohim in verse 1, and in verse 2, Yahweh/Elyon is proclaimed as king over all the earth, assuring the worshipers that all three names apply to the one deity. This psalm suggests to some scholars that Yahweh was ritually enthroned and proclaimed yearly at the appropriate festival, usually the Feast of Tabernacles, as a dominate king. However, there is no direct evidence to support that the Israelites were celebrating an annual ritual enthronement of Yahweh as opposed to a mere acknowledgement of the fact that he *de facto* sits enthroned by virtue of his power and authority. In Ps 33:13–15, Yahweh sits enthroned in the *heavens* and looks *down* on all the works of men that he fashioned. In the blessing of Ps 20, his aid is mediated through the temple in Zion. How then could he be repeatedly enthroned by men? If he is eternal and immortal, humans could only celebrate who and what he is already.

In Ps 47 God goes up with a shout and the sound of a trumpet, answering to Ps 44:26 where the psalmist pleads with Yahweh to rise up and redeem his people. The people are shouting, singing "Praise! Praise!" joyously, and clapping their hands. God's presence is being celebrated for another year at

---

8. Campbell, "Psalm 78," 61, 75. He views Ps 78, which seems to have an affinity with Ps 46, as a unity (a psalm written entirely at one time by one author), a tenth century "theological interpretation of history" pertaining to the rise and rule of King David and the transfer of sanctity from Shiloh to Zion.

the Feast of Tabernacles. With the noise, the trumpet sound, and Yahweh going up, it seems more like a day of judgment than God being aroused to rescue Israel.[9] There may even be a double entendre in verses 3 and 4:

> He subdued nations under us,
> peoples under our feet,
> He chose our heritage for us,
> the pride of Jacob, whom he loved. (Ps 47:3–4)

In light of the *Sheol* language in the Korahite Psalter and Psalms 49 and 88, "the nations under our feet" could be a subtle suggestion that God had subdued the terrifying forces of the nether world.

The secular and ecclesiastical aspect of the psalm is seen in 47:9:

> The nobles of the nations assemble
> as the people of the God of Abraham,
> for the kings of the earth belong to God;
> he is greatly exalted.

The Masoretic Text actually reads, "The princes of the people gather, the people of the God of Abraham." The verse depicts the princes and officials belonging to nations that acknowledge the rule of Yahweh and his king David or Solomon. Each year at a certain time, possibly during the harvest feast, foreign officials brought the tithe and tribute to the Judean monarch. In that double sense, Yahweh is literally the king over the earth. The Hebrew hints at the possibility that those who submit to Yahweh and his king in faith may be adopted into the family of Abraham. In the Davidic era, there were many foreigners in Israel. David's own armor bearer was a Hittite. He had a Philistine guard and treaties with kings from Moab to Tyre. The peace in the latter years of David's reign was attributed to Yahweh who was seen to own (rule) all the "shields"/kings of the earth. It was a heady time for Israel.

Psalm 48

Whereas Ps 47 is about the eternal king, Ps 48 is about his holy mount:

> Great is the Lord, and most worthy of praise,
> in the city of our God, his holy mountain.
> It is beautiful in its loftiness,
> the joy of all the earth.
> Like the utmost heights of Zaphon is Mount Zion,

---

9. For literary connections between noise, arising, and judgment see Pss 96:11–13; 97:1–9; 98:5–9; 102:12–13.

the city of the Great King.
God is in her citadels;
he has shown himself to be her fortress. (Ps 48:1–3)

The phrase "far north," "sides of the north," or more correctly, "far reaches of the north" (*yarketay zaphon*) has caused much speculation. Since Isa 14:13 is the other place in Scripture where the same Hebrew phrase is used, a comparison is usually made,

> How you have fallen from heaven,
> O morning star [Heb: Hellel, or Shining One], son of dawn!
> You have been cast down to the earth,
> you who once laid low the nations!
> You said in your heart, "I will ascend to heaven;
> I will raise my throne above the stars of God [El];
> I will sit enthroned on the mount of assembly,
> on the utmost heights [lit.: far reaches *yarketay zaphon*] of Zaphon.
> I will ascend above the tops of the clouds;
> I will make myself like the Most High [Elyon]." (Isa 14:12–14)

Mt. Zaphon was made famous in Ugaritic mythology, in which the mountain was the place where the god Baal built his palace. There is considerable debate concerning Zaphon's actual location,[10] but it was considerably farther north than Dan or Mt. Hermon. The Canaanite El, often called "Bull El" in Ugaritic lore, was the father of the gods and head of the pantheon. He was an amenable old deity who ate and drank to excess, mourned his son's death by mutilating himself, frolicked with his wives, and said yes to just about every request brought to him, no matter how silly. Hellel appears in the Baal myth as a minor god who occupies Baal's throne for a short while, but the throne is too large and the responsibility too great.[11] Elyon, whose sanctuary was in Jerusalem in the book of Genesis, is the deity to whom Abraham tithed. Isaiah is mocking the kings of the earth who think they are divine.

No one in Palestine would have equated Mt. Zion, which was not the highest or wettest mountain in the Levant, with Zaphon. However, there were several clear biblical attempts to use Canaanite iconography to displace Baal with Yahweh. Psalm 29 is a prominent example. Baal was the storm god who was called "Rider on the Clouds," who thundered with his voice, and brought the rain that nourished the land. Psalm 29 begins,

---

10. For a good example, see Day, *Gods and Goddesses*, 107–16. He points out that there are a number of places in the Hebrew Bible in which Zaphon signifies the firmament.

11. Ibid., 166–71.

> Ascribe to the Lord, O mighty ones [Heb: sons of Elohim],
> ascribe to the Lord glory and strength.
> Ascribe to the Lord the glory due his name;
> worship the Lord in the splendor of his holiness.
> The voice of the Lord is over the waters;
> the God of glory thunders,
> the Lord thunders over mighty waters. (Ps 29:1–3)

Thus, the temporal grace, sanctity, and beauty of Mt. Zaphon is appropriated by Zion in Ps 48. The era represented in the psalm is one of stability and dignity for Judah, when the kings of the earth were seen to tremble at what Yahweh had done for Israel. The season is probably the Feast of Tabernacles.

If there is any question in the mind of the Judean pilgrim as to which city is God's chosen, Psalms 132 and 48 allay all doubts. The author lingers with love over the description of the city and its suburbs—temple, towns of Judah, towers, ramparts, and citadels, and in the midst of it all, God's presence. "Count the towers," he says to a people who once had no state of their own, and tell the next generation what Yahweh has done for us.

Psalm 49

Psalm 49 will be dealt with in detail in the next chapter. It does not mention ritual, sacrifice, location, or nationality. It is the ultimate redemption and the end of all religion. When the enemy invades, when the city walls are breached, when the Temple burns, when the people are dragged away by brutal enemies, when the fields languish, when drought dries up the springs, when all the friends and family have passed into eternity, when one can only hope to be decently buried in a foreign land—there is the "taking" of Ps 49. It is the one thing that the wicked cannot steal from the righteous poor. The king cannot breach the gates of redemption with his armies. The righteous need not fear that they will lose their way in the fog of eternity, that they will lack the necessary magic charms, that they will be wanting for the needed sustenance for the journey, that they will have to flee the curses of the wicked, or that Death will grasp their heel and pull them back. Yahweh is the Taker. When the pilgrimages are no more, the righteous die in peace and confidence.

Psalm 84

The connection between Ps 42/43 and Ps 84 is not difficult to discern. The author of Ps 84 also yearns for the courts of the LORD. Psalm 84 is clearly a liturgical pilgrim song. Linguistic connections between the two psalms include the phrases "the living God," "to see the face of God," and "your tabernacles."[12] In Ps 84, Yahweh's courts and altars are so lovely that even the little birds love to nest there. No bird would nest on the fiery altar of sacrifice, so the altars specified in the psalm may not be well attested in biblical lore.

To a Canaanite, the Hebrew phrase "the God of gods will be seen in Zion" (Ps 84:7 NRSV and Heb.) would refer to an idol. For an Israelite, the phrase may have referred to a theophany such as falling fire or it may have been the only means of expressing the state of being in God's presence. Throughout most of the year, Babylonian, Akkadian, Hittite, Ugaritic, and Canaanite idols lurked in the dark recesses of their temples, inaccessible to the average worshiper. The images needed to eat, sleep, be dressed, and be dusted by temple personnel, as well as be protected from capture by a foreign enemy. If the idol was dragged off by a hostile force to another city, the people were devastated, fearing that they had lost the aid and favor of the god. It was a great comfort to them to see the image in procession during the sacred feasts.[13] Israel was unique in being the only nation in the Ancient Near East which had no anthropomorphic image to parade around the city. They did, however, have the Ark of the Covenant. During the era of the Judges, the reign of Saul, and the reign of David, the ark was taken into battle as a talisman (1 Sam 4:5; 2 Sam 11:11). David used to sit before it and pray (1 Chr 17:16). It was only in the later reign of King Josiah that the ark was retired permanently to the Holy of Holies (2 Chr 35:3).[14] One might safely speculate that during the sacred feast days, or at least once a year, the ark was carried in procession by the Levites to the cheers and admiration of the people. This may also help to explain the concept of appearing before

---

12. Goulder, *Psalms*, 3, does an excellent linguistic study on the connection of all the Korah psalms.

13. Keel, *Symbolism*, 323.

14. It is interesting that during Josiah's reign the prophet Jeremiah prophesied that the ark would disappear, not be re-built, and would not be missed. Jeremiah was preparing the people for the New Covenant to come and for a day soon to arrive when the temple would no longer exist. Perhaps Josiah, a firm believer in the prophets, was co-operating with that vision when he retired the ark (Jer 3:16; 30:27–34; 31:31; 33:10–11; 15–16). During the Second Temple period when the sanctuary was sacked by Greek and Roman armies, the sanctuary furniture was rebuilt and restored several times, but the ark was not restored.

the face (or presence) of God and the assertion that "the God of gods will be seen (or possibly appear) in Zion."[15]

If the rains came during pilgrimage, there would be thanksgiving for the accumulation of pools and springs of water. If the rains had not yet begun, there might be intercession on the part of the travelers. In verses 8 and 9 the priest prays for the king, who is referred to as "our shield" here and in Ps 89:18. The psalm ends in a flourish of confidence and steadfast devotion to the sacramental space, which may have been the Temple courts on Mt. Moriah or the tent enclosure set up by David in the City of David which was located in the original fortress of Zion that King David had wrested from the Jebusites. They both held the precious ark, Yahweh's throne on earth.

> Better is one day in your courts
> than a thousand elsewhere;
> I would rather be a doorkeeper in the house of my God
> than dwell in the tents of the wicked.
> For the Lord God is a sun and shield;
> the LORD bestows favor and honor;
> no good thing does he withhold
> from those whose walk is blameless. (Ps 84:10–11)

The Korahites were gatekeepers and bakers in Jerusalem as well as singers. They were indispensable to the functioning of the temple services year round. In the final edition of the poem, the tents of wickedness may have been the illicit sanctuaries of Dan and Bethel.

Psalm 85

Psalm 85 is associated with the national festivals because it seems to be an expression of ritual and national repentance and intercession intended to ensure successful harvests and the fertility of the land:

> You showed favor to your land, O LORD;
> you restored the fortunes of Jacob.
> You forgave the iniquity of your people
> and covered all their sins.
> You set aside all your wrath
> and turned from your fierce anger.
> Restore us again, O God our Savior,
> and put away your displeasure toward us.
> Will you be angry with us forever? (Ps 85:1–5)

---

15. In agreement with Eaton, *Psalms*, 180.

Goulder makes a worthy point that there is a connection between Ps 44 and Ps 85. Both are national lamentation and both plead for restoration. As with Ps 44, Ps 85 acknowledges no wrongdoing, but appeals to God's mercy and to the covenant relationship of the past. The psalmist listens for an oracle to present to the king and the people, just as any priest might do during a major feast day. Verses 10–13 may actually be the oracle received, a word of encouragement and hope that would make the celebrants glad of heart:

> Love and faithfulness meet together;
> righteousness and peace kiss each other.
> Faithfulness springs forth from the earth,
> and righteousness looks down from heaven.
> The Lord will indeed give what is good,
> and our land will yield its harvest.
> Righteousness goes before him
> and prepares the way for his steps. (Ps 85:10–13)

Pointing to Ugaritic myths in which minor deities accompany Baal, Goulder sees love, faithfulness, righteousness, and peace as four semi-divine, angelic beings that accompany the ark during the procession of the feast, but to make such an assertion is to seriously underestimate the Hebrew penchant for abstraction and poetic allusion. These graces are first and foremost aspects of God's nature. Faithfulness will spring from the ground due to God's blessing of the ground. Righteous will come down in the form of rain. The result will be that the land will yield its increase and the people will receive what is good, meaning produce and sustenance. There may be an allusion to a blending of the graces in a metaphoric way with the result of an abundant harvest, fertility in the flocks, and provision of everything needed during the year. The most important endowment of the year will be peace (verse 8), but the gift is primarily to those with repentant hearts.

Pilgrimage itself may not be enough to ensure Yahweh's full blessing. The person in whose heart are the roads to Zion—the person who serves Yahweh all year long—will receive all the benefits of the gifts and graces.

Psalm 87

It is interesting that in the Korahite Psalter, the names Israel and Jerusalem were never used. The courts, or altars, and mountains of the LORD are mentioned in plural form in the construct state without specifying which of several sanctuaries are signified (43:3; 84:1, 3, 10; 87:1). The name Jacob, the Patriarch of the twelve tribes, refers to the whole of Israel (44:4; 46:7, 11; 47:4; 85:1). Judah is mentioned once (48:11), and the troublers and enemies are not specified (44:16). The king in Ps 45 is anonymous. The river that makes glad the city of God is nameless. The nature of redemption from *Sheol* is often metaphorical and fuzzy (44:26; 88:3). Zion is the one focal point that seems to be the very heart of the KP, and that is only mentioned in three psalms (48:2; 84:5, 7; 87:2, 5). If there is any passage in the KP that expresses the core of its purpose and presuppositions it is 87:2, "The Lord loves the gates of Zion more than all the dwellings of Jacob."

The word for "dwellings" above is the word used for "tabernacle" or "sanctuary," indicating northern Israelaen Hebrew (IH) when used in a plural construct form where a singular translation is appropriate. So one might retranslate the second half of the verse to read, ". . . more than the sanctuary of Jacob," meaning the sanctuary at Dan or Bethel. Bethel would be the better candidate since that is where Jacob their ancestor had his famous dream of seeing Yahweh at the top of a stairway or ladder. It was at Bethel that he set up a memorial and received his legacy from God. As stated aptly by Marvin Tate, it does not matter if the psalm was originally written for a northern sanctuary or not, because we have it now as hailing Zion in Jerusalem and that must not be dismissed.[16] The originators of the ancient biblical records all painted a picture of the Korahites serving under the orthodox priests and under Zadok the High Priest.

This is not the Zion into which only the pious Jew may traverse. This cosmopolitan city reflects the diverse nature of the United Monarchy in which Philistines, Tyrians, Egyptians, Babylonians, and Hittites milled around the sacred courts next to Benjamites, Judahites, and Simeonites. Phoenicians had a great deal to do with the building of the Temple. The psalmist invites the strangers who have joined themselves by covenant to the LORD to count themselves as having been born there. It is God himself who registers them in His book as having sacred citizenship,

> I will record Rahab [Egypt] and Babylon
> among those who acknowledge me—
> Philistia too, and Tyre, along with Cush [Ethiopia]—
> and will say, "This one was born in Zion."
> Indeed, of Zion it will be said,
> "This one and that one were born in her,"
> and the Most High himself will establish her,
> The Lord will write in the register the peoples:
> "This one was born in Zion." (Ps 87:4–6)

---

16. Tate, *Psalms*, 388.

This multi-national register reflects a model for the future expectation that all nations would eventually come and bow before Yahweh, bringing their riches as they acknowledge his glory (Isa 56:3–8). The transcendent nature of this Zion may be hinted at in the final verse,

> As they make music they will sing, "All my springs are in you."
> (Ps 87:7)

Not just the Korahites but all of the musicians are shown to be unimpressed with the heights of Zaphon or the abundance of water north of Dan. Their springs are "in Yahweh." All the foaming floods and billows of the north are irrelevant compared to the light of God's countenance (lit.: his "face").

Psalm 88, 49, and the Book of Job[17]

Psalm 88 is famous for its *Sheol* language, which permeates the entire psalm. It asks questions which are not answered in the psalm itself. The questions are the same as those asked in the book of Job (e.g., why do the righteous suffer and the wicked prosper?). In a study of the book of Job, one might mention in passing Ps 88. However, if one is exploring Ps 88, the ideology of the book of Job must weigh heavily in the analysis. In the psalm, Heman the Ezrahite has been brought to the edge of the pit. At night he cries out his lament with words and phrases such as trouble, *Sheol,* pit, no help, among the dead, slain, lie in the grave, whom you remember no more, cut off from your hand, depths of the pit, regions dark and deep, shades (*rephaim*, the souls of the departed), *abaddon*, darkness, and land of forgetfulness. In the morning Heman renews his complaint with phrases like: "cast me off," "hide your face from me," "close to death," "suffer your terrors," "wrath has swept over me," "dread assaults destroy me," "like a flood," "close in on me," "friends and neighbor shun me." Alas, there were no therapists in those days.

But Ps 88 is not about *Sheol*. Heman is asking, "Where is my healing, my vindication, and my redemption?" He has suffered from his youth. His pain has caused others to be disgusted by his affliction, perhaps deeming him to be ritually unclean and therefore untouchable, and they assume that God is punishing him because he is a sinner. Being "shut in" has robbed him of purpose, social and political respect, and the ability to express himself

---

17. Michael Goulder also combined a study of Pss 49 and 88 in his work *Psalms of the Sons of Korah*. However, his conclusions are sufficiently fanciful that a separate study would be required to rebut them all. In short, he argues that the inspiration for Ps 88 is the prayer of Joseph in the dungeon. He sees Ps 49 as indicative of the plans that invaders have to hold the officials of the Northern Kingdom hostage for ransom, that a battle is referred to in the psalm, and that the officials of the court of Israel are the ones in danger of being sheep led to the slaughter (p 195).

spiritually with joy and thanksgiving. Job has the same vexation. The *Sheol* theology in both books is similar. Escaping to *Sheol* is not the solution to life's problems, because it is a dreary place of helplessness, a pit deep and dark, where one is forgotten by God and cut off from his hand (Ps 88:5–6; 10–12; Job 10:21–22).

At this point, we need to understand that statements about *Sheol* in Job and Ps 88 are not answers—they are probing questions sent forth from reasoning minds, challenging God himself. Part of the moral lesson of the psalm and the book is that it's OK to question the Almighty. Job's friends not only rebuked Job falsely for being a sinner, but they thought it blasphemous to throw suffering in God's face and question his judgment. The questions that the sufferers were asking reflect frightening, age-old, ubiquitous traditions about the afterlife which get woven into the poetry of the tenth century Israel and are not meant to be literal, systematic, or permanent depictions of reality. Both authors seem to represent an era at the brink of theological transition when old Canaanite iconography was re-imagined, reinterpreted, and re-contextualized.[18] The primeval orthodoxy, rigid and unnuanced, asserted that the good do not suffer (Job 11:13–20; 20:4–5). Job in his exasperation argued that the opposite is true—the good suffer and the wicked have a wonderful time in this life. Even their graves are watched over when they die, and the clods of the earth are sweet to them (Job 21:33). Similarly, the dead, whether they were wise or foolish, all sink down into *Sheol* and do not return.

There is a sub-theme in Job that is almost hidden. Job does not feel that it is fair for God to condemn humanity when he is so powerful and we are so impotent. He calls for a mediator—a legal advocate with divine and mortal characteristics (Job 9:32–35). A family member or a friend captured in a battle could sometimes redeem or buy back the man's life with a ransom. Job senses that in the heavens there is one who will vouch for him, redeem him in a sense. This advocate will "lay down a pledge for me with yourself. Who is there who will give surety for me?" (16:18—17:5). Later, Job is even more forceful:

> I know that my Redeemer lives,
> and that in the end he will stand upon the earth.
> And after my skin has been destroyed,
> Yet in my flesh I shall see God;
> I myself will see him with my own eyes—
> I and not another. How my heart faints within me! (Job 19:25–27)

---

18. For instance, Job 3:8, 7:12, 9:13, and 26:12 represent a reworking of the ancient Ugaritic creation myth. Yamm the Sea must be conquered before creation can begin.

This profound and astonishing sentiment answers the question asked in Job 14, where Job speaks of the ability of an aged tree to renew itself (14:7–9). Humans, however, the very apex of God's creation, die and cannot rise up again and no one is sure what happens to them (14:11–12). Job is asking, "If mortals die, will they live again?" (14:14a). He is hoping that there will be a time of release when God will long for the reunion with the works of his hands, pardon all their sin and call his children out of *Sheol*.

The questions that Job, Qohelet, and Heman are asking are also asked in Ps 49, but Qohelet comes to a radically different conclusion. Scholars often compare Ps 49 to Qohelet (the book of Ecclesiastes)[19] because the two texts address the same issues, but Qohelet offers no solution except to eat, drink, and enjoy life now because tomorrow we die and share the same annihilation as the beasts.

> I also thought, "As for men, God tests them so that they may see that they are like the animals. Man's fate is like that of the animals; the same fate awaits them both: As one dies, so dies the other. All have the same breath; man has no advantage over the animal. Everything is meaningless. All go to the same place; all come from dust, and to dust all return. Who knows if the spirit of man rises upward and if the spirit of the animal goes down into the earth?" (Eccl 3:18–21)

Even though the question may comprise a hundred verses and the answer only one, nevertheless, the answer is the whole point of the literary effort. Job and Ps 49 deal with the same questions about suffering, betrayal, fear of death, death itself, afterlife, and redemption in all its forms.

---

19. Spangenberg, "Historical Context," 11.

6

Translation and Commentary of Psalm 49

> Memos reduce, minimize, routinize, and seek to control; this sung poetry leaves things open in respect, awe, astonishment.... Speech without ambiguity has no power to heal or transform.[1]

The Relationship of Psalm 49 to Wisdom Literature

IN THE ANCIENT WORLD, wisdom literature was common from Egypt to Mesopotamia, and Ps 49 fits comfortably into the genre. There seems to have been a flowering of such literature in the tenth century, but throughout the centuries, the concept of wisdom as a source of guidance and blessing grew in prominence until it was almost equal to cultural traditions late in Israel's history. For some, wisdom, rather than atonement by sacrifice, became the new "tree of life." Wisdom called to ordinary people from every street corner, not just to Israel, but to any person who had ears to hear. This cosmopolitan understanding helped to sustain Israel during years of diaspora.

Psalm 49 contains some of the key words and concepts that place it not just in the wisdom genre of Israel, but also of the broader Ancient Near East. Wisdom literature comprises any philosophical or lofty writing about divinity and virtue that urges the individual to improve his or her behavior or that leads to order, honor, and well-being. It may include ancient and secretive knowledge of religious rites and healing rituals, although the Pentateuch, which describes the minutiae of rituals, is not considered wisdom literature. The commonly recognized forms of wisdom literature include exhortations

---

1. Brueggemann, *Life of Faith*, 113.

from father to son, dialogues, debates, poems, formal exhortations, narratives with a moral, riddles, and collections of proverbs.² Typical topics of wisdom literature are life and death, foolishness and wisdom, learning and teaching, parables, and aphorisms (common sayings, such as *a fool and his money shall soon be parted*). Such texts have been found in Egypt, Sumer, and Babylon, giving the Israelites an ancient heritage upon which to build. The definition of the genre could be stretched to include creation myths, the earliest contact between the gods and humans, narratives dealing with the beginnings of kingship, religious rites believed to keep misfortune and divine displeasure away from the community, and the founding of culture itself. It involves mankind's quest for self-understanding.

Wisdom in Mesopotamia was associated with kingship and antediluvian (before Noah's flood) rites that helped establish and maintain order and proper worship of the gods.³ In the Babylonian *Epic of Gilgamesh*, the protagonist (Gilgamesh, a king in other Babylonian legends) does not address the rites, but attempts to recover the secret to immortality gained by the antediluvian hero Utnapishtim, the Babylonian Noah. Gilgamesh failed because of the machinations of a serpent, but he came away from the adventure laden with ancient knowledge that would benefit his contemporaries. Ancient people regarded the king as a mediator of culture, so Gilgamesh's contact with Utnapishtim centers him in this restorative role. Ethics are subordinated to the exotic rites of the royal religion; in other words, in the view of the people living at that time, performing the correct mystical rites was more important than being a good and ethical person.

> Every important Mesopotamian text that offers a philosophical reflection on divine abandonment presupposes that failure to accomplish the divine will through neglect of some unknown rite or prescription can be the cause of individual misfortune. The sphere of wisdom extends even to the crafts of the exorcist and diviner, because they, too, control arts given by the gods to attain that superior knowledge. Indeed, the fame of the antediluvian king Enmeduranki as recipient and giver of wisdom did not rest on his moral teachings but on the fact that he received the revelation of the arts of divination from Shamash and Adad, the two gods of Sippar, in primeval times.⁴

---

2. For a survey of Ancient Near East wisdom collections in contemporary literature and a description of the genre as a whole, see Clifford, "Introduction," xi-xiii. Included in the volume is Beaulieu, "Setting," 3-19. Also see Hallo, "Sumerian Literature," 1-7.

3. Beaulieu, "Setting," 3-19.

4. Ibid., 7.

Among the Israelites for centuries thereafter, Hebrew prophets often encountered and challenged the effectiveness of rituals. Genesis 1–3 and biblical wisdom literature explain the loss of immortality as the result of wrong choices and failure to recognize or understand the real enemy. The minutiae of rites and rituals described in the biblical books of Leviticus and Numbers are actually more reminiscent of Mesopotamian conceptualizations than later Israelite wisdom, which exhorted people to "number our days that they may gain a heart of wisdom" (Ps 90:12). Israelite wisdom promoted no arcane knowledge from antediluvian times. Instead, morality, ethics, personal moderation, and restraint are the focus of many Israelite wisdom texts. Others emphasize the brevity of life and the meaning of death. The depiction of death in Ps 49 reflects the angst of the *Epic of Gilgamesh* in the sense that the anguish of mortality is universal, but Gilgamesh lacked confidence and hope, while the psalmist had access to a divine "redemption" from eternal death. Redemption is the act of exchanging something valuable (e.g., money, life, service) for something or someone that is endangered or doomed. Rescue is different in that it simply requires effective action on the part of the rescuer.

The levitical atonement rites offered no certain definition of the eternal implications of "redemption," although one might argue that the life of the animal is exchanged for the cleansing of those making the offering. Ritual defilement includes puss and bodily emissions. The reward of cultic success was that the individual, family, and community would be blessed and favored by God and the covenanted citizen would not be "cut off from his or her people." There is no reference to a heaven or hell other than the fact that in the Primeval History (Gen 1–11) Enoch was "taken" because he walked with God. Most later biblical wisdom texts offer the rewards of life to those here on earth—health, long life, respect, the favor of God, and blessings for the community and later generations.

Psalm 49 is a deliberate challenge to the "retribution theology" of Deuteronomy in which evil is severely punished here on earth.[5] In Deuteronomy, bad people suffer and become diminished while good people are blessed and have abundant resources and children. Psalm 49, on the other hand, promises no vindication or relief from suffering or stress. The faith of the just person is frequently tested upon observing arrogant people living successful lives while those they oppress suffer. We should not rule out supernatural intervention solely on the grounds that it is not highlighted in this psalm. Job suffered as a good man, but in the end was vindicated by a divine restoration of all that he had lost. His abandonment by God was

---

5. Maire, "Dieu N'échappe Pas," 173–83.

simply a test. But whether the righteous person is delivered or destroyed, the book of Job supports a bodily resurrection of some sort (Job 19:25–27).

In the tenth century BCE, King David suffered greatly at the hands of his tormentors, often unjustly; in the face of this tribulation, he firmly believed that he would be justified on earth by triumphing in the end over his enemies. Many psalms, such as Ps 53 (the same as Ps 14), proclaim that God intervenes to create and sustain the righteous community and to shield it from evildoers who threaten the community's well-being.[6] Psalm 49 does not reject the possibility of present vindication, but finds a more certain hope in the ageless idea (needing no historical context) that whether the righteous suffer or are vindicated, whether the arrogant are successful or decline in wellbeing, whether God intervenes or not, he is just and will take the righteous to himself, sparing them the grimness of the eternal grave. Many scholars date Ps 49 to a later era. They conclude that the frustration troubling the psalmist makes the most sense against the backdrop of the Persian or Greek persecution. However, the religious nature and pilgrimage focus of the Korahite Psalter also fits comfortably in a pre-exilic context. No era of Israelite history was totally lacking in stress and danger.

Mention of the harp in verse 4 suggests that Ps 49 is a psalm used in festive liturgy. Although scholarly trends would tend to put it and most wisdom psalms in post-exilic times, wisdom literature is ancient and ubiquitous and could easily have existed in Israel in pre-exilic times. They could be associated with harvest festivals, could intersect with ritualistic worship, and could be a complex literature that is difficult to categorize.[7]

Translation and Commentary

To the director. Of the Sons of Korah. A psalm.

1. *Hear this, all you peoples; give ear, all you inhabitants [and ethnic groups] of the world;*
2. *Both the sons of Adam and the sons of men, the rich and the poor together,*
3. *My mouth will speak wisdom and the meditation of my heart understanding.*
4. *I will incline my ear to a proverb; I will declare my riddle on the lyre.*

---

6. Bennett, "Wisdom Motifs," 16.
7. Dell, "I Will Solve My Riddle," 445–58.

5. Why will I be afraid in the days of trouble [when] the malice of my treacherous foes surrounds me,
6. The ones trusting in their wealth and [who] boast in the abundance of their wealth?
7. Ah! Surely a man cannot ransom himself, nor give to God his price.
8. For [the] ransom of his life is costly. It will always be insufficient,
9. That he should live forever and not see the Pit.
10. But he shall see the "wise" die. The fool and the stupid alike must perish and leave their wealth to others.
11. Their graves [shall be] their homes forever; their dwelling places for all generations, though [their kin ritually] call upon their names upon their lands.
12. A highly esteemed man cannot linger; he is like the beasts that perish.
13. This is [the fruit of] their way. They inherit folly, but others following them are pleased with their sayings.
14. Like sheep, for Sheol they are appointed. Death will be their shepherd; but the upright will have dominion over them in the morning. And their form will decay. Sheol will be their abode.
15. Ah! God will ransom my soul from the power of Sheol, for he will receive me. Selah!
16. Do not fear when a man becomes rich, when the glory of his house increases.
17. For in his death, he will not take it all with him. His glory will not descend after him.
18. Though his soul in life he blesses and they praise you when you do well for yourself,
19. He will go to the gathering of his fathers forever; they will not see light.
20. A man in his pomp, yea he will not understand; he is like the beasts that perish.

The Sons of Korah was just one of three musicians' guilds. Its members stood center stage in the Davidic era, led by Heman, a singer and the king's seer (1 Chron. 6:33; 25:5). The other two guilds, led by Asaph and Jeduthun and situated on the right and left in the choir arena, seem to have faded in reputation throughout Israel's history.

1. *Hear this, all you peoples; give ear, all you inhabitants [and ethnic groups] of the world;*

The psalmist, in true wisdom fashion, is not limiting his message to his own nation. That may be because the psalm was written in an era when Judah, Israel, or both were being persecuted by wealthy and powerful heathen nations. Yet the language of the psalm seems more suggestive of personal enemies who may have been the epitome of all the arrogant rich who oppress weaker citizens. The beginning verses seem formal and restrained, but the final verses almost sputter with rage and warning.

2. *Both the sons of Adam and the sons of men, the rich and the poor together,*

Verse 2 has spawned a variety of translations and interpretations. What did the psalmist mean by "sons of Adam" and "sons of man," a phrase also found in Ps 62:10? Interpretations include "high and low," "low and high," "both ordinary people and people of importance,"[8] "both the earthborn and the sons of men, rich one and needy one together,"[9] and "of lowly birth or high degree."[10] The word *adam* is used in a variety of ways in the Hebrew Bible, often simply referring to humankind. A unique solution may be drawn from W. Wifall, who has found the phrase "son of man" in both Late Bronze Age Egypt and the Canaanite Amarna Letters. Sometimes the vassal princes of the Amarna Letters referred to themselves as king, sometimes as "man," meaning a male citizen with legal status. Wifall also points to a second millennium BCE pharaoh named Amenhemnet I who was called "son of man."[11] It is uncertain, however, that the average pilgrim or reader would recognize such esoteric allusion and would read simply, "all kinds of people," with or without legal status.

3. *My mouth will speak wisdom and the meditation of my heart understanding.*

---

8. Goldingay, *Psalms, 42–89*, 98.
9. Pietersma and Wright, *A New English Translation*, 571.
10. Dahood, *Psalms*.
11. Wifall, "Son of Man," 335.

"Meditation" and "understanding" are typical wisdom terms. The word for "wisdom" is feminine plural. G. Rendsburg calls for a singular interpretation of it as an example of the northern Israelite Hebrew (IH).[12] Such usage could be another hint that the author was raised in the northern regions of Israel. The author is not making an inquiry here. He seems confident that he has the answer.

> 4. *I will incline my ear to a proverb; I will declare my riddle on the lyre.*

The Hebrew verb translated here "declare," almost always means "open," but can also denote "declare," "deceive," or "be simple." The related question attached to the Hebrew word for "declare" is whether it refers to *presenting* the riddle or to *solving* it. Interpretations go both ways but the idea of presenting, opening, or declaring, the riddle is most consistent with the location of this phrase at the beginning of the psalm. A strong argument can be made for "open" if one compares Ps 78:2, "I will open my mouth in a parable, I will utter dark sayings from of old." The important point is that the author is luring the listener by suggesting that a mystery is being presented that intrigues and surprises.

> 5. *Why should I be afraid in the days of trouble [when] the malice of my treacherous foes surrounds me,*

The controversial phrase in this verse is the traditional rendering, ". . . when the iniquity of my persecutors surrounds me" (NRSV). The word for "foes" has the consonants of the name "Jacob" and can also designate the word "heel." Jacob was the one who grabbed his brother's heel and supplanted his position as the future patriarch, but translating the word as "heel" misses the mark. The word "foe" suggests trickery and betrayal.

The psalmist is not an ordinary man. He is probably a courtly priest and should have been highly respected by those of his same status level, yet he is threatened by a class of privileged men. Only a man who is powerful himself, such as a king, priest, military leader, or sage, would have such an abundance of rich and powerful enemies. The psalmist is surrounded, endangered, and probably frightened, but he is not defeated because God is on his side. He is undoubtedly hoping for triumph in the present life, but if that escapes him he knows that "life" with God is the ultimate wealth. The author is no minor personality. Triumph over his enemies could have national consequences.

---

12. Rendsburg, *Linguistic Evidence*," 56.

6. *The ones trusting in their wealth and who boast in the abundance of their wealth?*

The psalmist's foes are unwise braggarts because they do not consider how fleeting the good life can be. In Ps 59 King David compares his enemies to snarling dogs who come to the city at night to run about and cause trouble. He prays for God to laugh at them and curse them. Their attacks are scoffed at in the psalm, but they clearly have shaken the king, causing anxiety and rage.

7. *Ah! Surely a man cannot ransom himself, or give to God his price.*

This verse has been muddied in transmission and requires emendation or guesswork. Most scholars emend the opening "a brother" to "Ah!" That sets this verse, "Ah! a man cannot ransom himself," in contrast to verse 15: "Ah! God will ransom my soul . . ." Another choice is "A brother/kinsman cannot ransom a man."[13] The debate cannot be resolved with certainty, but the psalmist's point is clear: a rich man may be ransomed from many things in life, including an imminent death at the hands of enemies, but never from death itself.

The word "ransom" in this context may be an established religious reference. In the legal codes of the Pentateuch, a ransom was sometimes paid to redeem the life of a man whose bull killed another man, or a newborn male, or a prisoner consecrated to God. This applied to humans as well as to animals, as for example when a firstborn son was redeemed by the sacrifice of a lamb (Gen 22; Exod 13:13; 21:29–30; 30:11–16; 34:20; Lev 27:28–29). Psalm 49:7 may be a warning against wealthy individuals who continually spend their riches on religious and ritual practices, often something occult, in the hope of purchasing from God an extension of life. When death calls, their wealth is useless.

8. *For [the] ransom of his life is costly. It will be insufficient forever,*

If verse 7 was muddied, verse 8 has been mangled. It may be a gloss (a later editorial edition) because verse 7 flows easily into verse 9 if verse 8 is removed.[14] "For the ransom of life is costly, and can never suffice" (NRSV) is probably close to the psalmist's intent. John Eaton suggests ". . . he would never have enough to pay for it."[15] The most sensible meaning is found in those translations which denote the everlasting failure of the earthly ransom

---

13. As in Owens, *Analytical Key*, 3:340.
14. Witte, "'Aber Gott,'" 543.
15. Eaton, *The Psalms*, 198.

to redeem a soul from death and the pit. What a shock for those who spent their lives telling others what to do or buying their way out of trouble! They can rewrite their history and burn their papers, but they cannot undo their past. Death knows.

> 9. *That he should live forever[16] and not see the Pit.*

If the above phrase follows from verse 8, it clarifies the arrogant aspiration of the psalmist's wealthy tormentors; like Gilgamesh of old, they hope by their own resources to attain immortality. The Hebrew word for "pit" strengthens the impression that the grave is a negative and dreary place to go. A pit was nothing more than a big hole into which dead animals were thrown. When a vexed psalmist wanted to portray fear or dread of an untimely death, he would often use this word to refer to *Sheol* (e.g., Ps 88:4, 6).

> 10. *But he shall see the "wise" die. The fool and the stupid alike must perish and leave their wealth to others.*

The translation of this verse is not controversial, but it is often misinterpreted. Many have compared it to the teaching of Qohelet (Solomon in *Ecclesiastes*) that the final destination of both the wise and the foolish is death and decay. This is the conclusion by which Qohelet was driven to nihilism.

> Then I thought in my heart, "The fate of the fool will overtake me also. What then do I gain by being wise?" (Eccl 2:15)

> All share a common destiny—the righteous and the wicked, the good and the bad, the clean and the unclean, those who offer sacrifices and those who do not. As with the good man, so with the sinner; as it is with those who take oaths, so with those who are afraid to take them. This is the evil of everything that happens under the sun: the same destiny overtakes all. The hearts of men moreover are full of evil and there is madness in their hearts while they live, and afterward they join the dead. Anyone who is among the living has hope—even a live dog is better than a dead lion! (Eccl 9:2–4)

Psalm 49:10 has on occasion been interpreted as an affirmation of Qohelet's conclusion. The intent of the psalmist, however, is to satirize rather than to affirm the preacher's cynical outlook. Where Qohelet assigns to the wise and the fool the same destiny, Ps 49 juxtaposes the "fool" and the "stupid." Wealthy men who think themselves "wise" are really fools, even

---

16. This word comes from the same root as "director" or "leader" in the heading.

though people praise them for their sayings, and it is they alone who share the fate of beasts. The psalmist might actually be writing about the preacher or his class of peers in his poem! Death is portrayed not as the great equalizer but as the great separator.

11. *Their graves their homes forever; their dwelling places for all generations, though [their kin ritually] call upon their names upon their lands.*

This difficult verse has attracted analysis from many capable scholars. There are two approaches to the verse. King James Version reads, "Their inward thought is, that their houses shall continue forever, and their dwelling places to all generations; they call their lands after their own names." NRSV is very similar, but there is a broad consensus among scholars that two letters in the Hebrew word for "inward thought" should be transposed, changing the word to "graves." This puts the Masoretic Text in agreement with the Septuagint (LXX), Syriac, and Targums. An inscription found in south central Turkey offers a similar thought, "I am Panamuwa, son of Qarli, King of Y'dy, who have erected this statue for Hadad in my eternal abode [i.e., burial chamber]."[17]

Mark Smith approves the NRSV and RSV version for 11a, b: "Their graves are their homes for ever, their dwelling places to all generations, though they named their lands their own."[18] Smith cites P. Jouon to the effect that the phrase "eternal home" for the grave finds parallels in Phoenician and Aramaic inscriptions.[19]

Smith feels that the language of the psalm indicates summoning the dead.[20] He cites Ps 16 as an example of David's rejection of the ancestor cult. His translation of Ps 16:2–4 is somewhat elaborate, but it boils down to the fact that David will not pour out blood libations to the "holy ones" who are in the *ground* (rather than the *land*), even though everyone delights in them. His translation of Ps 49:11 is, "The rich maintain the ancestral cult first with their burials, their eternal homes. The rich wrongly comfort themselves by indulging in the custom of summoning their deceased ancestors."[21]

No matter how one translates the passage, the point is that the rich are living in denial. They have false ideas about how their life on earth relates to the existence awaiting them in *Sheol*. Their real estate holdings on earth are

17. Younger Jr. "Hadad Inscription (2.36)," 2:156.
18. Smith, "Invocation," 105–07.
19. Jouon, "Glanes palmyreniennes," 99–103.
20. Smith, "Invocation," 107.
21. Ibid.

vast, but the 6 foot grave is their final mansion. They get the promotion on earth, but their degradation awaits them below.

12. *A highly esteemed man cannot linger; he is like the beasts that perish.*

The word for man is "Adam," but there is no pronounced significance in that choice of words. One is reminded of Ps 8 (where we find a poetic balance between "man" and "Adam"), which celebrates the placement of humans above all the cattle, beasts, fish, and birds. Even from toddlers and suckling babies can God ordain strength. Only God and his angels are greater than humankind. Psalm 49:12, by contrast, emphasizes the fact that the strongest, wealthiest, and most highly praised people cannot linger on this earth, cannot buy more time with all their resources, and finally will share the (mortal) fate of beasts.

The word most interpreters render "honor" is not the usual one. *Yeqar* actually means "to be valuable," so John Owens and others render it "mankind in pomp," because these men are not honorable but are pompous. A more typical rendering is "For all their riches, mortals do not abide; they perish like the beasts" (NAB), although such a solution broadens the address to all people rather than just the pompous.

13. *This is [the fruit of] their way. They inherit folly, but others following them are pleased with their sayings.*

This verse has undoubtedly been miscopied in transmission. The first phrase reads literally, "This their way/path; folly/foolishness is theirs/belongs to them." Proverbs 1:31 has the phrase "the fruit of their way," suggesting the word "fruit" may have dropped out. The LXX reads, "This way of theirs is a pitfall to them, and afterwards with their mouths they will express contentment."[22] Eaton offers the paraphrase, "This the way of those who boast in themselves, the end of those who are pleased with their own mouths."[23] Meinrad Stenzel offers, "This is their way, they trust in themselves; their path, in their mouth/speech they have been very pleased." The opposition of "path" to "way" Stenzel supplies with a nod to the book of Proverbs, where "way" and "path" often accompany one another.[24] David Zucker proposes, "Such is the fate of those who are self-confident, the end of those pleased with their own talk."[25]

---

22. Pietersma, *English Translation*, 571.
23. Eaton, *The Psalms*, 198.
24. Stenzel, "Psalm 49," 152–54.
25. Zucker, "Riddle," 144.

Adding "the fruit of" may not be necessary, but it does maintain the basic meaning of the phrase. Verse 13b may indicate that the wealthy inherit "folly" rather than godhood or nether world status, or it may mean that they are foolish, in spite of what others think of them.

Verse 13c is also controversial. Does it refer to others that admire the rich man, or to others that live after he is dead, or does it mean his own end? Scholarly opinions vary. Since the point has already been made that pompous men are like beasts, the psalmist may be saying that those who follow a fool in his way become fools themselves. One might think of a cow or goat wearing a bell that attracts the other beasts in the herd. They might even follow the bell goat to their own doom.

14. *Like sheep, for Sheol they are appointed. Death will be their shepherd; but the upright will have dominion over them in the morning. And their form will decay. Sheol will be their abode.*

Again, the text provokes scholars to vigorous disagreement. Markus Witte is not stingy with his emendations. He rejects verse 14 as written in the Masoretic Text, maintaining that in the literal translation the meaning is "forced." He begins by changing "appointed" to "sinking"[26] since sinking down into *Sheol* is the fate of all. His final solution (my translation from his German): "Like sheep they sink down into *Sheol*. Death will shepherd them and rule over them. Also, the upright are appointed to be deceased, and *Sheol* will allow their form to waste away, the dwelling for everyone."[27]

At this point the verse produces two controversial issues. Should it read, "Death will be their shepherd" (Eaton, Lattey,[28] NRSV) or "Death will feed on them" (Craigie, NIV, KJV)? John Collins highlights the claim of Ugaritic mythology, repeated by Israelite poets for literary effect, that Death is a monster that devours humans (Ps 69:15 "Do not let . . . the pit close its mouth over me," etc.). Those who make this comparison have a compelling argument, but Collins examined the wording of Ugaritic devouring passages to discover that the verbs used in them are not the same as in 49:14. Observing that the first phrase mentions sheep, he chooses to translate "Death will be their shepherd."[29]

Many translations change the phrase "and the upright will rule over them in the morning" to "straight to the grave they descend" (NRSV). Such translations often involve transposing two letters. Thus, a few emendations

---

26. Witte, "Aber Gott," 542.
27. Ibid., 543, ". . . und ihr Bild lässt schwinden die Scheol [die Wohnung für jenes]."
28. Lattey, "Note," 288.
29. Collins, "'Death,'" 320–26.

of the text by the translator can radically change the meaning. Since the metaphorical use of the word for "morning" occurs frequently in the psalms and prophetic writings, there is no reason to drop the literal meaning unless one simply cannot accept the idea that ancient Hebrews believed in an afterlife. In the poetic writings of psalms and prophets, morning (or dawn) signifies a new work of God (Gen 1), a new plan (Isa 33:2), a new solution (Ps 30:5), a new opportunity (Job 11:17), a new revelation (Gen 28:16–18; Isa 50:4), a new way of looking at things (Ps 143:8), the coming of Messiah (Mal 4:2; Isa 9:2), Judgment Day (Joel 2:2), and the final eternal communion with God at death (Ps 49:14).

The language of Ps 49:14 resonates with the prophet Isaiah's taunt against the king of Babylon,

> Nations will take them and bring them to their place.
> And the house of Israel will possess the nations
> as menservants and maidservants in the Lord's land.
> They will make captives of their captors,
> and rule over their oppressors. (Isa 14:2)

The image of Death as shepherd coincides also with the title sometimes ascribed to the Canaanite deity Baal/Hadd/Hadad in his capacity as judge of the dead. KTU 1.108 begins,

> Thereupon he drinks, the *rapha*-being, king of the nether world;
> And he [El] drinks, the powerful and majestic!
> El sits with Athtart,
> El renders judgment with Hadd, the shepherd.[30]

15. *Ah! God will ransom my soul from the power of Sheol, for he will receive me. Selah!*

The psalmist has drawn attention to this statement by enclosing it in two exclamations. The "Ah!" draws our thoughts to verse 7, which most likely began with the same expression. The *"selah"* here parallels the same expression at the end of verse 13. The present verse is the psalmist's answer to the warning and exhortation of verses 7–13. It is the heart of the psalm, in fact, the heart of the Hebrew Bible, because it hints at an ongoing existence beyond the earthly body—an individual and communal survival of the righteous after death. It may not be the explicit hope of heaven and resurrection day, but when read in conjunction with Ps 17:15, 16:9–11, and 73:24–26 it anticipates a joyous union with God. It rewards the poor and

---

30. Levine and de Tarragon, "Dead Kings," 649–59.

oppressed for their faithfulness to God, it gives hope to those terrified of death, and it magnifies the eternal faithfulness of God.

The translation of this verse is not difficult, but its interpretation has been deeply divisive. Some insist that there is no hint of afterlife in the psalm, or in any psalm for that matter. John Goldingay denies that the psalm is reaching for the afterlife and asserts that to do so would be "the coward's way out." He claims that until Jesus Christ died and rose again, the idea of an afterlife had no basis. God's redemption is worked out here in this life rather than in some realm we cannot see and for which the Old Testament cannot produce any evidence.[31] Goldingay's argument does not take into consideration the abundance of explicit statements about resurrection, Judgment Day, and afterlife in later Jewish Second Temple literature, including the Apocrypha. Any ancient Israelite who took the stories of Enoch and Elijah seriously would have a basis for belief in an afterlife, unless they thought God took Elijah and dropped him in the sea. The concepts of afterlife and resurrection were alive and well when Christ's ministry began. Moreover, calling those people cowards who hope for an eternity alive with God puts Goldingay in a very small minority, not only among scholars but among humans in general.

The controversial aspect of redemption from death is covered well by Witte. He describes the various possible interpretations:

1. Deliverance from imminent death (Sir 51:2; Ps 88:6; Job 14:13; 33:23–30; Pss 24:11; 26:11; 40:19; 44:27; 78:42).[32]

2. From daily death (pre-mortal deliverance): illness, economic disaster, isolation from the community, etc. (1QH [Qumran Enoch] 3:19; 2:32–35; 15:14). There is no ransom from these calamities for the sinner.

3. From a bad or early death (Jer 12:2–3; Ps 73:18–20; Job 27:13–23).

4. From life (i.e., translation or rapture as in the cases of Enoch, Moses, and Elijah; (Gen 5:24; 2 Kgs 2:3; Sir 44:16; 48:9; 49:14). The key phrase is, "he will receive me," based on the Hebrew word for "take."

5. From eternal death (*aus* dem Tod, post-mortal deliverance from either annihilation or existence in *Sheol*).

This is the heart of Witte's article. He points to the relationship between verses 7 and 15 and to the contrast between verses 14 and 15. Both 7 and 15 refer to deity and "ransom." Both also begin with "Ah!" Death is a punishment for sin (Gen 3:22), so for the righteous there is a special hope.

---

31. Goldingay, *Psalms 42–89*, 2:107.
32. Witte, "Aber Gott," 550.

Witte rules out rapture here but not redemption through the price paid by the power of God, by the will of God and not of man.

The psalmist doesn't care how the price is paid. Relationship with God results in a taking out/up or reception. This is ultimately the only way to survive death. The author doesn't try to imagine what the afterlife is like. He just trusts in God's power and his own relationship with him.

Witte turns to inter-testamental literature such as the book of Enoch and the Wisdom of Solomon for evidence that immortality was a robust hope in the Second Temple era. Writings from this period are explicitly supportive of a continuing existence of the righteous dead in the eternal presence of God.

> The righteous who have died will condemn the ungodly who are living, and youth that is quickly perfected will condemn the prolonged old age of the unrighteous. (Wis 4:16; also 3:1–8)

16, 17. *Do not be overawed when a man becomes rich, when the glory of his house increases. For in his death, he will not take it all with him. His glory will not descend after him.*

The translation of the verse is amazingly uncontroversial, but as usual, interpretations vary according to one's preconceptions. Many established scholars see no eschatology at all in the psalm. The only victory is that the wise die in dignity because they are not deluded. Many have expressed doubts that an eternal redemption of the soul from *Sheol* can be found in the Hebrew Bible. I disagree. The HB/OT whispers its belief in the immortal soul rather than shouting it, but often the profoundest biblical mysteries are found in the whispers. In this psalm, eternal judgment by the God of Life is the author's only hope. He is well acquainted with the actions of the wealthy and powerful. He is an insider, one who has been hurt by them. It galls him to watch them damage others. They dress well, speak well, attend religious rites, receive great press, and look impressive in the market place, but their deeds are dark, and few understand their true nature except an omniscient deity who cannot be fooled.

There is no need to envy the wealthy. If all go naked to the nether world, the high and low born are on an equal footing. In the world, the wealthy are considered to be blessed and favored by God, but a horrid shock awaits those who have used their gifts for selfish gain. As expressed in the book of Job,

> Fire resides in his tent;
> burning sulfur is scattered over his dwelling.

His roots dry up below
and his branches wither above.
The memory of him perishes from the earth;
and he has no name in the land.
He is driven from light into darkness
and is banished from the world. (Job 18:15–18)

The author's enemy will surely go to his grave in peace surrounded by the most coveted grave goods. According to the regional lore, that foe will have a memorial set up after him. Sons and daughters will bring him food and wine offerings to keep him invigorated, and will summon him at yearly festivals. His estates will continue to grow, and lands may be named after him. The family will assume that the foe is in a good place, at peace. Perhaps he or she will eat and drink with his deity (probably Baal or Asherah), and he will join the court of the deity as a god or *repha*. At least, so some people of the day believed, but not the psalmist.

Young King Tutankhamen of Egypt is a prime example of a wealthy man whose grave was stuffed with glorious goods. His sandals, cheetah bed, game boards, storage chest, golden mask, a dagger formed from a meteorite, and all of his other treasures were uncovered in the early twentieth century, after lying in the darkness for thousands of years. Now those items are in museums, gawked at by the rich and the profane alike. The willingness of the Egyptian court to place all of those treasures in a tomb beyond the reach of the living testifies to a firm belief in some kind of an afterlife in which certain items have a double life, so to speak. They cannot be translated physically into the netherworld, but the ancients believed that they could sympathetically benefit the souls who go there. The psalmist rejects such a belief. A person's belongings pass from generation to generation, but the dead are on their own in the afterlife. Only God's favor will avail anyone a happy fate after death. The psalmist is reassuring himself that he is favored of God and does not need to fear the consequences of an enemy dying and afflicting him as a vengeful shade.

> 18, 19. *Though his soul in this life he considered blessed, and they praise you when you do well for yourself, he [lit. you] will go to the gathering of his fathers forever; they will not see light.*

The NIV solution is, "Though while he lived he counted himself blessed—and men praise you when you prosper." The wealthy man does not fear his eternal fate because his wealth gives him a false confidence of God's favor.

20. *A man in his pomp, yea he will not understand; he is like the beasts that perish.*

As reviewed above in verse 12, this verse has been examined by many fine scholars who resolve it by changing the received text. Again, emendations are reasonable, but not necessary. J. D. Pleins and Perdue emend "perish" to "are silenced." Pleins points out that the psalm then begins with "Hear" and ends with silence.[33] Other scholars offer "are slaughtered." An incantation from the Egyptian Book of the Dead, a book of magic sayings in use during the era of the development of the state of Israel, adds a stroke of humor and sarcasm to the translation "slaughtered." Ancient Egyptians who did not live a good life, who were not buried, or who were interred without proper incantations had much to fear. The dying dreaded that the demons and judges of the nether world would remove the soul's head and devour it. This fate was warded off with a green amulet and these words addressed to the *ka* (soul and protector) of the deceased:

> O Weigher on the scales,
> May *maat* rise to the nose of Re (the sun god) that day!
> Do not let my head be removed from me!
> For mine is an eye that sees,
> An ear that hears,
> or I am not an ox for slaughter,
> shall not be an offering for those above!
> Let me pass by you, I am pure, Osiris has vanquished his foes!
> (Book of the Dead, ch 105)[34]

Emended or not, verses 12 and 20 are an important refrain; the image of the wealthy, who undoubtedly offered many oxen on their own behalf, being led off silently by Shepherd Death, is both ironic and amusing, at least to the psalmist. I think he sees it in his imagination, like a political cartoon of today, and the thought seems to bring him some therapeutic pleasure.

Conclusion

Psalm 49 contains many aspects of Wisdom Literature: words such as "riddle" and "parable," the address to all mankind, the diatribe against false pride, the issues of life and death as a result of right and wrong choices, the ironic contrast between what should be smart humans and dumb animals, lack of reference to Israel as a nation, and lack of reference to Temple or

---

33. Pleins, "Death and Endurance," 20.
34. Lichtheim, *Ancient Egyptian Literature*, 2:123.

ritual. Wisdom Literature is well attested in the Ancient Near East, and each nation undoubtedly had some contact with the literature of their neighbors. The difference between Israel's literature and that of Mesopotamia is that Israel's was based on ethical choices and restraint in behavior rather than on esoteric knowledge, mythic tales, magic rituals, and charms. Iconic images borrowed from foreign literature are no indication that Israel lacked a unique and creative message. Rather, they used the common coinage of the era, either ironically or poetically, to further their own unique points. The psalm was not lightly dashed off in a moment of emotion. It displays signs of careful literary planning such as planned structure, repetition, interlocking semantic fields, sound play, and other signs of literary skill. There are at least twenty-eight terms that the psalmist uses repeatedly.

In addition to putting the psalm in the genre of wisdom literature, calling the psalm a "riddle" lures the reader to want to be wise in the reading of it. The reader will stretch his or her mind to understand the riddle and will see the irony of the wealthy looking good on earth only to be led away by the King of Terrors like a dumb ox about to be slaughtered. Silk sheets and selfishness on earth lead to worms and dust in the afterlife.

Although the psalm is addressed to all mankind, both low born and high born, women, and even foreigners, the target audience of the theology laid out here is not the average sinner. The psalmist seems to have saved his sharpest darts for the wealthy Although he may have been an upper class Judean elitist himself, he considers himself to have the moral high ground and the approval of God. He is still trusting in God, not in his status, and he is not throwing others in the ditch to advance himself. He is not oppressing the poor, and he knows beyond all doubt that his elite status means nothing to the God of the universe.

7

The Struggle for Orthodoxy

Who Defines Right Practice?

A NAIVE READING OF the Hebrew Bible suggests that the Israelites were favored by God because they were his faithful people. A closer look reveals that the Israelites were more syncretists (people who blend religious beliefs) and apostates (people who pervert or reject an accepted religious tradition) than faithful followers, at least according to the prophetic record. From the fourteenth century BCE on, there were many foreigners in the land, each serving his or her own deity. There was never a smooth, linear progression of thought about monotheism, death, *Sheol*, and the afterlife. The progression of ideas is always discontinuous and ragged, and Israel's theological journey was no exception. Monotheistic Yahwism, as expressed by prophets and historians and as encouraged by the final editors of the Old Testament, was probably the minority view. However, according to the narrative, Yahweh always had his seven thousand souls, even in the North, that did not bend the knee to Baal.

Mark Smith and his wife Elizabeth Bloch-Smith[1] have a number of interesting and controversial theories. For example, they take exception to the contrast between "folk religion" and "true Yahwism" because they note that the Canaanite element in Yahwism was not limited to the common folk. Some kings, prophets, and priests of Israel and Judah were also syncretists and apostates. They argue that elements considered to be folk religion were more integrated into the mainstream than is generally acknowledged. That is a valid point; the most vehemently forbidden Canaanite practices, including child sacrifice, divination, dark magic, covenants with dead spirits, worship of idols, and worship of the starry host, were observed by the courts of both north and south from the days of Solomon through the time

---

1. Smith and Elizabeth Bloch-Smith, "Death and Afterlife," 277–84.

of the last king of Judah. "Syncretistic religion" is therefore a better term than "folk religion."[2] In other words, according to Smith and Bloch-Smith, there was no one true Yahwism. "Official religion" cannot be separated from "popular" religion. "Monotheistic Yahwism" needs to be distinguished from "polytheistic Yahwism," which many in both Israel and Judah assumed was a legitimate expression of the faith. They also argue that the ban against consorting with the dead was a late development in Israel, from the mid-eighth century onward.

In arriving at this conclusion, they make some suppositional leaps. They assume, for example, that unless a practice such as offering non-tithed food to the dead is explicitly forbidden, it must have been considered acceptable. To the explicit commandments against consulting the dead (Lev 19:31; 20:6, 27; Deut 18:10), they assign late dates of composition. On the other hand, if Israel's religion was in fact relayed through genuine prophets of Yahweh, then true Yahwism did exist, whether it was the majority understanding or not. The message of "true Yahwism" is found in the writings of the prophets, historians, recorders, and redactors that preserved the message. The fact that the message displays some inconsistencies does not detract from the general unswerving message.

As we learned in chapter 2, long before Israel secured its control over what would later become the high country of Judah, the tradition of calling forth and feeding deities and ghosts was firmly rooted in the Ancient Near East. In some cases, blessings were asked of these spirits. Fear of spiritual curses and vengeance ensured the continuation of these practices for many years to come. Israel's understanding of the afterlife was somewhat unique from the very beginning of its existence as a distinct people, but by no means was its theology monolithic or unconditioned by its Syrian heritage. Quite to the contrary, Israelite belief and practice could be quite eclectic. There was, however, constant pressure from certain leaders to be the only monotheistic nation in the entire region, a pressure that was often resisted at the grass roots. Prophets defined the religion, scribes and prophets preserved the orthodox writings, prophets rebuked wayward kings, and reformers kept the traditions renewed.

---

2. Even in the wilderness narrative, compromises were made. Archaeological discoveries point to the fact that the lifting of the bronze serpent on a pole as a means for healing was a Midianite practice. The instruction to craft such a talisman was attributed to Yahweh in Num 21:8, but later there would be an aversion to serpents, which were worshiped all over the Near East. The taboo regarding images of anything in heaven, on earth, or in the waters below (Exod 20:4; Deut 5:8) would surely include serpents and dragons, which were both mythological and divine. The later psalmists, authors, and redactors would never attribute such an instruction to Yahweh.

The crisis that the author of Ps 49 had with his powerful enemy could well have been between conservative forces in Jerusalem, those who thought any departure from the Mosaic Law was heresy, and those who followed David's revelation that animal sacrifice was much less important to God than right attitude. I guess every generation has its version of conservative thinking and progressive thinking. Progressives tend to welcome change, conservatives often resist. When politics and theology merge in a culture, the battle between ideologies and religious practices can be fierce.

The Patriarchal Era (c. 2000–1450 BCE)

The early Syrian Patriarchs of Genesis (Abraham, Isaac, and Jacob) had no scroll or written scriptures to follow that we know of. Oral tradition could be very effective in preserving family histories and genealogies. As for their customs, they lived out their daily lives according to the law codes of Eshnunna, Lipit-Ishtar, and Hammurabi. Other than some peculiar family traditions, they had only the Syro-Mesopotamian myths, traditions, and literature to help them sort out their attitudes toward death and immortality. The only source of major diversity from the local traditions about the afterlife would be the perception that some individual family member had received a personal divine revelation which could easily be passed on orally through the generations. For instance, Jacob was a committed monotheist like his grandfather. When he returned to Canaan from Haran with his wives and children and a company of servants and employees, he paused to have everyone bury all the little idols they had brought with them. His wife Rachel had to give up the family idols that she stole from her father. Some of those idols represented family authority, special protection, and fertility to the owners. The lure was so strong that Jacob had them give up their earrings to make sure they couldn't melt them down to make new idols (Gen 35:2–4).

In Genesis, references to *Sheol* are vague. The Patriarchs hoped to die peacefully after a long life, to be buried in the family tomb with proper mourning, and to be gathered to their fathers (ancestors). Scholars disagree as to whether that gathering refers to joining one's relatives in the nether world or to the physical family cemetery or both. The problem with the patriarchal record is that Genesis was composed long after that era ended, after the Israelites had conquered Canaan and had developed their own scribal tradition (Gen 7:2; 12:6; 13:7; 14:14; 36:31; 47:11; Deut 2:12). The Israelites never did put their stories on clay tablets. They wrote on animal skin scrolls in what we call today paleo-Hebrew letters. Specific memories about the fear of death or demons would be difficult to recover. Abraham affirmed his trust in Yahweh and the promise that his seed would inherit the land by refusing to bury his family members in his hometown of Haran in northern Syria. He bought a burial plot from a Hittite that became the new focus of family burial—the new homeland so to speak. When the third patriarch, Jacob, was dying, he said, "I am about to be gathered to my people. Bury me with my fathers in the cave in the field of Ephron the Hittite, the cave in the field of Machpelah, near Mamre in Canaan, which Abraham bought along with the field as a burial place from Ephron the Hittite" (Gen 49:28–30).

That statement doesn't tell us what Jacob expected on the other side. The important issue is what is missing. There is no plea for someone to libate for him, leave him food and grave goods, call out his name, or raise up a stone in his honor. Jacob's story was not utterly without ancient magical rites. The "mandrakes" (herbs associated with fertility) his wives sought may have been a superstition. The stakes that Jacob put out before the sheep to make them reproduce in a certain way was a kind of sorcery. These would be common practices of the day. Yet, the patriarchal stories do not uncover any association with foreign beliefs and traditions regarding afterlife.

The raising of stones for historic memorials was practiced by just about everyone in the Patriarchal Age. Some of the standing stones can still be found in isolated desert locals. Archaeologists are not certain what they represent, whether gods or ancestors. Jacob set up a memorial stone in Bethel when he was running from his brother Esau. After his famous dream of a ladder reaching from earth to heaven, he set up a memorial stone, anointed it with oil, and called it "El Beth-El" (Gen 35:7), meaning "God, the House of God." Jacob was not worshiping his ancestors as some have claimed. It was God who initiated the contact, God who made the promise, and God who was at the top of the ladder. Jacob was looking up, not down.[3] Later such standing stones were so frequently associated with polytheism that later Judean reformers banned them altogether.[4] The break with typical West Semitic practices and beliefs about death and afterlife was total. The best hope for a desirable afterlife lies in keeping the communal covenant with its civic and family duties and its rites and rituals, and avoiding all association with idols and foreign gods.

Worse than the fear of death was the fear of being "cut off" from one's people for covenant-breaking. As typical as the Hebrews were when they left northern Syria, living by law codes written before Abraham and Isaac, they

---

3. The story is also a foil against the Tower of Babel narrative, in which mankind attempts to build a pyramid that would reach heaven. They failed. God came down to disperse the whole project, so it was never finished (Gen 11:1–9).

4. Avner, "Sacred Stones," 31–41.

quickly developed into a unique clan with very different views of creation and Godhood. For a good portion of them, at least, gone were the demon judges, the invocation rituals, the magic amulets, the dangerous journeys, the sharing of religious feasts with ghosts and gods, necromancy, séances, the sympathetic relationship between grave goods and the afterlife, and magic incantations and rituals. However, they did expect to see their relatives there. It is unclear if they expected to sleep with their ancestors, but that is an unlikely scenario because everyone in the Near East believed in the immortal soul. Some souls would be content, others miserable, depending on the culture and the kind of death, but no soul ceased to exist.

If we are willing to look forward to the New Testament, those of faith can take a peek at the afterlife of Abraham, Isaac, and Jacob and the other patriarchs. Jesus Christ said of them (quoting Exod 3:6, 15), "But about the resurrection of the dead—have you not read what God said to you, 'I am the God of Abraham, the God of Isaac, and the God of Jacob'? He is not the God of the dead but of the living" (Matt 22:31–32).

He also said, "Your father Abraham rejoiced to see my day, and he saw it and was glad." Speaking of the living, Genesis has one important character that did not die. Enoch was an early ancestor of Abraham. "Altogether, Enoch walked with God; then he was no more, because God took him away" (Gen 5:24). This taking away while the man was alive may have contributed greatly to the confidence that God could take a soul out of *Sheol*.

Exodus, Leviticus, Numbers, and Deuteronomy

These four books plus Genesis comprise the Torah or Pentateuch. The last four describe the escape of the people of Israel from Egypt and their forty years of wandering in the wilderness of Sinai. During that time, Moses and others set out various kinds of laws. There were civil laws telling neighbors and townspeople how to get along. They emphasized traditional, common sense, community fairness. If your neighbor's ox gets loose, help him get it back under control. Don't pass around false stories. Try not to beat your servant to death. Treat your wives fairly. Here's how to treat a concubine and her children. Earlier foreign law codes dealt with similar issues with similar solutions. In all of those ancient law codes we can see where cultural worldviews caused justice to go astray compared to our standards today.

There were many sexual laws. Death to anyone who sleeps with his mother. Stoning for a man and woman caught in adultery. An unmarried priest's daughter who was found to be pregnant could be burned at the stake. Sex with animals was an abomination. There were also laws about the "sacred" versus the "profane." Profane refers to things that spiritually defile a person. No, this did not include the sexual bans. The purity laws were all about ritual defilement and cleansing—having sex or a night time emission, having a seeping sore, menstruating, or eating the wrong foods were all things that made a person "unclean." Leprosy, skin conditions—it had nothing to do with the condition of a person's heart before God. The defilement could be passed on from person to person by touch, so those needing help often didn't get it. The rules for cleansing could be inconvenient and take weeks. It would certainly be disruptive to a merchant or busy farmer, so Israelites took pains to not break the purity laws and to not touch another who was in the state of being unclean.

In the New Testament, a woman with a chronic issue of blood pressed through a crowd to touch Jesus as he was passing by. She touched the hem of his garment and was instantly healed. Until that healing, she led a life of isolation, not due to the fact that she was ill, but because she was ritually unclean and could be a serious inconvenience to others.

The laws for priests were very stringent. They could only marry a virgin. They could not approach a dead body or give aid to someone in an unclean state. Guilt was often communal. If a citizen sinned and got away with it, people feared that God would punish the whole community. The punishment described for mortal transgressions was physical death at the hands of the people. In that way, they passed the guilt away from themselves.

The Exodus narrative records that when the Israelites left Egypt, they were not all monotheists. A "mixed multitude" went with them—other captive Asiatics wanting to return to Syria, Lebanon, or Canaan (Exod 12:38). When Moses disappeared on Mt. Sinai (also called Mt. Horeb), the people reverted to manufacturing a golden statue of a bull, representing their familiar god, Baal, or his father Bull-El. Later on in their wanderings, they reverted to sacrifices to the dead associated with Baal Peor (Ps 106:23). In spite of the miracle of deliverance, provision of water in the Sinai wilderness, manna appearing on the ground, and birds falling out of the sky, the Israelites still grumbled and turned to the old deities (Ps 106:19–33; Amos 5:25–27).

As for the necessity of family cemeteries, Moses, Aaron, Miriam, and an entire generation of Hebrews are said to have been buried in the Sinai Peninsula in unmarked graves and without the wailing, gashing of bodies, and food offerings typical of other Near Eastern cultures. No hint of a dangerous journey to the nether world is registered. There seems to be no fear of souls being devoured or tortured by demon gods. The mourners did not cut themselves or shave their heads. There is no mention of the soul needing to be judged as righteous in order to continue existing in the afterlife, nor did thousands of bones need to be carried to the new land in order for the souls to find rest.

Deuteronomy 13 commands the death sentence for anyone who entices others to go after foreign gods or who offers their child in sacrifice to a god (Lev 20:1–3). Judgment was severe against any who practiced witchcraft, who turned to mediums to consult the dead, or conjured up spirits for sorcery, divination (using objects to procure predictions and instructions), or spells (Deut 18:10–11). A barrier was placed in the Mosaic Law against anything paranormal or occult, between the dead and the living. The idea behind this ban was that spirits that respond to sacrifices and incantations did not represent Yahweh or his angelic messengers. Like the serpent, their agenda would not be to aid the people but to ensnare them and turn them away from Elohim. This was a difficult shift in practice for a people who expected to honor their ancestors for generations to come. In their world, interaction with the world of deceased spirits was the norm. Not bringing food and drink to uncle Yakim or Grandma Rachel, nor consulting them for aid was almost unthinkable. And not doing so stirred the constant fear that vengeful ghosts might wreak calamity on the neglectful. It was a hard sell to a people full of superstition and fear.

Two important aphorisms developed in the Torah literature: one is that a person cannot see the face of God and live (Exod 33:20). The other is that without the shedding of blood there is no forgiveness of sin (Lev 17:11; Heb 9:22). These two concepts had a profound grip on the ancient people and still resonate among conservatives today.

Joshua-Judges

According to the Book of Joshua, Israel's ancestors worshiped idols in Syria before Abraham migrated to Canaan. Joshua challenged his followers,

> Now fear the Lord, and serve him in all faithfulness. Throw away the gods your forefathers worshiped beyond the River and in Egypt, and serve the Lord. But if serving the LORD seems undesirable to you, then choose for yourself this day whom you will serve, whether the gods your forefathers served beyond the River, or the gods of the Amorites in whose land you are living. But as for me and my household, we will serve the Lord. (Josh 24:14)

There were just too many syncretists to obey the laws in the Torah which demanded that they be put to death. In spite of the Jordan River drying up for them to cross dry shod, when Joshua led a renewal of the covenant with the Israelites at Shechem, they were still not wholly committed to monotheism. Once again, he had to order them to cast away their foreign gods. When the land began to be under Israelite control, a troop of soldiers from the tribe of Dan stole an idol and its priest and set off for the fertile city of Laish, north of the Sea of Galilee. They changed the name of the city to Dan, after their patriarchal ancestor. They set up the idol and chose their own priests without regard to the Law of Moses. Their extreme geographical isolation undoubtedly caused them to be less worried that the other tribes would rise up in wrath and declare war on them.

After the initial violent invasion of the land, Israelites and Canaanites lived in peace for almost three hundred years (Josh 13 and Judg 11:26). One of their aristocrats married a Moabitess who became so famous, a book of the Bible was named after her. Ruth's sister-in-law was also from Moab because an Israelite family settled there during a famine. However, this closeness with foreign neighbors is exactly what the author of Deuteronomy feared. Intermarriage causes compromise, compromise brings in foreign ideas and practices, and the resulting transgressions bring God's wrath on the whole community.

In Joshua and Judges, God manifested his favor to the people only when they called on him and him alone. We read about angels appearing as his messengers between heaven and earth. Only one major theological development arose in the era of the Judges, and that came through an old prophet named Samuel. In his conflict with King Saul, Samuel said,

> Does the LORD delight in burnt offerings and sacrifices as much as in obeying the voice of the LORD? To obey is better than sacrifice, and to heed is better than the fat of rams. For rebellion is like the sin of divination, and arrogance like the evil of idolatry. (1 Sam 15:22–23)

This stunning statement was an indication of how Samuel would influence David and his spiritual court.

Job

The law code of Deuteronomy offers scant information about the afterlife. Its importance for the present discussion, then, lies primarily in its "Theology of Retribution." According to this perspective, righteous people will "live," thrive, and prosper in the land. Sinners will suffer dire diseases, plagues, infertility, defeat, and exile in this life (Deut 27–28). This understanding of suffering as the product of moral failure is the foil for the book of Job. Job's comforters represent belief in the distant, stern, mighty deity who is unconcerned that humans are crushed like moths. Yet, because of who He is, no one may accuse him of being capricious and unjust (Job 4:18–21). Goodness will be rewarded; rebellion will bring wrath and destruction (11:20; 20:12–29; 22:21–30). God's vengeance will begin here on earth and follow the sinner into the afterlife. He will be marched off to the King of Terrors (an image similar to meeting Nergal or Mot); his name will be forgotten and his seed destroyed (18:5–21).[5]

Against the accusations of his friends, Job desires a day in the court of God to seek his vindication. His long protestation of innocence in chapters 29–31 is reminiscent of the long list of sins not committed that must be proclaimed by a deceased Egyptian in the presence of forty-two gods. His resumé of righteousness is impressive. He at once doubts, desires, and affirms the possibility of an advocate, a heavenly being (like the Akkadian Ishum) who stands in God's presence and who will plead for him.[6] In Job's speech, the powers of Abaddon and Mot (Canaanite gods) are satirized as being nothing compared to the wisdom of God (28:22–28). The mysterious fourth friend, Elihu, seems to mock Job's hopes of a Redeemer (33:24–30). Elihu's God does not despise men, but he is still perfect in justice and therefore metes out punishment that any reasonable observer can understand (36:1–15).

The mystery of afterlife is paramount in the epic. Job is a book from which we draw a great deal of our understanding of afterlife in the Hebrew Bible. Scholars too often resort to the book as a systematic resource on the theology of death in ancient Israel. There are many statements that emphasize the gloom, hopelessness, permanence, weakness, worms, separation from God, and the "king of terrors" (Job 10:21, 22; 17:12–16; 18:5–21).

> Why then did you bring me out of the womb?
> I wish I had died before any eye saw me,
> if only I had never come into being,
> or had been carried straight from the womb to the grave!
> Are not my few days almost over?
> Turn away from me so I can have a few moments joy
> Before I go to the place of no return,
> to the land of gloom and deep shadow,
> to the land of deepest night,
> of deep shadow and disorder,

---

5. See Sarna, "Mythological Background," 315–18 for the relationship between Job 18 and Canaanite mythology.

6. Job 9:33–35; 13:3, 14, 15, 18; 14:14–17; 16:19–21; 19:23–26; 23:3, 10; 27:1–6.

Where even the light is like darkness. (Job 10:18–22)

The reality of life after death is never the issue. The issue is the quality of that life. We find echoes in chapter 18 of the ancient need to be remembered and invoked, and for posterity to continue the family name. But to treat the book as a comprehensive textbook on the afterlife of both the wicked and the righteous is to miss the author's entire point. In fact, within the book itself, there are divergent views presented as to what happens to the righteous when they die.

By the time Job was written, two other great epics were known in the ANE, *The Epic of Gilgamesh* and *The Baal Cycle*. There are allusions to both in Job's pages, and both have a great deal to say about the nether world. Job is an epic that not only competed well with those older classics, but also outlasted them by thousands of years. The epic presents questions in the form of a drama about the prevailing Israelite views of the day, which were saturated with foreign mythology. It is no accident that *Sheol* as depicted in Job is gloomy and hopeless. The contrast between Job's lament and the hope expressed in 19:26 is jarring. Such a literary device may be designed to gain the reader's complete attention and to provoke discussion. God does not answer Job's questions, but he does vindicate what Job has said.

There are three important paradigms or thought-reforms promoted in the drama. The first is that the righteous can suffer. Conversely, the wicked may lead a life that is admired and envied by others. People in misery deserve the pity and aid of friends and family rather than quick and simplistic condemnation. The second is that the righteous will ultimately be justified by a mysterious heavenly redeemer/advocate. We learn three things about this entity in Job 19:25. 1) He already "lives," (exists in the heavens, see 16:19), but his main work will apparently be in the future, "at the last." 2) He will "rise up," an eschatological word, upon the "dust," a word often suggestive of the hopeless grave (Gen 3:19, Ps 90:3).[7] Perhaps he will brood over death with creative power the way that the *ruach elohim* brooded over creation. 3) He will plead for the righteous as if in a judicial proceeding. He does not need to inquire as to the innocence or guilt of the defendant. He already knows. Job does not confirm whether this vindication or plea for mercy is a post-mortem event.

The third doctrinal paradigm is that, unlike the sinner whose skin is devoured by the first-born of death (18:13), Job is confident that he will be restored in skin and flesh and will see God with his own post-mortem eyes (19:26). Job's purpose is to declare a vibrant hope for ultimate redemption and vindication.

---

7. Tromp, *Primitive Conceptions*, 33; Pss 22:30; 30:10; 32:33; 55:16; Jer 17:16.

David and Solomon

A lot could be said about the diverse views of afterlife between King David, the writer of so many Psalms, and his son, King Solomon. Both men were wealthy, good looking, talented, and charismatic, but they diverged in their relationship with Yahwism. David believed in prophecy, miracles, the power of the *ruach elohim* (the Spirit of God), the essential need for God's favor, the need to repent and acknowledge sin, and in the ability of sin to taint God's blessing in our life. When he did sin with Bathsheba, and the babe that was the result of his transgression died, David declared, "I shall go to him, but he shall not return to me" (2 Sam 12:16–23). David was certain that his child was out there where they could be united. There was nowhere in the universe where God could not find his children:

> Where can I go from your Spirit?
> Where can I flee from your presence?
> If I go up to the heavens, you are there;
> if I make my bed in the depths, you are there.
> If I rise on the wings of the dawn,
> if I settle on the far side of the sea,
> even there your hand will guide me,
> your right hand will hold me fast.
> If I say, "Surely the darkness will hide me
> and the light become night around me,"
> even the darkness will not be dark to you;
> the night will shine like the day,
> for darkness is as light to you. (Ps 139:7–12)

For David and those connected by covenant and relationship to Elohim, *Sheol* could not be a place where "even the light is darkness." It is possible that it was David's priestly court that wrote the book of Job and the above psalm to be a foil against the traditional fears, to alleviate the fears of those who were facing death.

Solomon began well. The authors of 1 and 2 Chronicles took great pains to describe the awe-inspiring worship at the consecration of his great Temple. Jerusalem bloomed into a cosmopolitan city with activity everywhere as Temple and Palace took shape. As we saw in chapter 3, when it was finished, there was an epic celebration. It was all so perfect, what could possibly go wrong?

Solomon married many princesses. Royal elites, both foreign and native, were seen on all the street corners of Jerusalem and the City of David. They wore their finest garb as they rode around in colorful chariots. Taxes rose to help pay for it all. Slave labor began to be abused. Worse yet, foreign idols proliferated in the city. All of the foreign practices detested by Moses and the prophets of Israel became part of everyday life—including child sacrifice. The Bible doesn't explicitly say that Solomon personally sacrificed his own children, but he "went after" gods despised by the prophets. He set up places of worship to Ashtoreth, Molech, and Chemosh (known for requiring child sacrifice) on the hills east of Jerusalem, and his wives burnt incense to these and all of their patron deities (2 Kgs 11:1–8). The beautiful gift of the Promised Land began to unravel, and so did Solomon himself. The book of Ecclesiastes is the testament of a bored, jaded king who abandoned the faith of his father and turned to foreign ways. This influenced his attitude toward death and afterlife. Solomon believed that we all died like dumb beasts, and that nothing on this earth was permanent or meaningful. He negates the Theology of Retribution promoted by the authors of Deuteronomy and 1 and 2 Chronicles (that God blesses the righteous and judges the wicked). He rejects the idea that life is sufficiently meaningful to be remembered by future generations (1:11); that anything in life can really change for the better (1:9, 15; 6:13); that wisdom brings happiness (1:18); that wealth brings fulfillment (2:11); that God favors the wise over the fool in both life and death (2:16; 9:2); that humans are better than beasts in the eyes of God; that life has a higher purpose (2:22–24; 4:3); that the righteous are "taken out" of *Sheol* (6:6; 9:5); that prophecy is real (6:12); that women can be virtuous (7:28); that divine providence can change the effect of time and chance upon a person's fate (9:11). Solomon's language reflects annihilation or an agnostic attitude toward afterlife whereby we can't know anything about it, so enjoy this life here while you can. David's revelation of a Messianic hope must have seemed naïve and incredible to Solomon, because for all of his "wisdom," he saw no grand purpose in Israel's existence and expressed little hope for the future. There is no sense in Ecclesiastes that one could call upon God in a time of trouble to find joy, comfort, and miraculous deliverance.

> And I saw something else under the sun:
> In the place of judgment—
> Wickedness was there,
> in the place of justice—
> wickedness was there.
> I thought in my heart,
> "God will bring to judgment both the righteous and the wicked,
> For there will be a time for every activity, a time for every deed."
> I also thought, "As for men, God tests them so that they may see that they are like the animals. Man's fate is like that of the animals; the same fate awaits them both: As one dies, so dies the other. All have the same breath; man has no advantage over the

animal. Everything is meaningless. All go to the same place; all come from dust, and to dust all return. Who knows if the spirit of man rises upward and if the spirit of the animal goes down into the earth? (Eccl 3:16–22)

Other Conflicting Views

After Solomon died, Judean kings regularly set up foreign cultic stations and followed regional practices "under every green tree,"[8] Shortly after 721 BCE, victorious Assyrian invaders filled northern Israel with foreigners who embraced worship of Yahweh but also continued in devotion to their own gods. Thus, the abundant archaeological evidence such as pillar figurines in Judean gravesites may reflect either a foreign presence or foreign influence. Orthodox, monotheistic Yahwism was still the practice of the minority—a theological elite and a handful of faithful families such as that of Joshua. Deuteronomy 13:12–17 warns against this sort of syncretism, demanding that if idols or foreign gods were set up in an Israelite city, the rest of the nation was to rise up, declare *herem* (total cultic destruction) over it, and kill every man, woman, and child in the city. Not a single item could be taken as booty. This injunction was never carried out because there were too many syncretists. In Elijah's day, writes the historian, there were only seven thousand in the north who had not bowed the knee to Baal (1 Kgs 19:18). Since Baal's other name was Hadad, and Yam's other name was Nahar, few Israelites would question if Yahweh was identified as having another name such as Baal or El. Nor would many have been startled if the priesthood declared the promiscuous Asherah to be the consort of Yahweh.

When young Josiah became king of Judah (640–609 BCE), there was an abundance of Baal altars and Asherah poles yet to be destroyed, as well as idols and horses dedicated to the starry host to remove from the temple.[9] Passover had barely been kept since the days of the prophet Samuel (2 Chr 35:18). Male prostitutes and women weaving for Asherah were evicted from the Temple in the reformation. Josiah removed the Topheth, a cultic cemetery, to forestall the child sacrifice that had been practiced since the days of King Solomon (2 Kgs 23:10). Not even King Hezekiah, in his zealous attempt at reform, had been as diligent. Isaiah's prophetic rebuke suggests that when some Israelites did practice ancestor worship, it included dark spirits,

---

8. 2 Kgs 16:3; 17:17, 31; 21:6; 23:10; Jer 32:35.

9. Day, "Asherah," 406. Day lists the references to Asherah worship from Judg 3:7 to Josiah in 2 Kgs 23:4, 6, 7, 14, 16. Both Joshua and Amos accuse the Israelites of polytheism and syncretism in the wilderness (Amos 5:26).

black magic, sexual rites, and infant sacrifice (Isa 57:3–10). The prophets believed that although idols were vain and powerless, the spiritual impetus behind such worship came from malicious, demonic entities.

Josiah led a renewal of the Yahwistic covenant with the nation, but it only endured through his reign, less than thirty years. Jeremiah, a prophet whose ministry continued after the death of Josiah, debated with the people of Judah who survived the attack of the Babylonians. They feared that all their misfortunes, including enemy invasion, were due to the fact that Josiah had forbidden the cultic worship of the Queen of Heaven (Jer 44:17–25).

Probably the most effective weapon in the forging of a canonical, monotheistic Yahwism was the time spent in exile in Babylon. Here the Jews were separated from their temple and the foreign feasts that had often led them into syncretistic practices. In Babylon they polished their records and legends, drawing them into a series of books that defined their faith and reviewed the significance of their history. The pen of the scribes was ultimately mightier than the sword of Josiah.

The point for our present purpose is that syncretistic borrowing in early Hebrew religion was neither uncommon nor, in the eyes of the average Israelite, illegitimate.[10] The fact that *anyone* in ancient Israel attempted to follow a single deity who forbad any crafted image is really remarkable. In contrast to the surrounding cultures, monotheistic Hebrew scribes wrote about the creation of the world without reference to demons or monsters. Monotheistic priests could face an uncertain future without resorting to divination and magic. Contact with the dead was kept to a minimum.

The injunction against sacrificing to goat demons in Lev 17:7 indicates that syncretistic worship was a very live issue, even in Israel's distant past.[11] In spite of the obviously contested nature of Israelite religion, the surviving biblical literature is fairly consistent in its rejection of syncretism.

---

10. See Cox, "Water Spilt," 1–9 for a review of Israelite traditions and beliefs.

11. Demons may also be found in 2 Chr 11:15 and Isa 13:21; 34:14. The NIV translates as "satyrs" as "wild goats" and "Lilith" as night creatures. Owens, KJV, and NASB prefer "satyr" or "demon." *TWOT* rejects the need to read demon into the usual word for a male goat. The context of 2 Chr 11 supports some kind of goat idol set up by Jerobaom I, which later would have been considered a demon by some. The Isaiah passages translate well as "wild goat."

8

Irrepressible Life or Certain Doom

Psalms 88, 22, and 16

As we have seen, an "early" way of thinking about death is reflected in the unrelenting misery of Ps 88 in which an unhappy death is variously designated as "the lowest pit," "the darkest depths," "Destruction/*abbadon*," "place of darkness," "the land of oblivion," a place where God's wonders are cut off, a place where the shades cannot rise up to praise Yahweh, a place where His steadfast love is not proclaimed. He may be describing a near death experience or a close brush with death, but more likely he is describing long term sickness and debilitation so severe that, as in the case of Job, his friends thought that God's judgment was cursing his life. The depressed and vexed author is calling upon every negative stereotype of death, judgment, and *Sheol* that he can think of, and wails in his despair like Gilgamesh and Enkidu. Death, illness, and rejection are poetically hyperbolized as literal death. In Israelite literature, death, afterlife, and the grave are closely intertwined, as if the afterlife were a metaphysical extension of physical death, corruption, and burial. There is no "taking out" in Ps 88, no redemption for anyone except to be blessed on earth.

An alternative way of thinking about *Sheol*, which oddly may emanate from the same time period, is found in Ps 22. The psalm begins with a wail of despair so profound that Jesus Christ quoted it while he was dying on the cross, "My God, my God, why have you forsaken me?" The psalm proceeds to describe a man who, like the author of Ps 49, is surrounded by genuinely malicious men, whom he calls bulls, lions, and dogs. These spiteful men have the author at bay. He is surrounded, and they mock and taunt him. The description that follows is that of a dying man, in fact, that of a man who is being crucified. They cast lots for his clothing, they pierce his hands and feet. Beginning with Ps 22:22, the psalm shifts gears into total triumph and rejoicing. The sufferer has been rescued from the grave. He testifies of it before the people of God in the congregation or assembly of God. There is feasting and worship that transcends the nation of Israel and reverberates down the generations of time. Even the dead can worship because they are not really dead:

> All the ends of the earth
> will remember and turn to the LORD,
> and all the families of the nations will bow down before him,
> for dominion belongs to the LORD,
> and he rules over the nations.
> All the rich of the earth will feast and worship;
> all who go down to the dust will kneel before him—
> those who cannot keep themselves alive. (Ps 22:27–29)

Psalm 139: In the Secret Place I am Found

We have already seen that in Ps 139, there is nowhere where the deceased can hide from God. His beloved redeemed cannot be lost or abandoned. God can pursue them throughout the universe, into eternity if need be, or into hell itself to retrieve them. Light and dark are the same to God, night will shine like the day. Further, the psalm describes a deity who dwells in a dimension where time does not matter or exist.

> My frame was not hidden from you
> when I was made in the secret place (Heb: "in secret").
> When I was woven together in the depths of the earth,
> your eyes saw my unformed body.
> All the days ordained for me were written in your book
> before one of them came to be. (Ps 139:15–16)

The Hebrew does say that the pre-mortal David was formed in the depths of the earth. We must not imagine a well-lit workshop where angels design humans and then place them in wombs. David could not possibly know where we are originated, but he clearly believed that God knew him before he was conceived. Lest this seem too superstitious to us, I dreamed of my second child before he was conceived, and I welcomed him into the family. My friend Mary had a friend who saw Mary's future baby boy in a vision well before the child was conceived. Mary had a cute but unique face. The friend told her that her little son would look just like her. When the child was born, he did in fact look like his mom. The first thing anyone said about him, including me, was, "Mary, he looks just like you." Even at the age of eleven he was the image of his mother.

In this psalm, humans are not like dumb beasts, unless they turn away from the wisdom that draws them to God. God is with them before birth, during gestation, and even unto death. The humblest human is worthy of his care.

Claiming that *Sheol* denotes only the grave solves the problem of the negative picture of *Sheol* in the Scriptures. If all men go there and none return and it is the same for all, where is the justice of God? If *Sheol* is the cold, dark, gloomy place often described in the Hebrew Bible, how are humans special In God's sight? The simple answer, that *Sheol* denotes the grave only, may be too minimal for a process that is long, complex, and diverse. Desmond Alexander is one scholar who rejects the notion that *Sheol* is compartmentalized with lower, dank, regions for the wicked and other areas for the righteous. Rather, it is the final abode of the wicked only.[1] Apparently, for some, it was the place where all went for eternity. That may have, at some point in history, been the majority report. But a bright new concept of "taking out" of the righteous arose with the Davidic prophets. Therefore, attempts to find a unified theory of *Sheol* will meet with frustration.

Isaiah 8:19–22, 9:1: History's Most Incredible Prediction

No prophet was more antagonistic to magic, superstition, spirits, or divination (fortune telling) than the eighth-to-seventh century BCE firebrand, Isaiah. He decried the foolish mimicking of Canaanite values and the grasping of temporary fixes for long term political and spiritual problems. The people of his day were obsessed with death and how to make peace with it. His poetic prophecies are both theological and political, encompassing long passages that often become separated from their contexts by translators and exegetes, making interpretation difficult. A strict monotheist, he viewed the Canaanite practices as a highway to "death" and to the worst of whatever the afterlife had to offer.

Isaiah 8 deals with a historical conspiracy between Northern Israel and Syria against Judah, which was ruled by the idolatrous king Ahaz of Judah. Although Ahaz was not walking in monotheistic light, God's time of judgment for Judah still lay further in the future. In chapter 7, Isaiah waylaid Ahaz's retinue on the road and promised the king that God would break the northern conspiracy that threatened him. As an assurance, he invited Ahaz to ask for a miraculous sign. Ahaz, for political reasons, refused

1. Alexander, "Life after Death," 43.

to ask. Isaiah offered the sign of a young woman[2] conceiving and bringing forth a son. He also predicted that the Lord would use the king of Assyria to break the conspiracy (7:18; 8:7). In chapter 8, Isaiah took a pen and tablet and called two faithful priestly officials of Jerusalem to go with him as witnesses while he "approached"[3] the "prophetess" and prophesied the conception of a child, a male, whose name would be Emmanuel, "God With Us" (7:14; 8:8). He assured these two officials in writing that the northern conspiracy would not stand (8:9–10). Anticipating the pressure they would surely feel to perform an inquiry of the dead for the king and military, he warned them to fear only God and not man (8:12–13), and he admonished them to seek Yahweh and not to fall into Canaanite ways that would bring only death and curse:

> When men tell you to consult mediums and spiritists, who whisper and mutter, should not a people consult their God? Why consult the dead on behalf of the living? To the law and to the testimony! If they do not speak according to this word, they have no light of dawn. Distressed and hungry, they will roam through the land; when they are famished, they will become enraged and, looking upward, will curse their king and their God. Then they will look toward the earth and see only distress and darkness and fearful gloom, and they will be thrust into utter darkness. (Isa 8:19–22)

The text of this passage is bristling with difficulties. One problem centers upon the interpretation of "mediums," which commentary writer J. Watts renders "fathers"—"to seek out the fathers and the diviners."[4] Here he stands alone due to the consistent use of the word in conjunction with "spiritists." The word can signify either a familiar spirit or the medium who summons it. Necromancy, the consulting of the dead for strategic information, is clearly the issue in these verses. Watts's use of "fathers" is not far off in the sense that the fathers being consulted are probably deceased ancestors.

The next problem centers around the interpretation of *elohav*, which is grammatically plural but capable of either singular or plural translation. A variant reading in 1QIsa makes the word "God" grammatically singular. Most translations choose the singular "God," as in "should not a people inquire of their God?" (NIV, NKJV, Oswalt, NRSV, KJV). The HCSB opts for

---

2. The LXX reads "virgin."

3. The word here is literally "approach" rather than the usual euphemisms for sex "go in to" or "know." Lev 18:6, 14, 19 and 20:16 use *qarab* "approach" for sexual contact or exposure.

4. Watts, *Isaiah, 1–33*, 24:125.

"their God" but offers the alternative "their gods" in a footnote. The root of the problem is the phrase: "Why consult the dead on behalf of the living?" In fact, NIV inserts the "why." The phrase is literally "[inquire of] the dead on behalf of the living?" Academic literature abounds where the linguists debate the translation possibilities. In the end, a guide would include common logic—what did Isaiah consistently preach? Where did he stand theologically? Which translation makes the most sense grammatically, both to us and to the ancient reader?

Isaiah is predicting the destruction of Jacob (Northern Israel) and he is warning the two priests of chapter 7, who are still with him, that Judah and Jerusalem are not immune from disaster and captivity. In verse 16 he tells his friends to protect his writings and his teachings until the crisis is passed. Desperate days are looming when the only safe haven will be Yahweh's protection and favor. God has his people covered. Consulting the dead will lead to famine and destruction.

The word "dawn" or "light" in verse 17 ("If they will not speak according to this word, they have no light of dawn") causes difficulties because the LXX reads δωρα, from Heb "gift" or "bribe."[5] Other translations have also been proposed for the MT word; however, the context favors "dawn," since it contrasts well with the theme of gloom, anguish, and darkness that continues from 8:20 and 8:22 into 9:1–2. And this is where the worm turns in the whole passage:

> Nevertheless, there will be no more gloom for those who were in distress. In the past he humbled the land of Zebulun and the land of Naphtali, but in the future he will honor Galilee of the Gentiles, by the way of the sea, along the Jordan—
> The people walking in darkness have seen a great light;
> on those living in the land of the shadow of death
> a light has dawned. (Isa 9:1–2)

From there the passage expands into the most extraordinary prophecy of all time. A male child will be born, a gift from God, he will be a king related to King David, he will inherit David's throne and kingdom, he will be a ruler of peace, he will be granted titles attributed to God himself in the Scriptures (Mighty God, Everlasting Father), his government will never be overthrown. The light of this king will be recognized in Galilee of the Gentiles. Many will turn from darkness to light.

---

5. Ibid. Compare Isa 47:11. Lit.: "Evil will come upon you. You will not know its dawning." Many versions follow Köhler and Baumgartner in translating "not be able to charm away" (NIV, NRSV). HCSB: "But disaster will happen to you; you will not know how to avert it."

Although difficult passages like Isa 8 and 9 present challenges for the expert Hebrew linguists, the metaphors are not difficult to understand. Light and darkness referred to in these verses are theological and end time metaphors, declaring that anguish will come to all those who consult ghosts and wizards regardless of their nationality. In Isaiah's day Northern Israel had been taken away by the Assyrians, never to return as a formal state. It truly seemed that Yahweh had turned his back on them forever. Yet in that land where the Israelites used to dwell, some transcendent light will dawn, bringing redemption and safety to those who dwell there, Jew and Gentile alike. The political and historical context becomes so interwoven with last day themes that it is difficult to limit its application to the eighth century Assyrian threat. The "dawn" of 8:20 seems more apocalyptic than historical.[6]

The subtle brilliance of this passage is that 8:21–22 are written as if the protagonists are not just a people in crisis but are shades already in *Sheol*. They look up as if they are below the earth. They curse their king and their gods (or perhaps their invoked ancestors).[7] Isaiah's aversion to the ancestor cult is so profound and his reasoning so developed that, regardless of what an occasional scholar would suggest, it is highly unlikely that he would accept any form of necromancy.

Deuteronomy: Healing Comes Last

Although the author of Deuteronomy seldom addresses the question of afterlife directly, Yahweh's power of life over death is never in doubt:

> The LORD will judge his people
> and have compassion on his servants
> when he sees their strength is gone
> and no one is left, slave or free.
> He will say: "Now where are their gods,
> The rock they took refuge in,
> the gods who ate the fat of their sacrifices
> and drank the wine of their drink offerings?
> Let them rise up to help you!
> Let them give you shelter!
> See now that I myself am He!
> There is no god besides me.

---

6. Christian theology finds the fulfillment of chs 7–9 in Jesus Christ as Messiah and Savior of mankind.

7. Psalm 107:1–16 contains a similar double entendre.

> I put to death and I bring to life,
> I have wounded and I will heal,
> and no one can deliver out of my hand." (Deut 32:36–39)

Verse 38 lampoons the belief that the deity actually eats the burnt offering, the cakes, the bread, and the libation of water or wine. Verse 39 assures the reader that those gods/shades are nothing; Nergal, Mot, Ereshkigal, Anat, Ningizzida, the Egyptian reptilian gods and goddesses, the demons of the underworld, and the Babylonian horned dragon beast called Marduk can neither aid nor destroy the one trusting in Yahweh. The word "rise up" in verse 38 conjures the image of gods and shades who are asleep or are coming forth from the grave. Verse 39 is the climax of the passage. As noted by many scholars, the killing and wounding are mentioned first; the "making alive" comes after. The word heal comes from the same root as "*rephaim*." Whether the issue is an individual or a nation in need of healing, whether deliverance from individual death or deliverance from national destruction, whether earthly relief or salvation in the afterlife is meant in this passage, God is sufficient. We are in his hands for good or for ill!

Hannah: A Poem about Reversals

The Deuteronomist's perspective is echoed in that of Hannah, a barren woman in the era of the Judges. Her inability to provide a child to the family caused her to be harassed by her husband's other wife. When she came to the tabernacle at Shiloh and prayed for a child, she was rewarded with a little boy who became the prophet Samuel. She wrote a psalm of thanksgiving, glorifying God for a miracle:

> The LORD brings death and makes alive;
> he brings down to the grave and raises up.
> The LORD sends poverty and wealth;
> he humbles and he exalts.
> He raises the poor from the dust
> and lifts the needy from the ash heap.
> He seats them with princes
> and has them inherit a throne of honor.
> For the foundations of the earth are the LORD's;
> upon them he has set the world. (1 Sam 2:6–8)

Once again, the distress comes first. "Weeping endures for a night but joy comes in the morning." In Gen 1, night comes first; the day ends with light. Think of Anne Frank in WW II. She spent years of her short life hiding in a closet. She never went to university, acted in a movie, married, ran for office, yet she is remembered by school children worldwide today—while her killers, so arrogant and self-assured at the time, are despised and forgotten.

In fact, the ultimate end of a distressing situation is where God manifests his covenant love. This song of reversals could simply be using the concept of *Sheol* and life in the same sense used by the author of Ps 88 and Ps 30:4, in which *Sheol* is a metaphor of personal anguish. But the passage should not be limited to this single meaning, because the notion that a text has only one, exclusive meaning is a modern way of thinking. The other improbable reversals of the chapter are offered as miracles springing from the forgiving grace of Yahweh. Hannah was not seeking healing from the *rephaim* or from a host of healers of the nether world. Her body was "dead," but Yahweh brought it to "life" and in doing so altered her emotional state and her status in the family and community. There is significantly no mention of sacrifice, herbs, ritual, figurine, or amulet. In a world awash with superstition and fear of otherworldly entities, Hannah's recourse to intense prayer to Yahweh alone is the very point of the narrative.

It could be argued that there is no proof in verse 5 of a belief in Yahweh's power to literally snatch souls from *Sheol*; however, even if death, life, and *Sheol* are simply metaphors for divine activity here on earth, many sages likely perceived a metaphysical reality behind the metaphor. A dead womb was brought to life. The basic fears of daily life in the ancient world are mentioned in Hannah's psalm: defeat in war, hunger, infertility, death, poverty, disenfranchisement, and lack of status. The result of not trusting in Yahweh is to be "silenced in darkness," another *Sheol* metaphor.[8] In the Second Temple era, the book of Tobit would reiterate the same sentiment:

> Then Tobit said, "Blessed be God who lives forever, because his kingdom lasts throughout all ages. For he afflicts, and he shows mercy; he leads down to Hades in the lowest regions of the earth, and he brings up from the great abyss, and there is nothing that can escape his hand." (Tob 13:1–2)

---

8. For a further discussion on Deut 32:39 and 1 Sam 2:5, see Johnston, *Shades of Sheol*, 218–20 and Levenson, *Resurrection*, 171–72. Levenson points out that the wounding and healing do not necessarily happen to the same person. True, but the context and point of the message is that an individual's or nation's circumstance can be reversed. One is poor one year and rich the next or vice-versa. One has to *read out* the message of redemption in the periscope to deny the whispers of immortality. Cf. also Spronk, *Beatific Afterlife*, 12, 14, 18. Tertullian cites Deut 32:29 as proof of immortality. In the Targumim the verse is changed to, "I kill the living in this world and make alive the dead in the world to come."

Elijah and Elisha: Humiliating Baal

The story of two northern prophets, Elijah and Elisha, is often analyzed in discussions of immortality in ancient Israel. The creative power manifested by these two prophets covers every type of miracle.

- Baal was the weather god, but on top of Mt. Carmel during the drought, it was Elijah who declared whether it would rain or not (1 Kgs 17:1).
- The creative miracle of the jar of flour and the jug of oil that wouldn't empty was reminiscent of Christ feeding thousands with one lad's basket of fish and bread (17:14).
- The resurrection of the widow's son certainly was a demonstration of Yahweh snatching a soul from *Sheol* and giving life to dead cells (17:22).
- Elijah and others of his gifting also offered the kind of strategic military information to Northern Israel's monarch, Ahab, that kings usually sought from prophecy, divination, cleromancy, the ancestor cult, or the *Rephaim* (1 Kgs 20 and 2 Kgs 1:3).
- In 2 Kgs 5, the Syrian officer, Naaman, was healed of leprosy by the word of Elisha.

On Mt. Carmel, Elijah mocked the prophets of Baal who gashed themselves to elicit a response from the storm god. He called forth fire from heaven to consume the sacrifice. In the Baal myth, Baal's sister Anat challenged her Father El on Baal's behalf. She brags that she destroyed his servants Fire and Flame.[9] Fire was also a means of building Baal's house in the myth. It burned for six days. On the seventh, it was extinguished, but it had turned silver and gold into bricks and plaques.[10] Since Baal was the rain god, when the ancients heard thunder, they thought of him:

> Balu himself opens up the rift in the clouds,
> Balu emits his holy voice,
> Balu makes the thunder roll over and over again.
> His holy voice [causes] the earth to tremble,
> at his thunder the mountains shake with fear.[11]

Finally, Elijah trumped Baal by being taken into heaven in a chariot. That put him on a par with the god who was called in the myth the "Cloud

---

9. Hallo, *Context of Scripture*, 1:252.
10. Ibid., 1:261.
11. Ibid., 1:262.

Rider." In Ps 18:10–15 Yahweh is the Cloud Rider, wrapping Himself in the darkness of a fierce thunder storm, exposing the valleys of the sea. In Ps 104:3b we see Yahweh again as the cloud rider, but there the emphasis is on Yahweh's garment of light, as if the storm is over and the clouds are parting. Winds and flame are Yahweh's servants or messengers:

> O Lord my God, you are very great;
> you are clothed with splendor and majesty.
> He wraps himself in light as with a garment;
> he stretches out the heavens like a tent,
> and lays the beams of his upper chambers on their waters.
> He makes the clouds his chariot,
> and rides on the wings of the wind.
> He makes the winds his messengers,
> flames of fire his servants. (Ps 104:1–4)

Elisha was never taken bodily into heaven like his mentor, but both are said to have raised the dead. Even Elisha's bones were infused with a powerful life force. He was honorably buried in a shaft and chamber grave in which the deceased is lowered down a shaft into a carved out chamber. When Elisha had been dead long enough for his bones to be exposed, Moab invaded Israel. Israelite soldiers were fleeing the field with the corpse of a fellow. There was little time to bury him, so they lowered him into the shaft of Elisha's tomb. The minute the deceased man's body touched the bones, he was resuscitated and cried out (accompanied by a few unprintable words from his companions?)

Some scholars have used that story to claim that the Israelites supposed that the bones of any dead person had special powers which were incorporated into cultic rituals. Such an argument is pure conjecture, and leeches the story of the author's original intention in writing it. Elisha was portrayed as a prophet and a miracle worker. The fact that his dried, fleshless bones had such a life force still remaining would only serve to vindicate his religious diatribes against Baalism. Thus Yahweh makes His case against Baal in the very arena where Baal functions. Since Baal was known as the source of life, albeit temporary, for the *rephaim,* freeing them at the harvest feast from the barred gates of the nether world, the inevitable mental extrapolation by the target audience—the average Israelite—would lead to the conclusion that if Elisha could do such miracles through the power of Yahweh, then Yahweh had power to snatch a soul from *Sheol.*

Jonah: Up from the Gates of *Sheol*

Another narrative that obliquely whispers of Yahweh's power to snatch souls from *Sheol* is that of the prophet Jonah. The story is cleverly told, salted with images of death and the nether world.[12] Jonah received the call to "Rise, go . . ." warn Nineveh of impending destruction. Jonah is portrayed as a monotheistic Yahwist who lived in the days of Jeroboam II, a syncretist king who followed the idolatrous path of Jeroboam I. Jeroboam II received many blessings from Yahweh because the LORD's compassion for Israel was still active in those days:

> The Lord had seen how bitterly everyone in Israel, whether slave or free, was suffering; there was no one to help them. (2 Kgs 14:26)

Many Hebrew writings profoundly challenged the religious worldview of the Israelites, but none more so than the tale of Jonah. He prophesied when Northern Israel's king Jeroboam (793–782 BCE) was threatened by deadly Assyrian incursions. Assyria had already begun invading the nations to her south, and had developed a reputation for brutality. Assyria kept a record of their brutal invasions on baked clay in their archives, which we are able to read today. Their demolition was complete, much like a plague of locusts that darkens the sky when they blew through and left nothing behind but stubble. The locusts, however, did not destroy the people, whereas the Assyrians did. Even before the height of their empire, the vanity of their kings knew no bounds. Samaria wasn't their target yet, but the prophets knew that the day was coming. They were the potential enemy of absolutely every nation in the region.

Why would God call on the prophet Jonah to preach repentance to them? If they respond and repent, their own destruction would be diverted! Jonah did not want to go. Most people know the story. He ran away on a ship. A storm came and almost sank it. While the sailors cried out to their gods to save them, Jonah slept down below. He tells them it's his fault, and tells them to throw him overboard. A huge fish swallows Jonah and vomits him up on the Mediterranean coast, so he stomps off to Nineveh and prophesies their doom. Rather than throwing Jonah into a dank prison cell as some Israelite kings might have done, the king of Nineveh called a fast and repented of the offending deeds. There were plenty to repent of. And of course, God relented and turned back their destruction . . . for the time being. When Jonah protested, the Lord said:

---

12. Achtemeier, *Minor Prophets I*, 17:260.

"You have been concerned about this vine, though you did not tend it or make it grow. It sprang up overnight and died overnight. But Nineveh has more than a hundred and twenty thousand people who cannot tell their right hand from their left, and many cattle as well. Should I not be concerned about that great city?" (Jonah 4:10–11)

New concepts were introduced that Jonah could not have fathomed without a direct rebuke from Yahweh. (a) Yahweh, unlike other gods or goddess, is not confined to one particular location or region of the world—ostensibly where the Temple resides. (b) Lingering perceptions that the sea is an Ugaritic god named Yam, or that the Philistine Dagon is in charge of the ocean or that Baal controls the wind were demolished. (c) The idea that *Sheol* is a place where one cannot praise Yahweh or from which one can never be released was also challenged. (d) Jonah learned that Yahweh is a deity that has compassion for all people, not just one nation. (e) The portrayal of Yahweh as a bloody, vengeful deity who wants only to crush his enemies was softened.

The language of the story is as important as the narrative itself. It begins as Jonah flees from the presence of God. He "goes down" to Joppa to find a ship. He boards the ship (literally "*goes down on it*"); he "*goes down into*" the lower levels of the ship; he *lies down*; he *falls asleep*; when he is tossed into the sea, he *goes down to the foundation of the mountains*. Four times the verb "descend" is used in the tale. His sleep is like death—not even the raging storm can awake him. Three times the verb for "hurl" is used. Yahweh hurls a great wind at the sea. The sailors hurl all their cargo over the side. Then they hurl Jonah into the sea. First, however, they all call upon their gods. They may have appealed to the Great Lady Atiratu of the Sea, the progenitress of the gods, the one in the Baal myth for whom El would do most anything. Or they may have cried out to Baal, Dagon, Asherah, Ishtar, Yam, Mot, and the entire pantheon from Egypt to Hatti to Shinar. The captain awakens Jonah with the same call that he received from Yahweh, "Arise, call . . ."[13]

As the storm continues to grow worse, they cast lots to see whose god has aroused the sea. When it falls on Jonah, they inquire carefully who he is and from whence he came. They want to know which god they must appease. Jonah tells them his story and suggests that they toss him into the sea. Although waves are crashing over the deck, and the wind is tearing at the sails, they fear that by doing so they may bring down a curse of bloodguilt on their heads, so they try to row to land. When the futility of that

13. Ibid., 263.

approach becomes apparent, they pray to Yahweh to relieve them of guilt as they hurl Jonah over the side. The storm ceases. The sailors all admit that it was Yahweh, and not Baal or any other god, who stilled the storm and to whom they should offer thanksgiving, vows, and sacrifices. Thus, Jonah was an evangelist even in his disobedience!

Already in the tale, the language of death has been used to show that the further Jonah went into disobedience, the closer he came to a death-like spiritual state. Now he is literally sinking into the deep, the Yam of Ugarit, the place of the waters of chaos, the place of waves and breakers and floods, all terms of death-like distress. The ocean is where the hapless sink and are not buried. The *tannin* (sea monsters) are there, as is Leviathan, the Hebrew version of seven-headed Lotan, the "fleeing, twisting serpent of the Baal myth."[14] The remains of fierce Tiamat are imbedded in the very waves of the sea. The fish eat their flesh; they are never found, so no bread or libation can comfort the deceased. The hapless die alone, forsaken by God. It is a sailor's worst nightmare, a place of total fear, but Jonah is too angry to be afraid.

Yahweh appoints a fish to swallow Jonah and he sinks to the roots of the mountains. All things are possible with the God of the Hebrews, but it is unlikely that Jonah is kept alive by God for three days and nights, as suggested by some, in the belly of a fish that is cruising the ocean bottom. Suffocation would be inevitable.

> The engulfing waters threatened me,
> the deep surrounded me;
> seaweed was wrapped around my head.
> to the roots of the mountains I sank down;
> the earth beneath barred me in forever.
> But you brought my life up from the pit,
> O LORD my God. (Jonah 2:5–9)

We should understand that Jonah did not have a near-death experience. He *died* in this fish. He is imprisoned in the pit beneath the earth, in *Sheol,* but there he is able to praise Yahweh and appeal to him. When Yahweh hears his prayer in his eternal temple (equivalent to Baal's palace on Mt. Zaphon), he intervenes on Jonah's behalf. It is no wonder then, that Jesus Christ's three-day death and resurrection will find a parallel in Jonah's experience (Matt 12:40). The fish vomits Jonah up onto land in the same way that the tomb will disgorge first century Lazarus. Mot, the figurative swallower of all mankind, will have to release his captives on a future day of judgment. In an ironic twist, Isaiah claims that Yahweh will ultimately swallow death (Isa 25:8).

14. Hallo, *Context of Scripture*, 1:252, 265.

Conclusion

When the Israelites left Egypt, monotheistic Yahwism was actually the "foreign" religion. In Elijah's day, when only seven thousand faithful monotheists remained in Israel, it was arguably still the minority religion. Throughout the period of the monarchy the prophets lamented that the people had not fully committed themselves to Yahweh. Monotheistic reforms were short-lived. The portrayal of the Israelites passing through the wilderness as pure monotheists in Deut 32 is merely a euphemistic, broad brush treatment of a people who were relatively monotheistic under pressure from a strong leader. Whatever Yahwistic tradition the patriarch Jacob's family practiced when his family of seventy entered Egypt, by the time they left they fell easily into the worship of bull and goat demons:

> They made him jealous with their foreign gods
> and angered him with their detestable idols.
> They sacrificed to demons, which are not God—
> gods they had not known, gods that recently appeared,
> gods your fathers did not fear. (Deut 32:16–17)

Turning the hearts and imaginations of the populace was no easy task and was far beyond the capability of any one man or family or generation of leaders. Narrative by narrative, psalm by psalm, *Sheol* became more real and more of an issue to be dealt with. The theological questions became more poignant, then more sophisticated: what happens to the soul of one who dies in the desert, at sea, or in battle? What is the relationship of the Temple to life and death? Why do the righteous suffer? What is *Sheol* and who goes there? Does any soul ever leave? Who has the power to open the gates? What happens if a soul is not fed and provisioned? The answers became more diverse but also more definitive. The narratives came with no systematic theological handbook or confessional expansion that could be applied to all generations in all regions of the country. There was no pope to issue a proclamation, no denominational headquarters to rein in theological deviation. Nevertheless, there emerged a literary and prophetic pattern in which the Ancient Near Eastern gloom of *Sheol* became balanced in Israel/Judah with the rising hope of escape. Yahweh was depicted as the true Lord of all that Baal, Asherah, and the Asiatic pantheon were alleged to rule; He is the Lord of creation, the Lord of life, the Lord of weather, the Lord of death, and the Lord who holds the key to the gates of *Sheol*.

When ancient Israel was faced with the choice of life or death, the nature of that life seemed far more tied to physical existence in the land of promise, but several passages can be read both ways. If they *can* be read on two levels, they probably *were* at some point in time, and may well have been *intended* to be:

> Keep my decrees and laws, for the man who obeys them will live by them. I am the Lord. (Lev 18:5)

> This day I call heaven and earth as witnesses against you that I have set before you life and death, blessings and curses. Now choose life, so that you and your children may live and that you may love the LORD your God, listen to his voice, and hold fast to him. For the LORD is your life, and he will give you many years in the land he swore to give to your fathers, Abraham, Isaac and Jacob. (Deut 30:19–20)

> In the way of righteousness there is life;
> along that path is immortality. (Prov 12:28)

> The path of life leads upwards for the wise
> to keep him from going down to the grave. (Prov 15:24)

The clear choice as presented in the Pentateuch is life and death here on earth in the "rest" (the land) provided by Yahweh. The choice in Proverbs approaches more clearly a transcendent meaning of life and death. In both cases, the way of life is obedience to Yahweh rather than the service of ancestors or other gods.

No one can say for certain when Ps 49 was written, but at almost every point in Israel's history there existed resources upon which the psalmist might have drawn in conceptualizing Yahweh as a deity who could raise the dead and snatch a soul from *Sheol*. The psalmist did not seem to care where or how he was buried. He had no illusion that grave goods or food would sustain him. He had no nagging doubt. His was a total confidence that needed no bolstering. In the words of Jon Levenson, Yahweh is portrayed as "the God of Life."[15]

---

15. Levenson, *Resurrection*, from the subtitle of his book.

9

Shared Semantic Fields

> "How a person lives his or her life is the most important investment one will ever make on the future-options exchange." Byron L. Sherwin

IN ATTEMPTING TO PROBE the depths of the heart and mind of the author of Ps 49, it is imperative to analyze the important contexts of his life and theology. Although certainty as to date and place of composition is beyond the reach of today's scholar, inter-textual echoes may be detected in four important bodies of literature: (1) There are conceptual and linguistic similarities between Ps 49 and Gen 1–3 that may reflect the ongoing contest between Yahweh and the tendency in Israel to favor the gods of Ugarit and Mesopotamia. (2) To enhance the historical and theological progression of Ps 49, it should be read in conjunction with the entire Korahite Psalter. (3) A multitude of scholars have recognized the similarity of thought and language in Pss 16, 49, and 73, which do not explicitly promote a theory of personal resurrection, but hint at a personal and blissful non-corporeal immortality. (4) A study of Second Temple/Inter-testamental literature (the Apocrypha, the Pseudepigrapha, the Talmud, and other rabbinic writings) may not verify with certainty what the biblical writers were trying to convey, but it shows where the antecedent discourse led the later generations.

The first three chapters of the book of Genesis share themes and phrases with Ps 49: Adam/*ish*; fruit/fruitfulness/eating the fruit of their ways; ground/dust/decay; God will take; live/die; misappropriation of trust; form/image; morning/light; beast/rule; fear/blessing. Although a close examination of these themes cannot prove an intentional association, it is possible that the author of one had the other in mind while penning their own masterpiece. At the very least, the authors seem to have shared a worldview or to have participated in a shared dialogue centered around the theme of life and immortality.[1]

Adam and ish. Although Ps 49 has reference points in common with the two creation documents in Gen 1–3, there are some significant differences to sort through between Genesis chapter 1 and chapter 2. In Gen 1, the word *ish* (man) is not used. Adam is called "the *adam*," the human creature; he is taken from the ground, *adamah*. Use of the definite article throughout the chapter suggests that *adam* is a category and not a name. In 1:26 the word is used without the definite article, but the application of the plural pronoun "them" again suggests a composite category:

> Then God said, "Let us make humankind (*adam*) in our image, according to our likeness; and let them have dominion over the fish of the sea, and over the birds of the air, and over the cattle, and over all the wild animals of the earth, and over every creeping thing that creeps upon the earth." (Gen 1:26)

The *adam* of Gen 1 is created already male and female with no agonizing wait or search for a mate, no joyous exclamation of "at last!" (Gen 1:27; 5:1–2):

> So God created man in his own image, in the image of God he created him; male and female he created them. (Gen 1:27)

> This is the written account of Adam's line. When God created man, he made him in the likeness of God. He created them male and female and blessed them. And when they were created, he called them man. (Gen 5:1–2)

Here both the man and woman are called Adam, and they are both made in the image of Elohim. Both are blessed, both rule over all the beasts and creatures of the earth, both are fruitful, both appear to be of the same status, and all is good. There is no evidence of an evil presence in the world to resist Elohim's creative goodness.

In Gen 2, the man is still called the *adam* until Eve is created as an *isha* because she was taken out of man, *ish*. A literal translation of 2:23 reads:

> This [one] at last, bone of my bones, flesh of my flesh, this [one] shall be called woman (*isha*) because out of man (*ish*) was taken this [one].

In chapter 1, *adam* is a category that includes both men and women. In chapter 2 it is the designation exclusively of the male. In Gen 5:3 the

---

1. For a discussion on the meaning of "associative field" and "universe of discourse" see Sawyer, "Hebrew Words," 218.

category designation falls away and Adam becomes the name of the first man. Therefore, the address to the sons of Adam and sons of *ish* (the generic term for "male" or "husband") in Ps 49:2 can mean all kinds of people, high and low, male and female, all over the world, and probably for all time. The differences between Gen 1 and 2 could be an oversight, but considering the care the editors took in transmitting their understanding of God, it is more likely that they were not concerned about the literal reconciliation of the two narratives or about the change of divine name or the difference in style. The final redactors chose not to iron out all the wrinkles that necessarily result from combining different documents with different perspectives. There is truth in both. Trying to reconcile them actually *suppresses* the inspiration in them.

Fruit, Fruitfulness, eating the fruit of their ways. Adam and Eve were blessed by Elohim with the ability to be fruitful (fertile) and fill the earth (Gen 1:28). This is of course an arboreal metaphor that echoes references to the fruit of the tree of the knowledge of good and evil. "Fruit" in the Hebrew Bible tends to symbolize the circumstantial results brought on by good or bad choices:

> Tell the righteous it will be well with them, for they will enjoy the fruit of their deeds. (Isa 3:10)

> Hear, O earth: I am bringing disaster on this people, the fruit of their schemes, because they have not listened to my words. (Jer 6:19)

Psalm 49 as it presently stands does not contain the word "fruit," but it may have been dropped out of one difficult, obtuse verse. A literal rendition of verse 13 reads, "This their way, their stupidity [is] in their end they are pleased with their portion." "Their way" is also found in Prov 1:31, "Therefore they shall eat the fruit of their way." Adam and Eve ate the fruit, but in actuality they made a significant choice and had to live and die with the consequences.

Ground/dust/decay. In Gen 2, the humans are fully separated from the "dust of the ground" when the breath/spirit of God is breathed into the man's nostrils. This dust is not the dry, dead dust of *Sheol*. Although it has not yet rained, a mist has arisen to water the ground and prepare it for later cultivation (Gen 2:6).[2] Rivers are already running through Eden and trees have been planted by Yahweh-Elohim to grow. After the humans' expulsion from the garden the same ground is cursed,[3] yielding only thorns, thistles,

---

2. Rain and rainbow are recorded in Genesis only during and after the Flood.

3. The curse on the ground is only temporary, being lifted after the Flood (Gen 3:17; 8:21).

and meager food and herbs. God proclaims that humans will return to the ground and once again become dust (3:19). "You turn man to dust," cried the author of Ps 90. For the author of Ps 49, the grave is the mansion of the arrogant rich forever, and there his form will decay (verse 14). The small opening where his withering remains are ensconced with food, furniture, jewelry, weapons, and finery is all he will ever get. Even many upright believers feared that worms and decay were the inheritance of all living creatures (Job 17:12–16; Ps 88:10–12; Isa 38:10–20). But for the righteous, there is something more. He may have considered that since the breath/wind/spirit of God is what exalted humankind from the dust in the beginning, there is no reason that God cannot revivify the dust of the righteous and restore that clay to its former image.

God took, God will take. The word "take" is theologically freighted in both Ps 49 and Gen 2:15. The psalmist does not specify what he means by his confidence that God will "take me." Most scholars who comment on the taking of the psalmist out of *Sheol* note that in Gen 5:24 Enoch, the seventh generation from Adam, was "taken" by God, generally interpreted as being taken alive up to dwell eternally in God's realm. Elijah also "went up," ostensibly taken by God into immortality, in a chariot of fire with fiery horses (2 Kgs 2).[4] Psalm 73 also expresses confidence as to being received or taken: "You guide me with your counsel, and afterwards you will take me into glory." As in the two psalms, no one knows whence Enoch or Elijah were taken, but since the experience appears to be an alternative to death, presumably they were taken somehow into resurrected life.

Live/die. The most obvious comparison between Ps 49 and the early chapters of Genesis is the contrast between life and death and the way that each is conditioned upon one's ethical standing before God. In Gen 3, Adam and Eve died spiritually and began to die physically for disobeying the command to abstain from the fruit of the tree; in Ps 49 the theme is also spiritual death that results in incontrovertible physical death for those who wrongly trust in their wealth; but for those wise enough to trust in God, there is held out the hope of being taken from the decay of death.

Genesis 1–3 and Ps 49 both qualify as wisdom literature. Genesis 1–3 is to a degree about the origin of all the civilized peoples of the Ancient Near East.[5] Psalm 49 is addressed to all those diverse peoples. The purpose of such literature is often to promote the value of wisdom over fleeting pleasure or wealth. In Proverbs, wisdom is depicted as a tree of life (Prov 3:18;

---

4. For example, Day, *Resurrection*, 99–105.

5. The narrative of Adam and Eve may well portray the Chalcolithic or early Bronze Age lifestyle before woven garments, music, and bronze metallurgy.

8:35, 36). By contrast, the foolish man who allows himself to be seduced by the loud and boisterous harlot is like a brutish, dim-witted beast led to the slaughter. He is on "the way to *Sheol*;" he is "going down to the chambers of death" (Prov 7:27).

> Now then, my sons, listen to me; pay attention to what I say. Do not let your heart turn to her ways or stray into her paths. Many are the victims she has brought down; her slain are a mighty throng. Her house is a highway to the grave, leading down to the chambers of death. (Prov 7:24–27)

In other words, the foolish who are seduced are "dead" while they live.

In both Genesis and Ps 49 there is a subtle riddle, the solution of which is a matter of life and death. In both books a shadowy ransom is supplied. The psalmist is confident that his soul will be redeemed. In Genesis, Yahweh-Elohim has prepared some covering for Adam and Eve that restores their relationship with him (Gen 3:21).

Misplaced trust. The culture addressed by the psalmist believed that there would be an eternal sympathetic connection between the soul, its grave goods, and the ritual invocation of the deceased. For some reason the psalmist did not accept that worldview, even though he may have seen it practiced daily in the world in which he lived. Counter to his culture, he believed that wealth did not prove a man's worth temporally or spiritually. He was able to discard practices and values that others cherished. He would explain that his trust was utterly in Yahweh-Elohim. In Genesis, the man and woman heard two voices claiming to be the one that had the power to preserve life. The second voice promised something akin to divinity. It removed the restraint of avoidance. The tree looked good, seemed to be a reasonable thing to eat, and it offered esoteric knowledge that would aid in personal growth, status, and success:

> When the woman saw that the fruit of the tree was good for food and pleasant to the eye, and also desirable for gaining wisdom, she took some and ate it. She also gave some to her husband, who was with her, and he ate it. (Gen 3:6)

Furthermore, the snake delivered. The couple did not die and God had to admit that they had "become like us, knowing the difference between good and evil." The question of which voice to trust became the question that would continue to plague the Middle East, at least in the eyes of the authors, for millennia. As shall be seen in the next section, the serpent plied his wares from nation to nation, generation to generation. The serpent's message was far more widespread than monotheistic Yahwism. Because monotheism was so counter-intuitive, the serpent was served with fear and devotion. Both religions had temples, priests, sacrifices, prophets, seers, and religious feast days. To the foreigners, Yahweh was just another Palestinian deity, who sponsored a particular people like the other gods and goddesses round about. To an outsider, Yahwistic religion looked similar to all the others, except that it was very exclusive. In fact, the monotheistic Yahwists had no images, no cult prostitutes, no magic, and no child sacrifice—a seeming disadvantage in the view of foreigners. The monotheists themselves looked to stories like the Exodus and the Conquest for their confidence that their deity was different. In the words of Rahab the harlot, the Canaanitess who married into one of the famous families in Israel,

> When we heard of it, our hearts melted and everyone's courage failed because of you, for the Lord your God is God in heaven above and on earth below. (Josh 2:11)

In time, trust in, and relationship with, Yahweh became more important in some circles than animal sacrifice and ritual (Ps 27:6; 28:7; 40:6–10; 50:13–50).

Form/image. The *adam* was created in the image of God. Since God is Spirit, lacking male and female parts, what that means is unclear but suggests that man and God share a similar intellect. Since part of that image was to develop an understanding of good and evil, the physical *form* of the *adam* was not God's critical image as much as "knowing good and evil" (Gen 3:22). But, in whatever sense our form and intellect reflect that of God, the psalmist declares that in the grave, the arrogant man will lose it. Rather than being a human with a spark of the divine, he will become like a beast. His physical form will decay (Ps 49:14c), and the image of God in him is already decayed; no amount of grave goods or ritual will avail him.

Morning/light. Both Genesis and the psalm contain the words "morning" and "light," although the semantic nuance in the two passages is somewhat different. In Genesis the morning is more literally connected to the beginning of a day. The light that dawns appears to be literal, physical light. The question in Gen 1 is simply how literally to take the reference to "day." In the psalm, the problem is similar. Are the mention of morning and light literal, or is there a subtler truth being signified? Light in the Hebrew Bible is frequently used as a metaphor for concepts such as divine presence, favor, understanding, and deliverance. The metaphor of "dew" serves a similar purpose. In Job 29:18–20 it signifies a good name and honorable life:

> I thought, "I shall die in my house (Heb: nest), days as numerous as the grains of sand (Heb: phoenix). My roots will reach

to the water, and the dew will lie all night on my branches. My glory will remain fresh in me, and the bow ever new in my hand." (Job 29:18–20)

In Ps 110:3 dew depicts the eternal youth or effectiveness of the holy king. In Ps 133:3 it is holy unity among the brethren. Morning, too, occurs frequently in Hebrew literature as a symbol, indicating newness and ushering in the blessings associated with life and dew.

Beasts/rule. Genesis 1 deals with mankind's relationship to the beasts. Humans are given dominion over every other living creature. Just as the sun rules the day and the moon rules the night, humans will "rule" the beasts with weapons, nets, fences, and cunning—domesticating and training them to help in everyday human labor. In Ps 49, the author mocks the ones trusting in their wealth and declares that they are similar to the beasts. These wealthy landowners, are those who "rule" during their earthly lives, but in the "morning" the true "rule" of the righteous will be revealed.

Fear/blessing. The word "fear" does not appear in Gen 3 until after the humans eat the fruit. They are embarrassed at their own nakedness and they fear that Yahweh-Elohim will punish them severely. The message is that sin and loss of innocence bring fear, shame, blame, death, and a host of negative consequences. Fear is mentioned twice in Ps 49. The psalmist seems to struggle with his fear of the trouble that his powerful enemies may make for him. Another possibility is that he chafes at the ever-present danger of war or disaster which might devastate the community. The wealthy seem to have a better chance of surviving due to the abundance of their resources. The psalmist reminds himself and the reader that it is the arrogant wealthy who have the most to fear. Those trusting in Yahweh can turn all their fears over to him and live the life of blessing in faith. The ritual service of the wealthy deceased will fade into the oblivion of generations.

There is a prime example of this concept in the New Testament. Jesus Christ shared a parable about a rich man who lived a luxurious life every day. In his day, he was a very important man who had global business ties and even consulted with the king on occasion. He dressed in the best garments, drank the finest wines, threw fabulous parties that everyone sought to attend. (OK, I'm adding a few imaginative facts here, but nothing that would actually contradict the first century parable in Luke 16:19–31.) His wife had the best purses, rode her own luxury camel, got her hair done every morning, and wore silken, flowing gowns. They had more cattle and sheep than anyone in the land, plus Arabian race horses and a big sailing boat.

When they rode down the long, shady path of their estate, they would see a ragged beggar named Lazarus sitting beside the iron gate. Lazarus was disgusting. He couldn't beg downtown because he had running sores, which the dogs occasionally licked, and he smelled really bad. No one would attend to Lazarus's wounds because that would put them into a status of being ritually unclean. Anyone who touched the beggar's helper would also become "unclean." It was not a matter of hygiene. The uncleanness was a subjective state in which holiness and normalcy were suspended. The person could not worship properly, move through society lest they spread this status, or conduct normal business. The remedy was a bath and a change of clothing at the end of the day.

So Lazarus sat by the rich man's gate and begged for whatever he could get. He was hoping for a few shekels to be tossed his way, or leftovers from the rich man's meal brought to him by a compassionate servant. The wealthy estate tossed him just enough crumbs to keep body and soul together.

The time came when they all passed from this life. Lazarus was buried in an unmarked pauper's grave outside the city. The rich man had a pleasant plot on a hill. A marble monument marked the place where his bones rested. His funeral was well-attended, and many wonderful things were said about his life. The irony is that when he looked around at the place of his eternal abode, the rich man found himself in agony in a hot and dry place, devoid of all the luxuries to which he was accustomed. His earthly closet full of iron weapons, the stuffed lion head that hung on his wall, the coin collection, that expensive bottle of chardonnay, the summer home—all were sold off at auction. He could now see his ancestor Abraham afar off, and to his surprise, there was Lazarus, the beggar, standing beside Abraham. Lazarus's sores were healed. Wow, he looked good. He was nicely dressed, had a thick head of curly hair, a mouthful of shiny teeth, and was even pleasant looking. "Father Abraham," the rich man pleaded, "Please send Lazarus to bring me a glass of water. It's really hot here. I'm dying of thirst." But Abraham answered, "Son, remember that in your lifetime you received good things, while Lazarus received bad things, but now he is comforted here and you are in agony. And besides all this, between us and you a great chasm has been fixed, so that those who want to go to you cannot, nor can anyone cross over from there to us." The man pleaded for Lazarus to be allowed to go to his father's house to warn his five brothers, but Abraham told him that if his brothers don't listen to Moses and the Prophets, they would not listen to Lazarus or anyone rising from the dead.

The rich man was not in the hot place because he was rich. It was because he was selfish. He was devoid of compassion and empathy. He had no time to alleviate the suffering of others. His luxurious life became his god. His grasping for social status, his religiosity in the market place, his hypocrisy, the mask of uprightness—all these things and more, plus a lack of genuine goodness brought him there. Even the good that he did was done for public approval or to stroke his own ego. Alas, in the New Testament, at least, and undoubtedly in the Old, the deepest, hidden secrets of the heart are laid wide open for afterlife review.

Psalm 73: Finding Comfort in Vexation

Most psalm scholars recognize a consistent pattern in the presentation of immortality in Psalms 16, 49, and 73. The debate raises the familiar question, are the psalmists referring to present deliverance from physical death or to a post-mortem deliverance from *Sheol*? Psalms 73 and 49 in particular have much in common.

We have seen that the author of Ps 49 is afraid of the trouble that his enemy may cause him. The increasing wealth of the wicked amazes and vexes him. It is not just that the wicked person prospers, but that his mantle of power and self-satisfaction passes to his posterity. This flies in the face of the common sense teaching that a just and perfect God will punish the wicked and bless the righteous on this earth. If we look deeply into history, we can see that the power of the wicked is sometimes fleeting, sometimes not. The traditional admiration of wealth as a gift of God and a sign of divine favor is overturned, because a) wealth is often gained through exploitation of the weak and the breaking of the Law of God, and b) life is complex and God's ways are mysterious. We shouldn't assume that the psalmist's polemic targets all powerful, wealthy individuals. Such is not the case. It is the arrogant wealthy who oppress Yahweh's people that the psalmist abhors. In that sense, he stands with the weak and disenfranchised because they are often wiser than those blinded by wealth and status.

> But as for me, my feet had almost slipped;
> I nearly lost my foothold.
> For I envied the arrogant
> when I saw the prosperity of the wicked.
> They have no struggles;
> Their bodies are healthy and strong.
> They are free from the burdens common to man;
> They are not plagued by human ills. (Ps 73:2–5)

The psalmist, by contrast, has constant trouble. He appears to feel as if God has singled him out for correction and humiliation. This perplexing circumstance confronts him with a compelling temptation,[6] one with

---

6. Alexander, "The Psalms," 13.

which he must grapple in the confines of God's very sanctuary. In this case, "Cult and Wisdom cooperate to overcome the crisis."[7] The psalmist came to his senses.

Both psalmists lament that the wicked are praised. Men speak well of them in the market place, the royal court, the temple, at their funerals, and on stelae to commemorate them. This in spite of the damage that they selfishly inflict on society. It's still interesting how even the most nefarious deeds are often wrapped in righteous window dressing. "We broke no laws." "Safety has always been our main concern." "We are banishing the free press because they are all liars."

"Their mouths lay claim to heaven, and their tongues take possession of the earth," cried the priest. "Therefore their people turn to them and drink up waters in abundance . . . This is what the wicked are like—always carefree, they increase in wealth" (Ps 73:9–12).

This author had to lay out his complaint in the sanctuary before the face of Yahweh before he could be reconciled to such a counter-intuitive reality. Both authors feel comforted to meditate on the end of the wicked. There will be a significant contrast between the appearance of their life and their final end. "When I tried to understand all this, it was oppressive to me till I entered the sanctuary of God; then I understood their final destiny." As with the humbled serpent, their splendor is demolished in the grave. In Ps 73 the wicked will "fall" "into ruin." They will be "destroyed," "swept away," "will perish," and come to "an end." When the psalmist realizes that his own lack of faith is as shallow and constricted as that of the wicked, he calls himself a brute beast. The author is also concerned about legacy, but he realizes that the riches left by the arrogant men are nothing compared to the wisdom that he can leave to his own posterity by right thinking and righteous speech (73:15).

The concept of "morning" is found in both psalms, albeit with somewhat different connotations. In Ps 49 the righteous will rule over the wicked in the morning, but the wicked will never see the "light." The author of Ps 73 feels he is punished every morning, but in the end, the wicked will be as unsubstantial as a dream or a shadow which is despised by God (verse 20).

Both psalms celebrate the concept of "ransom."

> Yet I am always with you;
> you hold me by my right hand.
> You guide me with your counsel,
> and afterward you will take me into glory. (Ps 73:23–24)

---

7. Irsigler, "Quest," 270.

There is no clear indication that this refers to mere deliverance from an imminent death. T. D. Alexander cites Hos 13:14 ("I will ransom them from the power of the grave; I will redeem them from death. Where, O death, are your plagues? Where, O grave, is your destruction?") and Ps 18:7 ("He drew me out of deep waters") as passages which scholars use to refute reference to afterlife in these psalms. Alexander makes a distinction between texts that cite definite terrestrial dangers and those that leave the door ajar.[8] He suggests that the "taking" in Ps 49 parallels that of Enoch and Elijah, but if the psalm is early and the Elijah narrative was not yet known, the psalmist's confidence would have to come from elsewhere.

The author of Ps 73 sets up a contrast between those who simply talk about God and those who draw near (verse 27). The near are those who are continually with him. God is forever their portion, their joy, their refuge. They meditate on his precepts and obey them.

In Sumer, many an official document was sealed with a wax depiction of a patron god literally holding the left hand or arm of a client worshiper.[9] The god is using his right hand. The patron deity is leading the client, ushering him into the presence of the head of the pantheon. This was a sufficiently common representation that it may have been what the psalmist had in mind when he penned his words. Yet, he makes it clear that in the heavens and the earth, there is no one other than Yahweh that he desires (verse 25).

Psalm 16: The Path of Life and Eternal Joy

Psalm 16 is often associated with 49 and 73. The Hebrew can be a challenge, but the modern translations come close enough to what is undoubtedly the message. Psalm 16 has four core components:

1) David believes that people who chase after other gods will only increase their own pain and suffering. "The sorrows of those will increase who run after other gods. I will not pour out their libations of blood or take up their names on my lips" (verse 4).

2) God has been good to David, and he is content with his lot. "The boundary lines have fallen to me in pleasant places; surely I have a delightful inheritance" (verse 6).

3) King David stays close to God, thinks about God all the time, and knows God loves him. "I have set the LORD always before me. Because his is at my right hand, I will not be shaken" (verse 8).

---

8. Alexander, "Psalms and Afterlife," 10.

9. Van Buren, "The God Ningizzida," 72–74; Fig. 1, B.M. 122125; Louvre, AO 4359.

4) The last Hebrew word in the psalm is "forever." God's joys and pleasures are eternal. *Sheol* will have no hold on God's faithful.

> Therefore my heart is glad and my tongue rejoices;
> my body will also rest secure,
> because you will not abandon me to the grave,
> nor will you let your Holy One [or faithful one or favored one] see decay.
> You have made known to me the path of life;
> you will fill me with joy in your presence,
> with eternal pleasures at your right hand. (Ps 16:9–11)

The topic of God's right hand appears twice in verses 8 and 11. In the first book of the Psalter, "right hand" appears seven times.[10] Perfect guidance is there, as are fullness of joy, stability (both personal and national), good health, and pleasures forevermore. The Ps 49 author would agree that these graces represent true riches. Psalm 16 also demonstrates the importance of making the right choice about who is worthy of libations and honor. The poem, bearing a heading which attributes authorship to King David, is controversial because the text has been poorly transmitted and the translation is difficult. G. Trull makes a strong appeal to accept David's authorship based on linguistic parallels with other psalms credited to David.[11]

The pressure to honor the deity of another must have been immense in politics. The fact that families were large and kept fairly close in those days also posed a problem, especially if the elders of the clan were syncretists. I'm not sure what kind of backlash a person might suffer if they snubbed another's religious ritual. Today, to be religiously exclusionary is highly unpopular. Many believe that all gods are the same.

David uses the metaphor of inheritance in Canaan with specified borders around each tribal allotment to say that, unlike the author of Ps 73 who has been vexed by troubles, God has been good to him. He is happy with his metaphorical "borders" and the good land allotted to him as his inheritance. In Ps 49, the wicked are very proud of their lands and fond of their wealth. David's flesh rests secure (16:9) because the maggots and decay of *Sheol* are no threat to God's "favored one."[12] David is credited with many psalms of lament due to vexation and anger about his enemies. The point of this psalm, which seems to flow naturally from the psalm just before it, is

---

10. Brueggemann and Miller, "Psalm 73," 49.

11. Trull, "Exegesis," 304–305.

12. The identity of the Favored One is controversial. Is it the author himself, some messianic personage to come, or just any righteous person? Trull envisions a messianic personality. See ibid., 307 for his review of five different interpretations of verse 10.

that he has made the right choice as to which deity to serve. He has lived the right ethical life, gotten onto the path of life ("you show me the path of life;" verse 11), and he will stay there "forever."

W. Quintens, in writing about Ps 21, reviews several inscriptions attributing eternal life to various kings; for example, Tuthmosis III ("I have placed you on the Horus throne of millions of years, so you may lead the living forever")[13] and Rameses IV ("You, Lord—Life, prosperity, health!—You will live forever!"). The gold crown mentioned in Ps 21:3, writes Quintens, finds parallels in several varied Near Eastern inscriptions due to its durability. It represents the gifts of divine life, length of reign, annihilation of enemies, and a connection with royalty. If Ps 21 parallels other royal inscriptions as Quintens claims, then we should expect nothing less than that the reference to a "crown of pure gold" (21:3) anticipates David's eternal existence.[14]

It is also worthy of note that Psalms 16, 21, and 49 have headings that put them in the same historical context. The psalms cannot be dated with any certainty, but the historical narratives of Samuel, Kings, and Chronicles place David, Asaph (David's seer and song leader), and the musical Korahites in the same era. The similarity of these three psalms indicate that they likely emerged from a theological movement based on reflection, relationship with God, and personal revelation. If this paradigm does not date to the tenth century, why construct the narrative to suggest that it did? In each of the three is found an expectation of escape from the gloom of *Sheol*.

---

13. English translation from Lichtheim, *Ancient Egyptian Literature*, Vol. II, 38. See Quintens comparison with Ps 21, "La vie du roi," 521–23.

14. See also, Quintens, "Le chemin," 233–42. Quintens calls for an interpretation of an "unlimited future" in Ps 16:10.

10

Serpents, Goddesses, and Gardens

JUST AS Ps 49 and Gen 1–3 appear to be connected, Gen 1–3 and the goddess cults might be connected. The debate about the connection between Ps 49 and Genesis 1-3 is about who the ultimate giver of life is and whether "life" includes immortality.

The "black-headed people" (what the Sumerians called themselves) are not, in the Genesis narrative, the first humans. Genesis 4–11 attributes the establishment of civilization in Mesopotamia to the pre-Sumerian descendants of Cain. Religion is active in a primitive way in the narrative of Gen 4. Even before the Flood, Cain and Abel are both offering the kinds of animal and agricultural sacrifices that would be considered orthodox in the later developing state of Israel. Cain's line is also said to spawn polygamy and the escalating violence of personal vengeance so common in the ancient world. After the Flood, the great cities of Sumer are said to be founded by the mighty hunter Nimrod (Gen 10:8–9; Mic 5:6). Little is explicitly said in Gen 1–11 about the religion of Sumer, but the cities there clearly are perceived as polytheistic.

When Abram turned to monotheistic worship of Yahweh in Genesis 12, his calling comes against the backdrop of a world dominated by the rule of Mesopotamian kings and the worship of multiple Mesopotamian deities. This portrait of the religious world of that day is confirmed by archaeology, which has provided artifacts, literature, and inscriptions that describe a polytheism that includes serpents of wisdom and goddesses of life. By contrast, there is no archaeological evidence of Yahwistic worship much before the thirteenth century BCE when the name Israel appears on a stela[1] and the name *Ywh* is found on a Nineteenth or Twentieth Egyptian Dynasty list.[2]

---

1. The Merenptah Stele, 1207 BCE.
2. *Ywh* of the land of the Shasu, in Redford, *Egypt, Canaan, and Israel*, 272–73.

Eve's very name (the Hebrew word for life) reflects the battle over which deity is the author of life. Isaac Kikawada notes that in Sumerian, *ti* means both "rib" and "giver of life." Ninti is a Sumerian goddess called "Lady of the Rib" and "Giver of Life." *Nin* means Lord or Lady.[3] Eve has subsumed Ninti's identity as the "Mother of all the Living." She is either the first woman to ever exist or perhaps the first female prototype of a wise, highly developed woman who exists in relationship with Yahweh. She is the mother-creator of all who trust in Yahweh rather than the Sumerian deities, the mother of all who participate in his covenant life. Contrary to the New Testament portrait of Eve as the first sinner and the bringer of death into the world (1 Tim 2:14), the author of the Primeval History (Gen 1–11) is emphasizing that Eve, the lady of Adam's rib, has the special status as a life giver with attributes similar to the goddess Ninti. It would be an error to think that a simple borrowing has occurred here. The borrowing is polemical, which deliberately modifies the old tradition in order to establish a new world view. Israelite theology uniquely holds that Eve is a human, representing Yahweh, and is no goddess.

Ninti was not the only ancient deity designated as a life-giver. Serpents, goddesses, and the sacred tree were common symbols of the life force throughout the Ancient Near East. The Ubaids, a pre-Sumerian race whose artifacts predate the city of Ur, made little figurines of creatures with naked human bodies and lizard-shaped heads.[4] Bumps on their shoulders may represent scales. Some females are nursing offspring. One infant has a short, lizard-like body, but another's lower body is that of a snake wrapped around the mother's waist. These upright, hybrid, reptilian creatures could well be the prototype for the talking "serpent" of Gen 3 who could peddle life and death with the aplomb of a politician.

When God rebukes the snake in Genesis, it is metaphorically reduced to a slithering beast who will eat dust, the very dust from which came the man and to which all humans will return. It is now the least of beasts, a predator hiding under rocks. Not only is this demotion reminiscent of Eve's drop in status, it reminds us of the arrogant rich man, so powerful and confident on earth, who is humbled in the grave as the worms eat his flesh. The average citizen of the Ancient Near East, however, did not understand the image nor absorb the lesson.

The Shasu are Bedouins who were despised by the Egyptians as nomads and raiders. Their territory was Edom and Moab around the Dead Sea. One of their cities was named "Laban," a patriarchal name in Genesis.

3. Kikawada, "Two Notes," 34.
4. *Sumer: The Cities of Eden*, 44, 158.

Coiled ceramic snakes were found in pre-Sumerian temples. The serpent deity Ningizzida became the personal patron deity of a major Sumerian king.[5] A fire-breathing cobra called the uraeus appears on the Egyptian crown as the symbolic source of pharaoh's royal power and wisdom.[6] Several Egyptian goddesses were also of a reptilian nature.[7] The Midianites of Palestine worshiped bronze serpents on poles.[8] Marduk, the spiritual "king" of Babylon, was a reptilian monster with double horns like the horned viper. Many of the Sumerian, Assyrian, and Babylonian gods, both in the heavens and in the Netherworld, were snake-dragon-viper beings.

Echoes of this serpent fixation may be detected in the Hebrew Bible. A Sumerian curse speaks of Ninki, the serpent god, arising out of the earth to sink his fangs into a human foot in order to take that foot from the earth (i.e., to cause the person to die).[9] This curse may also be resonating with Gen 3:15 in which the serpent bites the heel of the coming messianic Seed which in turn will crush the head of the serpent demon.

The bronze serpent in the wilderness of the Sinai Peninsula is another case of Israel negotiating with the serpent voice for life and healing. This event took place in Midianite territory on the way to Canaan, just before a horrific apostasy on the part of Israel (Num 21). The Israelites were marching toward their promise, but when confronted by a region of poisonous snakes, the Midianite guides knew what to do. The serpent on the pole was a charm against snake bite that worked so well that for centuries it sat in the temple with the Ark of the Covenant. Hezekiah destroyed it (perhaps at the urging of Isaiah) because it had become a pagan talisman, a source of esoteric knowledge of the sort forbidden by the Torah and the prophets (2 Kgs 18:4).

Gardens were also a common theme in ancient Mesopotamia. The Sumerian god Dumuzi was a gardener in the divine gardens. Well-irrigated botanical gardens were developed by kings for their personal pleasure. Trees were often found within the palace precincts (Song 5:1). The exotic species became a symbol of the king's widespread sovereignty over various peoples. The royal gardens symbolized the triumph over "chaos, decay, and death. Like temples, they are walled off from daily reality, with all its instability

---

5. Van Buren, "Ningizzida," 60–89.

6. Pritchard, *Ancient Near Eastern Texts*, 231: "I am come as the uraeus-serpent of Horus, flaming against my enemies..."

7. Wilkinson, *Gods and Goddesses*, 218–28.

8. Rothenburg, *Timna*, 150–52; and Rothenburg, et al., *Egyptian Mining Temple*, cited in Keller, *The Bible as History*, 149–50, and *Bible Review* 16.6, 20–21.

9. Kramer, *The Sumerians*, 313.

and irregularity and the threats these pose, and thus they readily convey an intimation of immortality."[10]

The icons of goddesses, gardens, snakes, a man and a woman, and the Tree of Life are sometimes linked together in ancient Mesopotamian thought. One twenty-third-century BCE seal[11] combines three icons found later in Gen 2: a sacred tree, snakes, a seated male deity, and a seated, worshiping woman.

Egyptian illustrations also contain a sacred tree that is melded with the depiction of the goddess. In one, the goddess is offering bread and drink to a man and woman.[12] The goddess's body is blended with the tree trunk. In another illustration, Pharaoh Tuthmosis III is drawing life-giving sustenance from a breast emanating from a sacred tree.[13] There is no evidence that the tree goddess is offering immortality, but she is giving some kind of life force separate from that offered by the usual patronage and protection of the personal or national deity. An Egyptian goddess named Qadesh or Qudshu seems to be derivative of Asherah/Astarte. In one illustration she stands on a lion; beside her stand the Egyptian God Min and the Canaanite god Resheph.[14] She holds in one hand a lotus, the Egyptian symbol of life, and in the other a serpent. Sometimes she is depicted with snakes in both hands. Min's erect penis indicates fertility. Resheph is holding the *ankh*, another icon of life force. In the New Kingdom, when the cities of Lower Egypt were inhabited by a large population of captive Asiatics, images of Asiatic deities commonly appeared in Egyptian iconography. Deities like Qudshu, Ishtar, and Asherah became blended.

Asherah was the most important early female competitor of Yahweh for the hearts and minds of the people of Israel. Her consort was Yahweh's male arch-nemesis, Baal. For many years, scholars doubted the reality of such a goddess because archaeological evidence confirming her existence was lacking. It was the discovery of the city of Ugarit in 1929 and the translation of the fire-baked clay archives that brought this goddess to the consciousness of the academy.[15] She is first mentioned in texts from the first dynasty of Babylon (*ca.* 1830–1531 BCE), which are written in the Akkadian language rather than Northwest Semitic (the linguistic precursor of Hebrew). Several names mentioned in the fourteenth-century-BCE el-Am-

---

10. Levenson, *Resurrection*, 86–87.
11. Mitchell, *British Museum*, 24.
12. Keel, *Symbolism*, 187.
13. Hestrin, "Understanding Asherah," 54.
14. Ibid., 55.
15. Day, "Asherah," 385.

arna letters, such as *Abdi-Ashirta* or *Abdi-Ashratum*, are likely invocations of Asherah.[16] In the Ugaritic tablets, she is called Athirat, the mother of the gods and the consort of El. Whereas in Mesopotamia she had been "the Lady of the Steppe," at Ugarit she was the Lady of the Sea (CTA 4.III.27, occasionally called Qudshu) for whom El would do anything.

In the Hebrew Bible, the word *asherah* and its plural form *asherim* are mentioned about forty times. The King James Version followed the Greek Septuagint in translating many of the instances as "groves" because a tree or grove of trees seemed to fit the context, especially in light of uncertainty as to the existence of a goddess by that name. The Mishnah also conceived of the *asherim* as groves of trees that invited adoration and idolatrous practices.[17]

However, in the mid-1980's theological debate led to a broad consensus that there are three uses of the word in the Hebrew Bible, and that "grove" and living tree are not among them. One use refers to a symbolic pole that resembled a tree, an icon of a stylized tree, or a tree that was pruned for cultic use. The *asherim* are often mentioned along with altars to Baal and even to Yahweh. The Torah warns against building an altar to Yahweh and planting an *asherah* or a cultic pillar next to it (Deut 16:21–22). This repudiation of the goddess icon by biblical authors is a testimonial against any official promotion of Yahweh having a consort. During the era of the Judges (post-Conquest but before the establishment of the monarchy), the Israelites began to intermarry with other inhabitants of the land, worship their gods (the *baalim* and the *asherim*), and follow their cultic practices (Judg 3:7). Gideon's father set up an altar to Baal with an *asherah* next to it. Gideon was instructed to repudiate his father's faith by tearing down the altar to Baal, cutting down the *asherah*, building a proper altar to Yahweh, and offering a bull. The wood of the *asherah* was to feed the flame of sacrifice (Judg 6:25–28). As is often pointed out, *asherim* were "made," "erected," "built," and "burned."[18]

The other two uses of the word are to denote the goddess herself (1 Kgs 15:13; 2 Kgs 21:7) and a standing idol representing the goddess (2 Kgs 21:7). *Asherim* are frequently mentioned alongside "graven images."[19]

> The king ordered Hilkiah the high priest, the priests next in rank and the doorkeepers to remove from the temple of the LORD all

---

16. Ibid., 386.

17. Ibid., 397. (*m. 'Or* 1:7, 8; *m. Sukk* 3:1–3; *m Abod Zar* 3:7, 9, 10) See p. 398, 399 for Day's review of the position of various scholars as to whether Asherah is or is not a goddess. Day is convinced that she is, but that she is separate from the goddess Astarte.

18. Ibid., 402.

19. Ibid., 403. (Deut 7:5; 12:3; 2 Chr 33:19; 43:3, 4, 7; Mic 5:13, 14)

the articles made for Baal and Asherah and all the starry hosts. He burned them outside Jerusalem in the fields of the Kidron Valley and took the ashes to Bethel. He took away the pagan priests appointed by the kings of Judah to burn incense on the high places of the towns of Judah and on those around Jerusalem—those who burned incense to Baal, to the sun and moon, to the constellations, and to all the starry hosts. He took the Asherah pole from the temple of the LORD to the Kidron Valley outside Jerusalem and burned it there. He ground it to powder and scattered the dust over the graves of the common people. He also tore down the quarters of the male shrine prostitutes, which were in the temple of the LORD and where women did weaving for Asherah. (2 Kgs 23:4–7)

The icon of the tree of life comes from Mesopotamia and dates as far back as the fourth millennium. In ancient iconography, it is often flanked by ibexes, goats, or rams. It is found on seals, ivories, cult stands, and pottery. Not too many years after the discovery of Ugarit, a thirteenth-century-BCE ewer was found in Lachish, an ancient city west of Jerusalem. During the 1980s, the ewer and other artifacts mentioning Asherah were much studied and debated because in several of them the name of the goddess appears beside that of Yahweh as if she were his consort. The translations are controversial, but even allowing for the variations of interpretation there does seem to have been a syncretistic practice spread widely throughout Israel that blended the worship of Baal, Asherah, the starry host, and the cult of the dead with the cult of Yahweh.

The artifacts mentioning Asherah and Yahweh also often depict ibexes, lions, fallow deer, rams, and a stylized tree. Ruth Hestrin writes:

> The sacred tree symbol was embedded in the traditions of the cultures of the Ancient Near East, and goes back to very early periods. Depictions of the sacred tree are found in Iran, Mesopotamia, Syria, Palestine, Egypt and Cyprus, as well as in the other Mediterranean countries. The tree symbolized the source of life and represented growth and revival.[20]

Other Late Bronze Age vessels from Taanach, Megiddo, Lachish, and other sites also depict sacred trees.[21] In some of the vessels, the two ibexes

---

20. Hestrin, "Lachish Ewer," 214.

21. See Lemaire, "Yahweh's Asherah," for a description of the discovery by William Dever of the inscription "Blessed be Uryahu by Yahweh and his Asherah; from his enemies may he save him . . . " (Lemaire's translation). This burial inscription was found in 1967 in a recently looted cave in Hebron. Lemaire felt that Dever's translation of the three-line graffiti needed a fresh examination. In 1975, the controversial pithos (storage

flank not a tree but a pubic triangle. Hestrin attributes the use of a pubic triangle instead of a tree to the fertility characteristic of the erotic goddess Asherah.[22] The same grouping of symbols is found on pendants worn by women. The fourteenth-century pendants have stylized breasts, pubic triangle, and tree, and the face of a goddess crowned with a Hathor wig (a wig with cow horns), which suggests a connection with Qudshu. In one case, the goddess has snakes curling behind her back. Hathor of Egypt was a cow goddess, but also a mother goddess who was known in Memphis as Hathor of the sycamore.[23] The goddess of the sycamore tree that suckled Thutmosis III was Isis, but the energy and protection understood to flow from goddess to worshiper is the same. In Hestrin's view, therefore, Qudshu, snakes, the Hathor wig, Hathor, fertility, the tree of life,[24] Asherah, Athirat, Elat,[25] lions, ibexes, and life force all comprise one deity with similar icons and functions.

Not all scholars agree that the author of Genesis is portraying Eve as a giver of life. Shawna Dolansky has carefully cited the ancient and persistent literary association of goddess, life-giving tree, snake, wisdom, fertility, and earth. In her view, the earth association is the reason why Adam originated from the dust by the hand of Yahweh, a male deity. In Dolansky's explanation, Eve was a goddess in some lost document, but in Genesis, she is fallen, humiliated, and essentially disenfranchised.[26] Positioning Eve as a former goddess is a radical stretch that misses the purpose of the author of Genesis, which is that Eve, the human mother of all the living, is *not* a goddess and had no hand in creation. The fact that she came forth from a man further limits her role as cosmic creative birth mother. She is the matriarch of a certain family of humans, but the life breath came from Yahweh. She is fallen, but as a victim of a global deception that also ensnared her husband. In Gen 1, man and woman are created on the same day in the same manner, with no reference to sin, hierarchy, or substance of origination. The point of the document is reflected in Ps 8:4–8, that humankind is created a little lower than the angels and all creation has been given into mortal hands. They are to rule and dominate the creation. In Gen 2 and 3, the narrative was deliberately written otherwise, risking the potential of contradiction, as a

---

jar) of Kuntillit Ajrud came into the dialogue with its eighth century BCE inscriptions, "I bless you by Yahweh of Samaria and his *asherah*," and "I bless you by Yahweh of Teman and his *asherah*."

22. Hestrin, "Lachish Ewer," 215.

23. Ibid., 219.

24. For a partial list of sacred tree illustrations on ancient artifacts, see Judith Hadley, "Drawings," 203–204.

25. Hestrin, "Lachish Ewer," 220–21.

26. Dolansky, "Goddess," 3–21.

warning and polemic against all things goddess and serpent. By submitting to the deception of the enemy as mediated through the snake and tree, both humans fall, but Eve particularly loses social dignity and status.

To equate all the sacred trees of ancient inscriptions with the tree of life in Genesis and to claim that the Genesis narrative is simply a borrowing from former icons is surely a misconstrual of the original author's purpose. The tree of life in Genesis plays a minor role in the story. It is the fount of immortality here on earth, but in the story it sits in the background untouched. The star of the tale is the tree of the knowledge of good and evil. It is a tree about choices, with which other sacred trees have nothing to do. The narrative of the tree of knowledge and the serpent has several purposes:

- It demonstrates that there is genuine evil in the world, which is so lethal it must be avoided. It shows that evil is very deceptive, purporting to offer life whereas its fruit is poison and brings death.
- It shows that there are sly entities in the world that challenge Yahweh's authority, claiming to offer more than what he promises.
- It moves the partaker beyond childlike innocence, opening a world of adult thought with adult consequences.
- It graphically demonstrates that it is a terrible choice to gain the whole world and compromise one's eternal relationship with God.
- It encouraged the generation that first read the story to conclude that goddesses and satan are dangerous.

The women of the ancient world confronted a host of fears and challenges from which they sought refuge in the cults of goddesses. Surrounded by a sea of icons, images, inscriptions, gods, goddess, and supernatural claims, it is little wonder that they reached for female figures who understood female issues.[27] That may well be why the author of Gen 3 had Eve, contrary to the gist of the Gen 1 account, as the first to listen to the serpent and taste the fruit. The presence of the garden, the gardener (Adam), the tree, the serpent, the man and woman, the fruit, the false offer of life that leads to death, the challenge to Yahweh's authority, and the cherubim guarding the way back to Eden all suggest that the astute ancient reader

---

27. See Ornan, "Twins," 57–60. The recent discovery of three amulets coming from the same mold portrays a worried woman who is carrying twins. The woman depicted on the amulet is wearing two amulets. One is a crescent around her neck, indicating the moon god Sin. On each thigh is a stylized tree flanked by ibises, indicating a goddess who is a patron of women, birth, and conception. One amulet was found at Revadim, ten miles east of Ashdod. It is Israelite, but one cannot be certain that an Israelite woman wore it.

would recognize references to unorthodox polytheism, and particularly, to goddess cults. The Genesis author may have understood that the tears and pleadings of a frightened woman could cause an orthodox man to be tempted who would not ordinarily be drawn to polytheistic practices.[28] The result of Eve eating the fruit was that she had to suffer the consequences of her scheme in later years. Granted, it is true that she conceived her first child after the expulsion from the Garden, but the goddess effect resulted in disaster. The first-born murdered his younger brother and was then was banished, so Eve's loss was compounded. That double death was in a sense symbolic of the two *kinds* of death dealt with in the narrative—spiritual and physical death. Abel died physically, but Cain's death consisted of separation from family and from Yahweh's focused presence. Cain "died" to Eve and family, but he also died spiritually in the sense that he left the place of blessing and covenant covering. To his descendants are attributed not only inventiveness and culture but escalating vengeance, violence, and polygamy. Furthermore, the goddess effect resulted in a pronouncement of more pain in childbirth rather than less.

Another example of an idolatrous action that resulted in disaster is Rachael's theft of the family *teraphim* (household idols) from her father. She hid them in the camel pack, then sat on it. She claimed to be having her menstrual period, implying that anything beneath her would be ritually be defiled (Lev 12:2), so even if her father suspected that the idols were in the pack, they were of no further use to anyone at that point. Yet when she got to Palestine with her family, she was pregnant with Benjamin. What should have been a joyous moment turned to tragedy. When the lad was born, she named him Son of my Sorrow because she was dying in the process of giving birth (Gen 35:18). Priests of Yahweh may have pointed to such narratives as warnings against turning to any goddess for comfort and deliverance.

Many scholars point out that tree metaphors are so common in the Ancient Near East that even Yahweh in Hos 14:8c compares himself to a green pine tree. The whole passage is very arboreal,

> I will heal their waywardness
> and love them freely,
> for my anger has turned away from them.
> I will be like the dew to Israel;
> he will blossom like a lily.
> Like a cedar of Lebanon he will send down his roots;
> his young shoots will grow.

---

28. A case in point would be Jer 44:17, 25 in which the women pressed for a return to devotion to the Queen of Heaven, a cult in which both wives and husbands participated.

> His splendor will be like an olive tree,
> his fragrance like a cedar of Lebanon.
> Men will dwell again in his shade.
> he will flourish like the grain.
> He will blossom like a vine,
> and his fame will be like the wine from Lebanon.
> O Ephraim, what more have I to do with idols?
> I will answer him and care for him.
> I am like a green pine tree;
> your faithfulness comes from me. (Hos 14:4–8)

The lure of the tree—why not? The results are usually immediate, for good or for ill. Turn away, cried the prophets and priests. Turn to the LORD, the tree of life. All that mankind could desire was embedded in his promises, but there is a price to be paid. One has to wait on God's timing, and waiting means exercising faith, often in the face of discouraging circumstances. God's promises are often slow in coming, like the growth of a great tree. But in the end the results can be breathtaking.

11

Redemption, Resurrection, and Social Justice

A Pilgrim's Progress through Time

THE IMMENSE AMOUNT OF research that has accrued on the topic of afterlife and resurrection in the Hebrew Bible has not settled the debate in scholarly circles. The orthodox Israelite beliefs emerged only with great difficulty from the framework of the longstanding Near Eastern world view. This was not a process involving clean, consecutive categories. As always in times of change, there was debate, resistance, dialogue, innovation, backlash, overlap, and foreign influences that complicate the picture.

The interpretive difficulties are augmented by the fact that there is a certain circularity involved in dating any work. Texts can be dated based on preconceived trajectories in language or ideology rather than by facts. Facts are often elusive to missing, which requires a lot of guesswork. An ancient text may have had one or more redactors (scribal editors) who imported into it the vocabularies and ideologies of their own eras. John Sawyer argues that Early Hebrew, representing writings up to about the fourth century BCE, has been for the most part lost and written over in the HB by redactors who lived after 400 BCE, which he calls the Middle Period, covering Mishnaic and Medieval Hebrew.[1] He reasons, therefore, that the intent of the original authors is extremely difficult to determine; our analysis should take into account post-exilic and post-biblical understandings and literature. Since the rabbinic writings explicitly promote the idea of a Day of Judgment and resurrection, Sawyer believes that we have good reason to read afterlife and resurrection into passages that defy interpretation, like Deut 32:39; 1 Sam 2:6; 1 Kgs 17:22; Isa 26:14, 19; 53:11;

---

1. Sawyer, "Hebrew Words," 219.

66:24; Ezk 37:10; Hos 6:2; Ps 1:15; 16:19; 17:15; 49:16; 72:16; 73:24; 88:11; Job 14:12; 19:25–27; and Dan 12:2.[2]

It isn't my intention here to grapple with dating issues, but a general developmental trend, may be perceived in the Hebrew Bible's references to afterlife and resurrection. Several stages are depicted in the canonical narrative and writings.

Stage 1: Being Gathered to One's Ancestors

The Torah and former prophets only hint in the vaguest terms that God can, and fully intends to, conquer the death sentence meted out to Adam and Eve (Deut 32:39). The taking up of Enoch is one of the passages in the Torah that sowed the seeds of a later doctrine of resurrection (Gen 5:22). Beyond the Torah, a related and even more explicit passage is found in Hannah's song in 1 Sam 2:6, "The LORD kills and brings to life; he brings down to *Sheol* and raises up." For the most part, however, the deceased of the Torah and historical narratives are said to be "gathered to their fathers." Whether the patriarchal narratives view *Sheol* as the physical grave or as a location for the souls of all the departed is a matter of discussion and debate. Whatever afterlife was understood to be, it was steeped in cultic rituals which to a large extent reflected the practices and ideas of the Canaanite environs. Afterlife was tied to tribe, family, and nationality. It was communal, covenantal, and (in the Torah) arbitrated through the male gender. The punishment for the worst offenses was to be "cut off from one's people."

During this early period standing stones, *teraphim*, and rituals of the ancestor cult were tolerated as long as they did not involve active magic or necromancy. Later association with polytheism brought condemnation from the Deuteronomistic school, the early and later prophets, and the scribal committee we call the Chronicler. Whether one could offer food to the dead that was not tithable is debated among scholars. The fact that a Mosaic law forbad it suggests to some that it was often done. Deviating from prescribed rituals and Mosaic law could be a capital crime equal to polytheism and was often punishable by death.

This is an era of new paradigms, when an entire ethnic group was redefining itself, and not always voluntarily. The multitude in the wilderness often wanted to turn back to Egypt. The spies brought "an evil report of the land." The polytheists forced Aaron to agree to the construction of a golden calf, and the descendants of Moses through Gershom and Jonathan offered blood sacrifices to idols in the city of Dan. On the other hand, families like

2. Ibid., 230–31.

that of Joshua, Caleb, Boaz, and the sons of Korah stood firm in the new vision of monotheistic worship.

Stage 2: The Canaanite and Mesopotamian Paradigm

As Israel settled itself into the new land, the influence of Ugaritic, Sumerian, and Babylonian literature, law codes, and religious practices still had a powerful hold on the imagination of the Hebrews. In passage after passage, well into the era of Jeremiah, *Sheol* is described in terms similar to the Babylonian Erkallu/Arralu or to the underworld of the Epic of Gilgamesh—a gloomy, dark, cold, wormy, dusty city with bars and gates to imprison all who go there for all eternity. They are cut off from God's aid and miracles. When a protagonist or author is emotionally depressed and wants to elicit sympathy for his situation, there is no comfort in the thought of being gathered to the forefathers. Descriptions of *Sheol* often equate with the grave itself or a metaphysical extension of the grave. All go there, including the righteous. God is not worshiped, and the dead are not remembered by him. This stage was actually very persistent in Israel.[3] Relationship with Yahweh is mediated through the rituals and the priesthood, which were legalistic and binding. Because God is just and perfect, suffering is a sign of sin. Good people are delivered from trouble. The descendants of the wicked die out so that their very memory decays and fades. Humans were made from dust and to dust they shall return. Death is the realm of *tehom*, the deep, inhabited by Leviathan, the Hebrew version of the Canaanite/Ugaritic seven-headed Lotan.

Stage 3: Animal Sacrifice is Not Sufficient

Overlapping that ideology throughout Israel's early monarchy was the theology attributed to the Davidic court, or at least to a school of thought originating in the Davidic era, during which ethical behavior, prophecy, confession of sin, repentance, gratitude toward God, verbal testimony, and musical worship were promoted over cultic practice. Animal sacrifices were subordinated to sacrifices of thanksgiving. The sanctuary represented a special focus of God's presence and was revered in the sight of the devout, but God was also understood to be everywhere. The temple of Solomon was not his place of abode, it was a place of worship where his Name was

---

3. See Hooke, "Life after Death–V," 236–39; Cox, "'As Water Spilt,'" 1–17; Birkeland, "Belief," 60–78; Rust, "Destiny," 296–311.

hallowed. His presence extended to the ends of the earth and even into *Sheol*. Wherever he was honored, light and dew and a new morning were there (Ps 139:7–16). This understanding of God's power and influence began to change the way some people viewed the gloom of death. Dermot Cox offers three justifications for this change of perception. (1) Since God is the creator and source of "life" it seemed harsh and illogical that death should be annihilation at his hands. (2) There arose a need to justify God's dealings with the righteous, making a difference between the fate of the righteous and the ungodly. (3) The concept of "the holy ones" and their intimacy with Yahweh became more defined. The language of the Psalms began to anticipate an afterlife with God (Psalms 1, 16, 21, 24, 40, 49, 50, and 73). In this environment, the book of Jonah, with its language reminiscent of death, and its prophet being spit up by a big fish, fit quite well.

The Temple stood throughout the entire monarchy; in the early monarchy it was still a center of national promise and pride. The Korahites relished their association with the worship there and the possibility of experiencing God's presence in a unique way. Thus, the wicked were expected to perish in the afterlife (Job 18:17–21; Ps 1:5–6; Ps 146:4), while the righteous would maintain their existence in God's presence. The word "perish" is not defined, but evidently represents separation from God and from the righteous community. In addition to individual redemption from *Sheol*, Israel's continued existence in the north and the south was assured for the Korahites because of God's covenant kindness and mercy.

Stage 4: Prophetic Clarity

In the era of the latter prophets, apocalyptic theologies became increasingly important as national vigor weakened. Mysterious prophecies of a messianic savior-king proliferated in Scripture, but so also did the worship of Baal and Asherah. Multiple references to the Baal myth salt the oracles attributed to Isaiah. King Solomon had early on opened the door to child sacrifice and polytheism, a door that opened and shut several times over the course of the rest of Judah's history. Solomon also set the stage for a northern Israel that would tolerate idol worship to appease the people. By the time of King Hezekiah's reign in southern Judah, the ancestor cult included magic, necromancy, and possibly infanticide, and had become highly repulsive in the eyes of the sages and prophets. The Temple was often an object of neglect or a place of syncretistic practice. Kings like Ahaz and Manasseh allowed it to fall into decay and disuse. Prophets like Isaiah, Micah, Amos, and Hosea warned that Israel was doomed to exile and ruin, while Judah's existence was in dire peril. God's loving vindication of his people became more transcendent, metaphorical, and spiritual and less about the earthly covenant community (Isa 35:5–8; Jer 3:14; 31:30–31). Animal sacrifice and cultic action fell out of favor with several latter prophets.[4]

A New Covenant was anticipated that would be different from the Sinai pact in that it would actually change the heart and attitude of the people, which the first covenant failed to do:

> "The time is coming," declares the LORD, "when I will make a new covenant with the house of Israel and with the house of Judah. It will not be like the covenant I made with their forefathers when I took them by the hand to lead them out of Egypt, because they broke my covenant, though I was a husband to them. This is the covenant I will make with the house of Israel after that time," declares the LORD. "I will put my law in their minds and write it on their hearts. I will be their God, and they will be my people." (Jer 31:31–33)

Jeremiah also predicted that the Ark of the Covenant, so crucial to the process of blood atonement, would disappear. It would never be found and would not be missed (Jer 3:16). That prophecy came literally to pass. The Holy of Holies was empty by the time the Babylonian army burned the Temple of Solomon in 586 BCE. After Judah returned to their cities in the post-exile, Second Temple era, the temple was occasionally looted by foreign armies. The furniture and golden utensils were refashioned and replaced, but the Holy of Holies never again contained such an ark.

As national prospects declined, the expectation of a global awakening spread throughout the prophetic literature. The Gentiles would acknowledge Yahweh even while the Hebrews failed to do so (Isa 9:1, 2; 24:14–16; 25:3, 7). "Therefore strong peoples will glorify you," Isaiah writes; "Cities of ruthless nations will fear you . . . And he will destroy on this mountain the shroud that is cast over all peoples, the sheet that is spread over all the nations; he will swallow up death forever" (Isa 25:7). Life, spiritual life, would come to the nations.

In the same general era, statements about afterlife and resurrection became more explicit,

> They [the earthly foreign rulers who oppressed Israel] are now dead, they live no more; those departed spirits (*rephaim*) do not rise. You punished them and brought them to ruin; you wiped out all memory of them. (Isa 26:14)

---

4. (Psalms 22:22, 25; 27:6; 40:6; 50:7–15, 22, 23; 51:16, 17; 69:30–33; Isa 1:10–17; 66:1–3; Jer 3:14–18; 4:4; 6:20; 31:27–34; Hos 6:6; 14:1–2; Amos 5:21–27).

So there will be no resurrection for the wicked oppressors, in spite of Canaanite practices and beliefs. However, Isaiah comforts the righteous people:

> But your dead will live; their bodies will rise. You who dwell in the dust, wake up and shout for joy. Your dew is like the dew of the morning; the earth will give birth to her dead." Isaiah claims that the LORD is coming out of his dwelling to punish the unjust sinners of the earth. "The earth will disclose the blood shed upon her; she will conceal her slain no longer." (Isa 26:19–21)

Hosea cries out,

> I will ransom them from the power of the grave (Heb: *Sheol*); I will redeem them from death. Where O death, are your plagues? Where, O grave, is your destruction? I will have no compassion, even though he thrives among his brothers. (Hos 13:14)

The New International Version (NIV) quoted above states definitively that God will ransom and redeem. The various Bible versions differ as to whether Hosea is making a statement or asking a question: "Shall I ransom them from the power of *Sheol*? Shall I redeem them from Death?" (NRSV). The NRSV ends the verse with "Compassion is hidden from my eyes." The ESB (Lutheran Study Bible) also makes it a question and ends the verse as does the NRSV. The New King James makes it a statement. Looking to the Hebrew in Owens,[5] we see no grammatical markers of a question, yet the commentaries correctly point out that the context is one of judgment against Ephraim (northern Israel) for sin. It's as if a glorious promise of national restoration and even end time resurrection of bodies on Judgment Day were dropped accidently into the middle of a declaration of judgment against the nation. As a prophet, Hosea knew well that in his day that Assyria was going to be the instrument of that judgment, and that northern Israel would not ever fully recover.

Either way, our point here is made. If God is saying to Ephraim, because of your sin, I will not save you from destruction and death, I will not raise you from the dead, I will not ransom or redeem you, then the opposite is true. If you serve me and love me, I will ransom and redeem you from death and destruction. The grave awaits those who ignore the warning. Redemption is the promise for those who hear and obey.

Psalm 1 is easy to read without any inkling of a possible link to resurrection, but in the Hebrew the words for "rise up/stand up" and "judgment" take on a new life, especially when read against the backdrop of a cultural

---

5. Owens, *AKOT*, vol. 4.

context in which afterlife and a day of divine judgment are open topics of conversation. There is an oblique hint of an end time theme in the verse, referencing a final Judgment Day:

> Therefore the wicked will not stand in the judgment, nor sinners in the assembly of the righteous. (Ps 1:5)

Stage 5: Late Development

In the late pre-exilic, exilic, and post-exilic eras, Jewish thinkers dwelled on the promise of national and cultic restoration, but that hope was blended with a belief promoted by the prophets and sages of a bodily resurrection. The most important passage comes from the book of Daniel, a Jewish prophet and sage who spent the major portion of his life as a captive in Babylon:

> At that time Michael the great prince who protects your people, will arise. There will be a time of distress such as not happened from the beginning of nations until then. But at that time your people—everyone whose name is found written in the book—will be delivered. Multitudes who sleep in the dust of the earth will awake: some to everlasting life, others to shame and everlasting contempt. Those who are wise will shine like the everlasting brightness of the heavens, and those who lead many to righteousness, like the stars forever and ever." (Dan 12:1–3)

Although the book of Job is not necessarily a late work, one particular passage is so explicit that it must have had a powerful grip on the theological imaginations of Israel all throughout its history.

> Oh that my words were written!
> Oh that they were inscribed in a book!
> Oh that with an iron pen and lead
> they were engraved in the rock forever!
> For I know that my Redeemer lives,
> and at the last he will stand upon the earth.
> And after my skin has been thus destroyed,
> yet in my flesh I shall see God;
> whom I shall see for myself,
> and my eyes shall behold, and not another.
> My heart faints within me. (Job 19:23–27, ESB)

Jon Levenson develops the theme of resurrection as a symbol of the preservation and restoration of the Jews as a people. He begins with biblical stories in which apparent, real, or threatened deaths of children are reversed, particularly by the impending birth of another. "Birth," he suggests, "can qualify the finality of death" and so in the HB birth is sometimes described by the metaphor of resurrection.[6] Levenson concludes that the deliverance from *Sheol* is not immortality, but the continuation of temple, family, and lineage. For some Jews, according to Levenson, there was a problem with the concept of the soul of the individual surviving without the body because they were seen to be a unity.

One difficulty with his interpretation here is that in Isa 56 eunuchs are promised a name better than children. Levenson fails to indicate how this promise comes to pass with no lineage and no stela to remind the world that the eunuch lived. His premise also raises the question of what happens to metaphorical immortality when time wears a burial inscription away or buries it in the sand. What happens in war when the child is not restored and the line ends? Such a remedy fails to resurrect such lives to give them eternal significance. When the Hebrew prophets and psalmists expressed their confident, timeless expectations of redemption from *Sheol*, was their concept of immortality really as limited as Levenson insists?

Levenson pursues his thesis in the poetry of the prophet Isaiah in which the young, divorced wife, the bereaved widow, and the barren woman (all representing Israel itself) are comforted for loss or lack of children (Isa 43–50; 54:4–6) by the promise of future uncountable seed. Israel should extend the pegs of her tent in order to accommodate all that will call Jerusalem and Zion mother. Exile equals death, but repatriation equals life. An element is missing in that equation, however, because Isa 49:21–23 suggests that the queens and kings of foreign nations will come to Zion offering their own children. Isaiah 66:18–21 repeats the theme with the stipulation that some Gentiles will serve as Levites. How do these metaphorical promises play into the concept of exile and repatriation unless the Gentiles actually become Israelites? A more reasonable way of viewing the Gentile passages is that the life, death, and immortality of these passages have nothing to do with being a restored Israelite but in being one that acknowledges that Yahweh is the source of life globally. The Zion of the latter half of Isaiah is not the literal mountain, although at one level a physical restoration is indeed being promised. Levenson challenges the reader to expand our concept of life and death, but we must also expand our concept of Zion.

Genocide, war, famine, death, and disaster threaten to annihilate the life of his people, but God reverses the impending death or doom and brings

---

6. Levenson, *Resurrection*, 117–18.

forth life.[7] Thus far, Levenson views the Scriptures as referring to restoration rather than resurrection. However, in Dan 12:1–3 he sees a definite account of resurrection.

Levenson's online article "Resurrection in the Torah: A Second Look" artfully examines the premise of immortality as the continuation of the family. Scanning various biblical narratives, he points to the repeated theme of the restoration of lost children. In the end, after emphasizing that the early patriarchs had no thought of their own individual immortality, he closes with some inspiring thoughts about eventual resurrection,

> The same is true of the doctrine of the resurrection of the dead when it finally comes into being. To affirm the fact of death without mentioning the promise of life is not only to give a partial picture. It is also to invert the priorities of many biblical texts, from a number of genres and periods, and to miss the tension out of which the doctrine of resurrection of the dead will eventually arise. For that doctrine upholds both realities—the fact of death and the promise of life—and again gives the last word not to death, but to life.[8]

Although we cannot be sure when various portions of the Scriptures were written and finalized, there is a world of difference between the understanding of life and death in the majority of the Hebrew Bible and that of the Hellenized post-exilic world. The author of Ps 49 stands somewhere in between. Fixing on a rigid, sequential progression of ideas may distract us from the point so aptly expressed by Levenson that in the Hebrew Bible death and life are both affirmed, but in the end, whether the topic is the continuation of family and clan or the immortality of the individual, life trumps death.

Resurrection in the Inter-testamental Era

> For to know you is complete righteousness, and to know your power is the root of immortality. (Wis 14:3)

By the time the books of the Apocrypha were being written, the concept of national restoration was giving way to the idea of individual immortality, but no single theological thought had won the day. Psalms 49, 16, and 73 insinuate individual immortality which results from having a righteous

---

7. Ibid., 180.

8. Levenson, http://www.ctinquiry.org/publications/reflections_volume_6/levenson.htm.

perspective on ethics, life, death, and God's redemptive power. In association with other literature, it becomes a bridge from one paradigm to another. The beliefs of the past, although open to interpretation, will be viewed by the generations of the future as inspired and crafted by the Spirit of God in such a way that ongoing revelation can urge a clear concept of individual immortality and redemption, leading towards the full-blown doctrine of resurrection in the post-exilic era.

A comprehensive survey of all Apocryphal, Pseudepigraphal, and rabbinic literature dealing with immortality and resurrection would be a thesis in itself and is too broad to deal with here. Our point, painted with the broadest of brushes, is that the gulf between the theology of works attributed to David and that of the book of Qohelet, attributed to Solomon, was not resolved in the Second Temple era. David believed in prophecy, a divinely-gifted purpose for his life, and the reward of an afterlife with Yahweh.[9] Qohelet bitterly despaired of hope in a blissful eternity. In the Second Temple era these perspectives were taken up most famously by the Pharisees and Sadducees, respectively.

The Wisdom of Jesus, son of Sirach (also called Sirach, Ben Sirach, Sirah, or Ecclesiasticus) portrays no hope of heavenly immortality (10:11; 14:12; 21:10; 19:3; 17:27–30; 22:11; 28:21; 44:9; 46:19). Retribution is individual and certain, but it catches the wicked here on earth rather than later.[10] *Sheol* is the end of all, but Ben Sirah does not clarify whether he means the grave or a place of eternal sleep. A sample of his statements shows that we are to enjoy what we can of life because God's blessing here and his reward of good things on earth is all we can expect:

---

9. Regarding the debate as to the existence of David and Solomon, see Shanks, "A Fortified City," 38–43, about a tenth century site between Bethlehem and Tell es-Safi/Gath being worked by Yossi/Yosef Garfinkel that reveals a casemate wall, a chambered gate, and an ostracon with proto-Canaanite letters on it. According to Garfinkel the potsherd bears the words "king," "judge," and "slave." Garfinkel claims that the fortifications and the ostracon may show that in the era in which the Bible places King David, Israel was a state with writing and a king as well as sophisticated architecture. If so, the claim that certain beautiful and progressive psalms came from David and his priestly court is strengthened. In the same issue is Nadav Na'aman's "The Trowel vs. the Text," in which he explores the contrast between the conclusions drawn from reading the el Amarna letters and the archaeological evidence in the field. The trowel suggests that cities like Lachish, Meggido, Shechem, and Jerusalem (to name a few) were barely inhabited, lacked walls, and were of little influence. The cuneiform letters discovered in the late 1800's tell a different story. Na'aman surmises that since so much of what must have existed in the Middle and Late Bronze Age has been obliterated over time, the same may be said for the city of Jerusalem.

10. Keller, "Hebrew Thoughts," 30. Also see Levenson, *Resurrection*, 194–96.

> How can dust and ashes be proud? Even in life the human body decays. A long illness baffles the physician; the king of today will die tomorrow. For when one is dead he inherits maggots and vermin and worms. (Sir 10:9–11)

> Who will sing praises to the Most High in Hades in place of the living who give thanks? From the dead, as from one who does not exist, thanksgiving has ceased; those who are alive and well sing the Lord's praises. How great is the mercy of the Lord, and his forgiveness for those who return to him! For not everything is within human capability, since human beings are not immortal. (Sir 17:27–30)

In several other statements, Ben Sirach takes up the theme, familiar from Isa 66:24, of unquenchable fire and imperishable worms. "Humble yourself to the utmost," he proclaims, "for the punishment of the ungodly is fire and worms" (7:17; 19:3; 28:23). The image here, however, seems to refer to chastisement against the ungodly in this life and the reference is metaphorical. Judith also threatens the nations that arise against Israel with fire and worms, but her retribution takes place on the Day of Judgment. Whether that day is historical and metaphorical or eschatological and literal is not so clear (Judith 17:17).

The author of the Wisdom of Solomon has a very different expectation, one with which the authors of Psalms 16, 49, and 73 would find common ground. He admits openly that his motive for writing is to refute the theological sentiments of the likes of Ben Sirach and Qohelet, "For they reasoned unsoundly, saying to themselves, 'Short and sorrowful is our life, and there is no remedy when life comes to an end, and no one has been known to return from Hades'" (2:1). This attitude, according to the author of Wisdom, leads to wickedness and sin, whereas "the souls of the righteous are in the hand of God, and no torment will ever touch them" (3:1). The righteous will only seem to have died and been punished; in truth they are immortal (3:2–4). Although this immortality does not necessarily involve a resurrection of the body, verse 8 seems to imply it: "They will govern nations and rule over peoples." The author of Ps 49 implied much the same thing in verse 14b. A similar thought is found in Wis 4:16:

> The righteous who have died will condemn the ungodly who are living, and youth that is quickly perfected will condemn the prolonged old age of the unrighteous.

Wisdom of Solomon 5 is even more eloquent in promoting immortality. The deceased oppressors will grieve as they recognize the reward of the righteous. The psalmists would have arisen from their seats with a shout of approval to read thus:

> What has our arrogance profited us? And what good has our boasted wealth brought us? "All those things have vanished like a shadow, and like a rumor that passes by; like a ship that sails through the billowy water, and when it has passed no trace can be found, no track of its keel in the waves; or as, when a bird flies through the air, no evidence of its passage is found; the light air, lashed by the beat of its pinions and pierced by the force of its rushing flight, is traversed by the movement of its wings, and afterwards no sign of its coming is found there; or as, when an arrow is shot at a target, the air, thus divided, comes together at once, so that no one knows its pathway. So we also, as soon as we were born, ceased to be, and we had no sign of virtue to show, but were consumed in our wickedness." Because the hope of the ungodly is like thistledown carried by the wind, and like a light frost driven away by a storm; it is dispersed like smoke before the wind, and it passes like the remembrance of a guest who stays but a day. But the righteous live forever, and their reward is with the Lord; the Most High takes care of them. Therefore they will receive a glorious crown and a beautiful diadem from the hand of the Lord, because with his right hand he will cover them, and with his arm he will shield them. (Wis 5:8–16)

Both Sirach and Wisdom of Solomon praise wisdom, but Ben Sirach sees it as a blessing to the wise here on earth whereas the author of Wisdom of Solomon sees it as a veritable reflection of God's nature and a gateway to immortality (Wis 7:24–26; 8:13).

The epic of the Maccabee family (Macc I–IV) affords another important example of expectation of retribution after death (2 Macc 6:26). The message is still nationalistic in the sense that it foresees the punishment all sinful Gentiles (while remaining silent as to the fate of righteous Gentiles). Jews, too, may be disciplined by God for wickedness, but his punishment for them is corrective and not permanent (2 Macc 6:12–17). In the story of the seven brothers and a mother who are martyred for their faith, a clear message agreeing with Wisdom of Solomon is developed. Martyrs will not only win a crown and a reunion of family in the afterlife, but their suffering will contribute to the redemption of other Jews. Their torturers will burn in eternal fire (4 Macc 9:9, 32). Other books are equally explicit. Second Baruch speaks of the earth giving up the beasts Behemoth and Leviathan on the day of Messianic restoration. The earth will become fruitful, and the righteous will glow with health:

> And it will happen after these things when the time of the appearance of the Anointed One has been fulfilled and he returns with glory, that then all who sleep in hope of him will rise. And it will happen at that time that those treasuries will be opened in which the number of the souls of the righteous were kept, and they will go out and the multitudes of the souls will appear together, in one assemblage, of one mind. And the first ones will enjoy themselves and the last ones will not be sad. For they know that the time has come of which it is said that it is the end of times. But the souls of the wicked will the more waste away when they shall see all these things. For they know that their torment has come and that their perditions have arrived. (2 Bar 30:1–5)[11]

The rabbinic writings also weigh in with clear affirmations of immortality and bodily resurrection. Levenson cites the midrash *Lamentations Rabbah* on Lam 3:23: "Rabbi Alexandri said: Because You renew us every morning, we know that Your grace is ample to bring about the resurrection of the dead."[12] The rabbis taught the existence of a personified Evil Inclination (Satan) which draws humans into sin and death, but God is able to strengthen them with a power to resist and offers redemption to spare them inevitable condemnation.

> Israel said to the Holy One (blessed be he!), "Master of the Universe, You know the power of the Evil Inclination, how powerful it is!" The Holy One (Blessed be He!) said to them, "Chip away at it a little in this world and I will remove it from you in the future," as it is said, "Build up, build up the highway, / Remove the rocks!" (Isa 62:10). Similarly, it says, "Build up, build up a highway! Clear a road! Remove all obstacles from the road of My people!" (Isa 57:14). In the World-to-Come, I will uproot it from you: "I will remove the heart of stone from your body and give [you a heart of flesh]" (Ezek 36:26). (*Num Rab* 15:16).[13]

Although many have set their hands to examining the Hebrew Bible references to death, *Sheol*, and afterlife, Spronk's work is unique in revealing the alterations introduced into biblical texts by the Palestinian Targums,

---

11. Translation from Charlesworth, *The Old Testament Pseudepigrapha*, 1:631. For a more developed treatment of the doctrines of immortality and resurrection in the Apocrypha and Pseudepigrapha, see Keller, "Hebrew Thoughts," 29–44 and Hooke, "Life after Death VI: The Extra-Canonical Literature," 273–86.

12. Levenson, *Resurrection*, 181.

13. Ibid., 224.

which are essentially paraphrastic translations.[14] Since Spronk's work is not readily available, and since the insights he offers on the topic of the Palestinian Targums are rare, several examples are reproduced here.

To Gen 19:26, in which Lot's wife was changed into a pillar of salt, the Targum adds, "until the day of the resurrection of the dead." In Gen 25:34, in which Esau despised his birthright and sold it for a bowl of pottage, the Targum adds "Thus Esau despised his birthright and concerning the resurrection of the dead he despised the life in the world to come." Gen 3:19 reads, "You are dust and to dust you shall return, but from the dust you will rise to account for the things you have done."

Deuteronomy 32:39, oft discussed in books and articles regarding resurrection, is changed to, "I kill the living in this world and make alive the dead in the world to come."

The Targum version of Deut 33:6a reads, "May Reuben live in this world, and not die in the second (death) in which the wicked die in the world to come."

The Babylonian Targum also made changes to passages such as 1 Sam 2:6, Isa 58:11, Deut 33:6a, Hos 14:8, and Isa 65:15, supporting the idea of eternal life in the world to come as opposed to the "second death." The concept of second death passed into the Book of the Revelation (2:11–17; 3:12). Hosea 6:2 becomes a clear statement about Israel's restoration in the resurrection.

Four Paths to Redemption in the Hebrew Bible

1. The Mosaic Law with its purity rituals and animal sacrifices. The blood sprinkled on the ark was essential for national atonement and covenant relationship. One problem with the Law was that quite a few of the civic laws were echoes of ancient Mesopotamian law codes that reflect the days of Abraham and earlier. The disciplines of that ancient era were rather brutish, and women certainly retained the status of inferiority in the family, community, and congregation. Ancient superstitions slip into the language, such as the sacrifice being "the food of your God," which is repudiated in the Psalms in no uncertain terms. The proverb

---

14. The Targums were known to have been in use in Palestine in the third century CE/AD. They are loose translations or paraphrases, sometimes with explanatory glosses or theological additions. Occasionally they employ a "converse translation technique" in which a passage is rendered as the opposite of what the original stated because the translator felt that God and his ways were inappropriate. See Metzger, "Important Early Translations of the Bible," 35–49, and Klein, "Converse Translation," 515–37. Metzger's article can be found at http://www.bible-researcher.com/aramaic4.html.

"eye for an eye, tooth for a tooth" is actually taken from the earlier law code of Hammurabi, a famous Babylonian ruler. The Mosaic code was an Israelite reworking and improvement of the way people were already living, but it included ritualistic things one does that almost magically removes the stain of unclean status. There were definitely commandments about ethical behavior, such as the Decalogue (the Ten Commandments), and the need to be generous to the poor, honest in business, kind to foreigners, fair in arranging inheritances, and caring to one's neighbor. However, human nature being what it is, the actual redemption was accredited to the rituals and sacrifices.

2. The Davidic path was about genuine inward ethics and doing what is right. The first commandment given to a human by Elohim after expulsion of the family from the Garden was to Cain. It was to "do what is right." There was no rulebook to follow at that time, so it was about fairness, humility, patience, family relationships, and obedience. The rule was imbedded in Cain's conscience, but he tuned it out. This path also included the sacrifices of praise, joy, and thanksgiving. These attitudes were not the side dish. They were the main course. Animal sacrifices were optional.

3. Scattered throughout the Psalms and prophetic writings are cryptic references to a coming king/suffering servant. Connecting all the dots is challenging, but not impossible. This king will be fully human but have aspects of the divine in his being (Isa 9). He will die an agonizing death that sounds very much like a crucifixion, all the while being mocked by his fierce enemies. His persecutors will divide his cloak amongst themselves (Ps 22). He will be treated horribly and rejected, led to his death like a lamb to the slaughter, yet, unlike the arrogant, in some manner his brutal death will be accepted as a guilt offering by God, and he will "sprinkle" many nations. Afterwards, he will see the light of life and rejoice because he has born the sin of the people and justified many (Isa 52:13–15; 53:4–11). He will be a king and a priest after the order of Melchizedek, and will rule at Yahweh's right hand (Ps 110). He will be born of a virgin (Isa 7:14, LXX, NIV) of the house of David and will be called The Branch. The full power and revelation of the Spirit of God will rest on his shoulders. He will bring forth judgments of justice and righteousness (Isa 11:1–5; Zech 3:8–10). Basically this person will be rejected and die, by which he will provide a path to redemption for all nations.

4. A sure way to infuriate one's Judeo-Christian deity is to ignore mercy for the poor and withhold justice, social or local! If I wanted to buy a

candy bar and I presented coins that were engraved only on one side, my purchase would be voided. The final requirement in the redemption process goes back to the second point here:

> Though you bring me burnt offerings and grain offerings, I will not accept them. Though you bring choice fellowship offerings, I will have no regard for them. Away with the noise of your songs. I will not listen to the music of your harps. But let justice roll on like a river, righteousness like a never-failing stream!" (Amos 5:22–24)

The minor prophet Amos has declared that both the Mosaic and Davidic sacrifices are insufficient without social justice. No justice adds up to no redemption. The minor prophet Micah agrees:

> He has showed you, O man, what is good. And what does the LORD require of you? To act justly and to love mercy and to walk humbly before your God. (Mic 6:6)

Micah is the same prophet who predicted that the Messiah would be born in Bethlehem. He reams the officials and leaders of both Israel and Judah for their injustices. Such is God's empathy for the pain of the oppressed:

> Listen, you leaders of Jacob, you rulers of the house of Israel. Should you not know justice, you who hate good and love evil; who tear the skin from my people and the flesh from their bones; who eat my people's flesh, strip off their skin and break their bones in pieces; who chop them up like meat for the pan, like flesh for the pot? (Mic 3:1–3)

Isaiah lays it out in even stronger terms:

> "The multitude of your sacrifices—
> what are they to me," says the LORD.
> "I have more than enough of burnt offerings, of rams
> and the fat of fattened animals;
> I have no pleasure
> in the blood of bulls and lambs and goats. . . .
> Your hands are full of blood;
> wash and make yourselves clean.
> Take your evil deeds out of my sight!
> Stop doing wrong, learn to do right!
> Seek justice, encourage the oppressed.
> Defend the cause of the fatherless,
> plead the cause of the widow." (Isa 1:1–11)

If there is one burning, all-encompassing, non-optional set of requirements in the Old Testament, it is this: justice, mercy, humility, love of God, love of mankind, virtue, generosity, and care for anyone, anywhere weaker than us.

There are no mint juleps or yachts in the hot place, but there may be quite a few politicians and world leaders there.

12

The New Testament Paradigm of Kindness

The Concept of Hell in the Early Church

IN FIRST CENTURY PALESTINE, there was a broad spectrum of ideologies and literature to inform a curious Jew, all with different views of ethnic relationships, cleanness, rituals, and afterlife. One non-biblical work that was held in high esteem was the book of Enoch. First Enoch 46:1–5 predicts a Messiah called the Son of Man who will judge every throne and king. Not one unrighteous ruler will escape his wrath. "Darkness shall be their habitation, and worms shall be their bed; nor from that their bed shall they hope to be again raised, because they exalted not the name of the Lord of Spirits."[1] He warns that the angels will wreak punishment on unrighteous rulers. They will be bound in chains, and their deeds will be forgotten. The righteous, however, will be allowed access to the Tree of Life in that day of recompense. The actual place of torment is described in 1 Enoch 10:4–7 and 2 Enoch:

> And those men carried me to the northern region; and they showed me there a very frightful place; and all kinds of torture and torment are in that place, cruel darkness and lightless gloom. And there is no light there, and a black fire blazes up perpetually, with a river of fire that comes out over the whole place, fire here, freezing ice there, and it dries up and it freezes; and very cruel places of detention and dark and merciless angels, carrying instruments of atrocities torturing without pity. (2 Enoch 10:1–6)[2]

---

1. www.book-ofenoch.com
2. www.pseudepigrapha.com

Palestine was a diverse and divided region when Jesus began to preach. There were Pharisees, Sadducees, Essenes, Zealots, Hellenistic (secular) Jews, orthodox Jews, Greeks, foreigners, scribes, Levites, priests, and Roman rulers. The Dead Sea Scrolls for the most part were already written, predicting a Teacher of Righteousness and a cosmic war between the Children of Light and the Children of Darkness. Into that mix appeared the one who would later be called Messiah. The early chapters of Matthew tell of the birth of Jesus Christ, his announcement as Messiah by John the Baptist (Matt 3:13) and his temptation by the devil (Matt 4:1–11). For the purpose of this chapter, we should note that the devil began his temptation in the wilderness, but ended at the pinnacle of the Temple in Jerusalem, indicating that Satan can lure his marks in church or synagogue as well as in the wilderness experiences of our lives. Christ's victory over that temptation was actually a replay of the temptation of mankind in the Garden. The first man Adam brought death to all, whereas the last Adam brought redemption to the whole human race (1 Cor 15:45). This time the Kingdom of God would be within. God's very presence is within us, transforming us even more into his image and likeness.

Shortly after that victory, we find Jesus was sitting on a rocky hillside, preaching to a mixed crowd who, for good or for ill, were struggling to grasp the sense of what he had to say (Matt 5–7). In these chapters, Jesus rejected good behavior and works that were for outward show but did not reflect an inner righteousness. He described God's various reactions to such inadequate good deeds. In the case of money given, God may just withhold any heavenly reward because the giver has already received his praise from men (Matt 6:1–2). Long, wordy prayers, said to impress others, will receive no answer from God. Gifts given to the synagogue or church by a giver who has harmed others are a waste of time and goods (Matt 6:1–4). The giver must make amends for his hurtful deed before the gift is actually counted by God.

Beginning with the Beatitudes, there are several rewards mentioned for right living. They include earthly as well as heavenly blessings. "Blessed are the meek, for they will inherit the earth," and "Blessed are the poor in spirit, for theirs is the kingdom of heaven" (Matt 5:3–12; 6:4, 6, 18, 33; 7:7). These rewards are not spelled out in detail, but rewards are by nature pleasing and good.

It is important to understand who Jesus was speaking to. Some may have been doubters, foreigners, or sinners, but most were average synagogue attenders. Many will transition over to being followers of Christ when His full message is revealed. They will then be house church members. The Jews of Jesus' day were depending on several things to pave their way to a blissful afterlife: a) circumcision, which places them securely into the covenant of

Abraham; b) the rituals of the Law of Moses, such as the food restrictions, which gave them a sense of righteous behavior; c) attendance at the temple in Jerusalem, which seemed to affirm God's presence and favor over Jerusalem; d) the temple sacrifices, which promised atonement for sin; e) and the long tradition of belief that they were a special people, holy by nature and favored of God. On the mount that day, Jesus opened a new understanding of what God additionally requires of them, and what the consequences would be if they don't live up to the commandments he laid out for them that day. If a follower of God is consistently generous, helpful, forgiving, and kind, they will attain a status of greatness in the kingdom of heaven (Matt 5:19). If they do not manifest these qualities, there could literally be hell to pay, for the Sermon on the Mount also carried within it many dire warnings for *all* those who do not live according to God's laws.

> You have heard that it was said to the people long ago, "Do not murder, and anyone who murders will be subject to judgment." But I tell you that anyone who is angry with his brother will be subject to judgment. Again, anyone who says to his brother, "Raca," is answerable to the Sanhedrin. But anyone who says, "You fool!" will be in danger of the fire of hell. (Matt 5:21–22)

The fire of hell is actually "the fire of Gehenna" in the original Greek. The first mention of Gehenna is in the book of Joshua. It was a valley near Jerusalem called *Geh Ben Hinnom*, or The Valley of the Son of Hinnom. It was mentioned as being part of the allotment of land to the tribe of Judah in the days of the prophet Joshua. Later mentions are more sinister. It included a site called Tophet where children were sacrificed to the foreign gods Molech and Chemosh. Babies were "passed through the fire" (burned alive). The Judean monarch King Ahaz participated in the dark rites of this place. Later kings did nothing to stop the practice of child sacrifice at Tophet until the reformer Josiah desecrated it (2 Kgs 23:10; 2 Chr 28:3; 33:6; Jer 7:31; 32:35). In the book of Isaiah, Tophet became a metaphor for the burning judgment against the king of Assyria (Isa 30:27–33). In Christ's day, it was a garbage dump where worms and fire were constantly present, making it an apt metaphor for both earthly and eternal punishment. Jesus uses this metaphor as if it is a foreboding of the afterlife for all those who will not forgive others and who let their grudges lapse into fulminating hate. In Jas 3:6, fire indicates earthly ungodliness, and the name Gehenna refers to hell itself, the very source of all evil. In the book of Revelation, that same hell is called "the Abyss," and it's full of fierce demons.

Gehenna turns up two more times in Matt 5, warning against sins of the eye, meaning what we see can spark what we think, which leads to what we do (with our hands and bodies). In Matt 10:28 and 18:9, we again see a reference to death of the soul, but "death" signifies a separation from God and a sentence of eternal punishment. We are to fear the devil, for he has power to "kill" both soul and body in the fire of Gehenna. (See also Mark 9:43–50 for a restatement of that sermon, referencing unquenchable fire, worms, and salt that has gone bad.)

Another description of hell is "outer darkness," with "weeping and gnashing of teeth" (Matt 8:8:12; 22:13; 25:30, NKJV). This doesn't literally match fire and worms, but the despair described is the same. It's just not where anyone wants to go.

Kindness vs Outward Piety

Who does the New Testament say goes to hell, and why? Well, the answer to that is complicated. Of course, we are commanded to be cautious about judging others, in spite of the fact that some of us have private opinions as to who we might expect to find there. An ancient Jew whose scriptural focus was the Law of Moses might expect the usual candidates to be: all Gentiles who are not fearers of God; the usual sinners who break the Ten Commandments; those Jews who do not keep kosher; who do not wash their hands properly before eating; those who charge high interest for loans to other Jews; and idolaters. If you were a follower of Jesus Christ, you would assume that everyone that does not openly accept and acknowledge Jesus Christ as Messiah and Lord. You would also condemn the sinners listed in Mark 7 such as liars and drunkards.

A deep study of all New Testament references to heaven and hell tell a deeper story. It's true that John 3 assures us that we must be "born again." This experience is a regeneration, a spiritual rebirth, a real renewing of the soul that changes the things that drive us. To be born again, one must only believe and "open the door" to the Holy Spirit's invitation. Paul clarifies that "it is by grace that you have been saved, through faith—and this not from yourselves, it is the gift of God—not by works, so that no one can boast." There is nothing we can do to deserve to be "saved." The price has been paid—our redemption is a free gift. Acknowledging our unworthiness, we are bought with the price that Jesus Christ paid on the cross.

But then we must read on, because the other side of the coin—works—is in the next phrase: "For we are God's workmanship, created in Christ Jesus to do good works, which God prepared in advance for us to do" (Eph 2:8–10). So our salvation was foreseen, planned, and approved by God, perhaps before time began, but so were our works. In fact, in the

Gospel of Matthew, Jesus declares in no uncertain terms that the flip side of the faith coin is a requirement to live a life of care for people who are in need: those who need clothing; those who are in prison; those who are ill; those who are strangers in need of a place of safety and rest; those who are hungry. Of course, these categories simply represent anyone who is in desperate need who cannot help themselves. Jesus warns that there will be a separation on Judgment Day. Those who lived selfish lives and turned away from the needy will be the banished ones. The kind-hearted will be at his right hand for eternity. Jesus did not equate himself with the mighty and wealthy of the earth in this passage. He identified with those hurting ones who need our aid, the ones we often look down on. To deny them is to deny Christ (Matt 25:31–46).

The Judgment passage shares an outlook with the parable of the Good Samaritan. There was a traveler who had been robbed and beaten and thrown into a ditch. We don't know his nationality, age, or race. We don't know if he was Jew or Gentile, good or bad, religious or atheist. He was just a man in the ditch who needed help. A priest and a Levite came by but wouldn't help. They were simply obeying the Torah, which forbad the "holy" temple servants to touch this bleeding man. Due to his wounds, he was ritually "unclean," so if they aided him, they would be "defiled" and be in violation of the levitical taboos for priests and Levites (Lev 21:4, 10–12). The Samaritan was from the north where the nation of northern Israel used to be, very close to the Galilee of the Gentiles described in Isa 9:1. Samaritans had a skewed version of the Torah. Because they had their own Pentateuch (Torah) and were not all ethnic Israelites, they were despised by regular Jews. He undoubtedly knew about the ritual defilement beliefs of the Jews, and yet he did not hesitate to help the man. He made sure that the victim was fully cared for, beyond what he himself was able to do at that moment. It was the Samaritan's kindness, rather than the supposed holiness and proper theology of the priest and Levite, that Jesus praised (Luke 10:25–37).

It was the most religious and orthodox of the Jewish leaders that aroused Jesus into a fulminating fit. His list of accusations was long: they made too many rules for people to follow; all that they did was for public display; they were enamored by status and titles and public respect; their brand of religion actually repelled those who might have been seekers; they obsessed about trivial ecclesiastical matters but totally missed what was important to God; they looked wonderful on the outside, but within they were full of corruption, greed, and self-indulgence; they built white-washed tombs for themselves, not acknowledging the death and corruption within. Jesus saved his juiciest epithets for these scribes, Pharisees, Sadducees, priests, and Levites. God had been watching these types turn his gift of religion on its head for over a thousand years. Jesus was furious when he finally had a chance to dump divine wrath on the lot of them. They were hypocrites, children of hell, blind fools, filthy dishes, whitewashed tombs full of dead men's bones, snakes, a brood of vipers. These types of religious leaders have no clue what God is really looking for in people. According to their own Messiah, they are all hell-bound (Matt 23).

A word of warning here—do not for a moment think that this raging fury could not also apply to Christian leaders today, or even politicians. Sometimes in our blind rush to fulfill the letter of the law, which can result in bondage, we miss the true spirit of the law where life and freedom reside (Rom 7:6).

The Dangers of Being Too Comfortable

There is a parable in the Gospel of Luke, chapter 12, which would resonate well with the author of Psalm 49. It's called "the parable of the rich fool." He did well in life. Drove the right car, kept out of debt, paid his employees on time, and sent his kids to the right schools. He had several barns where he kept his crops after harvest. One year was so bountiful, he didn't know what to do with it all. "I know," he said to himself. "I'll tear down these barns and build bigger ones." His old barns needed upgrading anyway, and the new ones would look really snappy from the road up the hill. "And I'll say to myself, 'You have plenty of good things laid up for many years. Take life easy, eat, drink, and be merry.'" But God had other ideas. That night the man had a heart attack and passed away. Jesus ended the parable with, "This is how it will be with anyone who stores up things for himself but is not rich toward God" (Luke 12:16–21).

Jesus made it clear that it wasn't the man's wealth that was the problem, but that he was spiritually impoverished. He did not give God credit for his good blessings, and he never considered doing anything with his abundance other than please himself. Like the rich man who saw Lazarus standing beside Abraham, he was selfish. He gave little thought to eternity. Quite a few individuals and companies today are storing their abundance in barns off-shore in hidden accounts, but the same principal applies. Those funds are not taxed. What are they for? Do they make the world a better place? Be assured that if the Bible has any truth in it, God Almighty knows every account number and he doesn't cook the books. We insure our cars, our homes, our lives, but we live as if we will never die or as if the manner in which we live our lives has no eternal consequence.

The parable of the ten virgins (Matt 25:1–13) is not about sinners, seekers, or unbelievers. It describes people loosely affiliated with church or synagogue who actually believe that there is an accounting after death, but they are careless in their lives. They don't take eternity seriously enough because they are having too much fun here on earth. The virgins of the parable are all waiting for a summons to a wedding that they have been invited to. They are all waiting in one place. They have been there all day and have no idea when the summons will arrive, but they know if it comes at night, they must be ready with lamps lit and trimmed. Five of them were foolish and didn't take oil with them to the place where they were to await the call. Five took jars of oil. It got to be late. All of them fell asleep, but at midnight a messenger alerted them that the Bridegroom was on his way. "Trim your lamps," said he. "Be ready, because he will be here soon." With great anticipation, they all turned up their lamps and combed their hair. But because the groom didn't get there right away, five of the lamps began to flicker. The five women pleaded with the others to give them some oil, but the wise ones answered, "Sorry, ladies, but there may not be enough for us and you. Go buy your own. There's an all night market on 5th and Madison." So you can guess the rest of the story. While the five were out purchasing more oil, the Bridegroom (meaning the Second Coming of Christ) appeared. The five wise women hopped into his carriage. When they got to his mansion, they entered with great joy and celebration, and the doors were shut . . . and locked. The other five were too late. With or without oil, they weren't prepared for the sudden appearing of the Kingdom Groom. For Jesus Christ, eternity is serious business.

Even after his death, Jesus was warning his churches about being lukewarm, and it was the same warning given in the tales of the rich men. In the book of Revelation, the prophetic author receives a message from the post-resurrection Jesus Christ for the angel appointed to guard the city of Laodicea (in what today is Turkey),

> So because you are lukewarm—neither hot nor cold—I am about to spit you out of my mouth. You say, "I am rich; I have acquired wealth and do not need a thing. But you do not realize that you are wretched, pitiful, poor, blind and naked. I counsel you to buy from me gold refined in the fire, so you can become rich; and white clothes to wear, so you can cover your shameful nakedness; and salve to put on your eyes, so you can see." (Rev 3:16–18)

These souls in peril of hell will be sitting in their Christian church when the messenger arrives to read the scroll written by John! That very day they may have taken holy Communion or baptized new believers. How many churches today would deserve such a message? Being hot for God doesn't mean that you have to jump and shout in church, although being noisy in celebration of God's goodness is very biblical. It doesn't mean giving away all your goods and joining a convent. It means that whatever financial or emotional state we are in, God is our ultimate love, and obeying his commandments as the ultimate goal of our lives. Since wealth was the core of the rebuke in the message, it seems apparent that the offending sins were greed, pride, an obsession with earthly distractions, and selfishness, as in the cases mentioned above. Again, Jesus warned, "Not everyone who says to me, 'Lord, Lord,' will enter the kingdom of heaven, but only he who does the will of my Father who is in heaven" (Matt 7:21).

It's Not about Being Rich and Powerful

The theme of the warnings in Ps 49 and the above parables is wealth. Jesus made it clear that the sins associated with wealth are addictive and are a lethal danger to the soul. It is easier for a camel, he said, laden with all kinds of goods on its back, to squeeze through a short, narrow gate in the city than for a rich man to enter the kingdom of heaven. Why? Because wealth fosters pride, greed, selfishness, and earthly distractions just for starters, not to mention the usual sins and temptations that plague mankind. Faith and belief are our initial doorway into God's kingdom, but humility and virtue will keep us there. An attitude of gratitude and an open hand will enable us to afford the riches and gold that Jesus commanded us all to buy.

The Futility of Wealth in the Kingdom of God

But don't the evangelists of today tell us that God wants us to be rich? Send money to a particular ministry and God will reward you with an abundance of wealth. They have testimonies on TV to demonstrate the truth of what they say. They have a pocketful of Scriptures to back up their claims. And yet, Jesus Christ pointed to John the Baptist as one of the greatest men on the planet during the time of his ministry. John was the cousin of Jesus. You can read about John's arrival on the planet in a prophetic announcement by the Old Testament prophet Isaiah, who wrote his words around (by loose count) seven hundred years before John and Jesus were born. In Isa 40:1–11 we read that a forerunner would come who would cry out in the wilderness to prepare the way for the advent of the Sovereign LORD, coming in power like a mighty king and a gentle shepherd. "What shall I cry?" asked the voice. "That all flesh is as grass," was the answer. "The grass withers and the flowers fall, but the word of our God stands forever" (verse 8). Jesus pointed out that John, the messenger of the covenant, never darkened the door of a king's palace or mansion. He ate locusts and honey in the desert and wore rough clothes. He probably had matted hair and gnarled hands.

Why would Jesus want us so badly to be rich when he himself pointed to the lilies of the field as God's idea of natural beauty? Not only were they more perfect in God's sight than all of Solomon's riches, but their lack of compulsion about the events of this world were also advisable spiritually. Jesus loved their simplicity. They don't fret about clothes, cars, bank accounts, yachts, titles, status, big houses, or Wall Street portfolios.

> For whoever wants to save his life (not just the physical life, but everything that defines our life) will lose it, but whoever loses his life for me and for the gospel will save it. What good is it for a man to gain the whole world, yet forfeit his soul? Or what can a man give in exchange for his soul?" (Mk 8:35–36)

Is this not the very question that the author of Ps 49 asked in his riddle? Before Jesus was born, a king named Herod the Great (73 BCE to 4 BCE) was crowned by the Roman emperor. Herod literally wanted to gain the whole world. Metaphorically speaking, when the devil took him to the temple in Jerusalem and offered him status, wealth, and power, he said, "I'll take it!" He had the power of life and death in his hands, and he used that power in a paranoid, bloody, murderous reign. His wealth was pretty much unlimited. And yet, as with the man who wanted to build bigger barns, eternity came calling for him too early. According to a lurid description of Herod's death by the first century historian Josephus, Herod died delirious and screaming. He had difficulty breathing, putrid breath, and convulsions, conditions miserable enough, but complicated by a maggot-infested genital gangrene that no one could cure. Yes, that's right. The worms of hell and the fire of pain ate his private parts from the inside out.[3]

Degrees of Punishment?

The most frequently asked question today about the biblical hell is, what about all the people of other religions who never had a chance to know about Christ's salvation? After all, the Old Testament tells us that to get to the good place, you have to be circumcised. The New Testament requires that we acknowledge Jesus Christ as Lord, or it's the hot place for us. We

---

3. Josephus, *Antiq* XVII, VI, 5.

can't be good enough to get to heaven and there is no other name on earth by which we might be saved (Acts 4:12). There are several answers to this, although one seldom hears them from the Christian pulpit.

Jesus claimed to be the door to the sheepfold. Of course, we are not sheep, but he is speaking metaphorically. He is the Gatekeeper of the Kingdom of God. He has the keys to death, hell, and the grave (Rev 1:18; 20:13). After all, coming to earth, healing the sick, raising the dead, dying on a cross, and being resurrected is not exactly chopped liver. No one gets into the Father's kingdom without his say-so. But he may have a nuanced rubric about who qualifies that doesn't square with our way of thinking. For one thing, he said that those who know God's will but are careless about doing it will feel the full weight of God's displeasure. But those who don't do God's will because they don't know any better will be granted mercy (Luke 12:47–48). This explains how the citizens of Nineveh in the book of Jonah found mercy and grace in the sight of God. They repented when they heard the word of God. But had their hearts been cold and unresponsive, if they, like Herod, rejoiced in the evil and harm they visited upon the nations they wanted to oppress, they may never have been given the chance to repent and be delivered from destruction. God foreknew their response. The book of Acts 17:30 tells us that God can overlook our egregious ignorance if we have not been exposed to the truth.

Jesus came to save the world, to spread God's mercy abroad, to release us from chains of bondage, to make our life better. His purpose is not to search for excuses to toss us away. It is not God saying no today, it is us, mankind, too busy, too successful, too miserable, too distracted to say yes. But God's yes is there for all, Jews, Gentiles, Muslims, Hindus, all who will answer the call to repent of sin and walk in God's love.

13

Afterlife Today

Afterlife in the Atomic Age

IN FORMER CHAPTERS OF this book, we took a pilgrimage through times of long ago, describing in a somewhat neutral way the changing afterlife beliefs of an ancient Syrian family with Mesopotamian roots. They immigrated to Canaan with a new understanding of who God is and what he wants of us. The stakes were high as to getting the message right—the reward was continuation as an ethnic group, complete with a homeland and an official state government. Included in the package was the promise of "life" versus "death." The energy of life begins here on earth for both the community and individuals and extends into eternity. The ultimate reward is individual eternal redemption and a "taking out" from the grim fate of hell.

Many will say that the Bible is a story book about ancient beliefs and not relevant today. That is why I thought it would be beneficial to add one more chapter to this book to see if the biblical claims have any relevance today. In recent years I have done a good deal of study on afterlife issues. Fortunately, there a growing body of evidence on the topic, which includes research by doctors, psychologists, hospice workers, and journalists. The research is conducted with scientific protocols, but in the end, the whole body of study depends on anecdotes—stories told by those who have been over there and back. We need not apologize too profusely about this lack of test tube lab proof because good forensic detective work has always required good listening skills. Modern intelligence work often begins with gossip, rumors, and stories, and in our courts we listen to witnesses portray their version of what happened and when. In my research, I have collected quite a few stories, some from books, some from my own life, some from people that I have interviewed. I am sharing a few of these here to suggest that the biblical claims about afterlife are not merely ancient myths.

Is There a Blissful Afterlife?

Research on the topic of Near Death Experiences (NDE's) has exploded in recent decades. Most of us have been exposed to the list of typical events when the soul leaves the body. No one person experiences all of the usual events, because no two experiences are alike, but with thousands of testimonies collected in books and on websites, trends have emerged. They often see a tunnel which leads to a Light Being who often doesn't speak. The soul feels love and peace, but more than that, they see a review of their life that includes their thoughts, hidden intentions, the effects that they had on others, the things they did right, and things they did wrong. They see what needs to change, and they usually return with a whole new outlook on life. Some see cities of light where all souls are at peace. Some see realms where souls are stuck, because they can't let go of earthly attachments and desires. Others have distinctly negative experiences. They actually see hell.

The separated soul may see relatives rather than a Light Being, and the relative or the Voice tells them they have to go back, that it's not time for them yet. This oft heard phrase, "It's not your time yet," indicates that there is some kind of divine plan for these individuals. Someone knows when the right time has arrived and "punches the clock" as they say. I have a friend who told me that her husband had an NDE and was given a choice of whether to go or stay. Often there is a barrier like a river or door. Christians may see angels or Jesus Christ. One woman saw little sparks flying around her and realized that they represented her future grandchildren, which would not be born if she didn't go back.

Another trend is that people who are lying in hospital beds, broken in body and wracked with pain, often have miraculous healings. They don't always recover immediately, but when they have finished their rehabilitation, the results are spectacular.

One of the most amazing NDE's with healing occurred in 1959 when a twenty-seven-year-old woman named Betty Upchurch (later Betty Malz) went on vacation to Florida with her family.[1] Her appendix became inflamed there. A young doctor in a small hospital told her that she had appendicitis and needed immediate surgery, so she went to a larger hospital. There she got one misdiagnosis after another. The penicillin they gave her wasn't helping, so she flew to her home in Terre Haute, Indiana with the intention of checking into a hospital there. The problem is that when she got home, she just went to bed, thinking that all would just fade away. Three days later she was on fire with infection. Another trip to the hospital finally resulted in a

---

1. Malz, *My Glimpse of Eternity*.

proper diagnosis—her appendix had exploded, and since it was eleven days since the first diagnosis, her organs were covered with peritonitis and some of them had begun to disintegrate.

Betty lingered in the hospital for some time, during which she clearly heard music that didn't come from any natural source. There were two more operations and several blood transfusions, and finally, after six weeks, pneumonia. Betty's family got the call that she had died. Her father entered her room to see a sheet pulled up over her head. Betty found herself walking up a grassy hillside with an angel beside her. They came to a pearly gate, which the angel nudged open. Inside, Betty saw golden streets and a Presence all of light, which she identified as Jesus. Then, it was time to go back. In her room, Betty saw a Bible verse lit across the room. It said, "I am the resurrection and the life; he that believeth in me, though he were dead, yet shall he live." As she reached out with her spirit hand to touch the light her body was transformed. She sat up and pushed the sheet away. Her father had been standing beside the bed groaning the name of Jesus. He was astonished to see her revive. That wasn't the end of the story. Betty's insides had been what the doctor described as a mass of goo. Normally, she would be an invalid even if she had somehow lived. The infection was gangrenous by the time of her first operation. But Betty felt wonderful and began eating regular meals right away. In spite of being told she would never be able to have more children, she had another daughter which she named April Dawn.

Stories of Brief Good-byes and Crisis Revelations

Three stories were shared with me by a couple that I knew some years ago. The woman is also named Betty. The first tale took place in the early 1930's in Milwaukee. Betty's grandmother received a visit from her brother one morning. She had some fresh cookies on hand, so she poured some milk, and they had a nice visit. When the family came home that night, she said, "Uncle George was here this morning." That night, they got a call from a relative that George had passed away that morning. Since he lived across the state, there is no way he could have driven to Milwaukee and back and then died.

Betty's father had an interesting experience when his wife died. He went to the funeral home, and there was Dorothy his deceased wife behind the counter. She was smiling at him. She waved and laughed, then turned and walked through the parlor. Betty swears that neither her grandmother nor her father would make up such stories. She had her own experience with her mother. They knew that she was dying, so they made what they figured would be the last visit to her in southern California. She was not responsive or cognizant of their presence, however. They had to leave due to other obligations before she actually died. Halfway across New Mexico, they looked up into what had been a cloudless sky to see one unusual cloud. Betty pointed it out to Evans. He said, "That looks exactly like your mother." Betty said, "We have to stop." They called and found out that she had just died.

A prolific author and pastor named Charlie Shedd shares a compelling story that occurred when he was in Junior High School. He used to hang out with a couple of mischievous friends. The three dared each other to do things that were hurtful and dangerous. One night while Charlie was watching a game on TV, one of them called with a plan to rob a trolley that very night. They would have a gun, wear masks, and get away with a lot of money. It would be easy. While Charlie listened to this plot, he felt a firm hand tightly grip his shoulder and press him down. "And with it came a voice, a clear voice from deep inside me, 'Tell them you're busy, Charlie. You're listening to the game. Have some more popcorn.' And when that inner voice went silent, I heard myself say, 'Not tonight, guys.[2] I'm busy.'" The two friends carried out their plan, but panicked when the kindly old trolley driver recognized them, so they shot him. They wound up spending the better part of the rest of their lives in prison, regretting that they shot an old man that they knew and actually liked.

My aunt LaVerne had an NDE in the mid-1960's. I'm cobbling together accounts from two of her adult children here. She was at home with her son Paul, who was about 5, and her baby daughter when she felt something go terribly wrong in her abdomen. Sensing she was in trouble, she got her son to dial the operator, then she passed out. When she came to, she was staring at the floor, strapped to a huge circular hospital bed that was flipped upside down. (a Stryker circle-electric bed, which helps a comatose patient recover when they cannot be on their back for a long time.) Surgery revealed a large tumor blocking her colon, which was removed, but sepsis had set in and she was officially declared dead on the operating table. At that point she left her body. She saw her mother who told her that she would be OK and that it wasn't her time yet. She had to go back because her kids will have designated tasks to accomplish. Doctors were able to resuscitate her, but she remained in a coma. It was the orderlies who came to clean her room that found her waking up. Fifteen years later her doctor pronounced her cancer free. She ultimately had one more child and died at the age of 73.

2. Shedd, *Children*, 98–102.

I have only one personal story of possible communication from a deceased relative. My father was an airline captain who died in a crash in 1951. I was raised Catholic, but I jettisoned my faith when I got to college, as so many do. One day as I was sitting in my dorm room in Haggett Hall at the University of Washington, my heart was bursting to know what was on the other side of death. A mental picture appeared in my imagination. It wasn't exactly a vision, but just a strong thought. I imagined my father standing on the crest of a hill that represented death. He looked back at me and winked. He seemed to be saying, "If you could see what I see, you would be happy." Then the image changed and I saw a flag pole, with my dad's leather flight jacket waving in the wind like a flag, but it was old and tattered, representing faded memories. I was moved to write a poem,

> Hands in pockets, head low,
> we watched him standing on the hill alone.
> A last look back; he winked,
> "I can see the other side."
> Then gone he was, his memory
> flapping in a dying wind.
> Where he went is where my soul is
> when I question the wind-breath;
> the sun cares not to teach, or cannot,
> and I wish my soul could find that hill
> on which our hopes are pinned.

I scribbled the poem quickly in pencil on binder paper. I almost erased the word "wind-breath" several times. I remember my eraser hovering over the word, wondering where it came from and what exactly it might mean, but in the end, I left it. I folded the scrap of paper and stuck it in my wallet, where it sat for many months, perhaps a year. That was in 1965, the year I committed my life to Jesus Christ. I immediately began reading the Bible and any theological matter than I could get my hands on. One day I read a paragraph in a book that mentioned the *ruach-Elohim,* the Spirit of God or Holy Spirit. The Hebrew word *ruach* means wind, breath, or spirit in Hebrew, and the book actually used the word wind-breath. The word wind-breath kept scratching at something deep in my mind. Where had I heard it? One day while I was walking along and thinking about the word, it occurred to me. I whipped out my wallet, opened the poem for the first time since I wrote it, and there it was. In 1965, before I knew anything about biblical Christianity, I was questioning the very Spirit of God, which was obviously breathing on me when I wrote the poem.

These stories are important because they suggest that we as Christians are worshiping the same deity that was described in the ancient biblical writings, both the Old and New Testaments. The God that king David sang about is the God I serve today. The descriptions of NDE experiences today do not at all conflict with the imagery that the prophets wrote about.

Are Demons Real?

In this limited space, there are two books I can recommend that demonstrate the reality of the demonic realm. The first is the life story of a former boxer named Curtis "Earthquake" Kelley. In his book, *Bound to Lose, Destined to Win*, he describes a horribly dysfunctional home life. He was child number seven of ten. His mother was a Christian, but his father was a voodoo priest who also practiced obeah (a West Indian type of sorcery), witchcraft, and Santaria, all guaranteed to open a paranormal door in a home and fill it with malicious spirits. Oddly enough, his father was also a Baptist preacher. By the time Curtis was four, he was hearing a voice that instructed him how to get into trouble and cause damage. His mother would see a goat spirit coming out of her closet at night, and the children would be chased by spirits around the house. No one got much sleep.

Kelley describes the demons he worked with before his conversion, and although I won't describe them here, he makes it clear that they are real, effective, and malevolent. The only thing they couldn't touch was a dedicated Christian. In his wayward days, Kelley had an NDE from a drug overdose in which he went straight down to hell. He says that golden hands pulled him out, and he was told that his mother's prayers and his future destiny as a minister in God's kingdom had saved him. He was resuscitated in the nick of time by his brothers.

Curtis was given a clear call and task by God, but for a long time he refused to obey. Then he had a stroke and another visit to hell. God brought him back but warned him severely that his particular call is serious business. During this same hospital stay, Kelley had another NDE, but this time he went to heaven. He walked on soft green grass until he came to a river. Across the water he saw his son Scott, who was killed in a car jacking incident. Scott told him he could not cross because it wasn't his time. Other friends and family there told him the same thing. He was commissioned by Jesus Christ to go back and warn the people that hell is real and sin will take them there. He also saw many children, some of whom had been aborted. Jesus told Kelley that doctors who claim to be Christians but who perform abortions are terrorists against the unborn. There was also a long diatribe by

Jesus against ministers who commit adultery or preach for fame and money. They idolize themselves, he said, not allowing any blemish on their bodies. The last words that Kelley heard as he was propelled back into his hospital bed was, "Take this seriously. You must take this seriously. My people are not taking me seriously. Keep your heart clean no matter what people say or do to you. Forgive them. If you can forgive the man who killed your son, you can forgive those who hurt you in the churches."[3]

Kelley's life was neither easy nor tidy. He stumbled and got up many times and was attacked by demonic entities often, but he sent them packing by using the name of Jesus.

An equally terrifying book about a dysfunctional family is Bill Bean's *Dark Force*. His father moved the family into a home that was haunted by several malevolent spirits. The parents resisted moving out to their peril. In the end, family wholeness and harmony were destroyed. Bill came close to having his life ruined by the negative energy there, but he gave his life to Christ, and he found that he gained a power to resist. Today, he has a deliverance ministry and can be seen occasionally on TV.[4]

Dr. George Ritchie and His Afterlife Tour[5]

One of my favorite NDE stories is that of George Ritchie because it covers a broad spectrum of afterlife possibilities. Of course, I can't prove that Dr. Ritchie actually experienced what he describes in his book, but I have no reason to dismiss it either. The story began in late September, 1943, when twenty-year-old Ritchie of Richmond, Virginia signed up to serve in the Army. He was stationed at Camp Barkeley in Texas. He deliberately delayed his planned attendance at the Medical College of Virginia in his home town in order to emulate his father, who had enlisted when we entered the Second World War. Ritchie was ecstatic to learn that the Army would send him to that same college, and they would pay for it, and he was determined to be there when classes began on December 22. Recruits trained hard that winter, sitting on the cold ground as punishment for lapses. An influenza outbreak hit the camp, filling the infirmaries with coughing, feverish recruits, some of whom contracted pneumonia and died.

---

3. Kelly, *Born to Lose*, 117.

4. Bill's website is www.billjbean.com. I reviewed his book on Eternal Gateways, http://janetkatherinesmith.blogspot.com/2012/10/the-haunted-beans.html.

5. Ritchie, *Life after Dying*, and *Return*. Also adapted from my blog, Eternal Gateways, http://janetkatherinesmith.blogspot.com/2010/02/george-ritchie-part-2.html. Also see blog title "Reviving Ritchie."

On December 10, Ritchie ran a fever which turned from influenza to double lobar pneumonia. During days of recuperation, he lost a lot of weight. The Army arranged a jeep to transport him to Richmond, but first he needed to gain back fifteen pounds and have a normal temperature. Ritchie feared that if he didn't show up on the 22nd, his place would be given to another, so he fought hard to recover. He also looked forward to Christmas with his family and girlfriend. He gained the required fifteen pounds, but as the day drew near, his fever was still spiking and dropping. The day he was to leave, it spiked to 106. During an x-ray he passed out. He was carried to a small, single room in the ward. The next day on December 21, he died.

In the first minutes after death, the now non-material soldier found himself in a strange little room with a bed and chair and the prone body of a young man in the bed. "But, the thing was impossible! I myself had just gotten out of that bed! For a moment I wrestled with the mystery of it. It was too strange to think about—and anyway, I did not have time."

All he could think of was getting to Richmond. As he raced down the hallway, no one at the infirmary would acknowledge his presence, so his soul went flying out of the hospital, across the desert, past farms and towns. He came to a stop at a café in a strange city. He tried to ask directions, but it was here that he finally understood—he was immaterial. He had to get back to the camp and find his body. Years later, he would find that same café again in the city of Vicksburg, hundreds of miles away from Camp Barkeley.

After a long, crazy, lonely search throughout the hospital, he found a small room where a sheet-covered corpse lay. The head was covered, but the arms were lying outside the sheet. On the finger of one pale hand was his fraternity ring. Dejected and confused, he lay across his body. Suddenly the room got lighter and lighter until it was so bright that he felt it would have scorched his living eyes. A man made of brilliance walked into the room.

"The instant I perceived Him, a command formed itself in my mind. Stand up! The words came from inside me, yet they had an authority my mere thoughts had never had. I got to my feet, and as I did came the stupendous certainty: You are in the presence of the Son of God . . . This Person was power itself, older than time and yet more modern than anyone I had ever met. Above all, with that same mysterious inner certainty, I knew that this Man loved me. Far more even than power, what emanated from this Presence was unconditional love."

Ritchie then entered into the "life review" described by so many who have returned from eternity. It should have taken hours to see all of the scenes that were presented at that time. Although the data was immense, the purpose of it all became clear. It wasn't to point out the minutia of his sins, but to ask, *what did you do with your life?* This was frustrating to a twenty-year-old male who had never given the purpose of his life a moment's thought. He realized that he was selfish. He saw "only an endless, short-sighted, clamorous concern for myself." He thought, "I became an Eagle Scout." The Voice retorted, "That glorified you."

When Ritchie understood that the purpose of living was supposed to be about love, he complained, "Someone should have told me! A fine time to discover what life was all about—like coming to a final exam and discovering you were going to be tested on a subject you had never studied . . . .I did tell you . . . I told you by the life I lived. I told you by the death I died. And if you keep your eyes on me, you will see more."

At one point, Jesus laughed at him. He pondered the waste of having recently bought a life insurance policy that would last until he was 70. "The words were out, in this strange realm where communication took place by thought instead of speech, before I could call them back . . . If I had suspected before that there was mirth in the Presence beside me, now I was sure of it: the brightness seemed to vibrate and shimmer with a kind of holy laughter—not at me and my silliness, not a mocking laughter, but a mirth that seemed to say that in spite of all error and tragedy, joy was more lasting still."

Then Jesus took Ritchie on a long tour. He describes in his next book (about his life after near death) how he saw a series of spiritual realms. First he was taken to a city with factory smokestacks and lights burning in all the windows. He saw ghosts everywhere. Disincarnate people hovered around the living, trying to control what they can no longer touch. He saw regret, addiction, suicide, rage, and perversion.

He also saw a hint of our technological future, growth in the arts, and finally a glimpse of a vast, bright heavenly city.

Before it was time for Ritchie's return to earthly life, the ward boy had alerted the doctor on duty that the patient was unresponsive. That doctor declared him dead and ordered that he be remanded to the morgue. The ward boy finished his chores and returned. He thought he spotted a movement and called for the OD (Officer of the Day) to recheck. The OD confirmed the death call. George Ritchie was dead and was to be prepared for the morgue. Depressed at the loss of such a young life, the ward boy suggested trying a shot of adrenalin straight to the heart. Although it was not an approved procedure, the doctor agreed to try it (remember, this is 1943). To their astonishment, George's heart revived, but he was still unconscious for three more days. The doctor claimed that nine minutes passed from the time they first declared Ritchie dead to when his heart began to beat again. He also affirmed that there was no natural explanation for Ritchie's complete recovery.

Weeks later, George was recovering and was on his way to med school. Because he was late and in ill health, he flunked out that year, but the following year he tried again and passed all tests. He married his girlfriend and became a medical doctor and later a psychiatrist. His experience utterly changed his life. He spent the rest of it serving others and sharing his testimony.

It took him many years to process and describe his experience in 1943 when he was only twenty years old. He describes Jesus more fully in this second book. He had blue eyes and chestnut hair parted in the middle. (Many people who claim to have seen Jesus describe the same coloration, and that in spite of the fact that in his earthly life he most certainly had brown eyes, olive skin, and black hair.) He was over 6′2″. "This was no sweet, gentle Jesus meek, weak, or mild. Here stood a robust male who radiated strength."

The young George Ritchie was shown five inter-dimensional realms. The beings in those realms could not see Ritchie and Jesus, nor could they see the other realms—they could only see their own. This fact alone was worth the price of the book for me, because I have studied these realms long before being aware of Ritchie's book, and I wondered why they were all so different and why souls are oblivious of other modes of existence. When Jesus was on earth, he spoke of "many mansions." Perhaps he was referencing what Ritchie called "realms."

The first realm was earth. After an exquisitely detailed life review, in which Ritchie understood that the whole purpose of life is to learn to love, he and Jesus just went up through the roof and flew at an impossible speed toward a large American city. There was no mention of them climbing into a UFO or flaming chariot, by the way. They just flew. In this earthly city he saw living humans and ghostly entities sharing the streets and offices together. The living, who were distinguished by an aura of light surrounding them, were utterly unaware of the ghosts, who had no such aura. Ritchie saw people who died in the thrall of addiction, unforgiveness, greed, selfishness, a desire for control, suicide, etc. They were all chained to the earth by their unresolved obsessions, emotions, and the consequences of their actions, but they couldn't touch, change, or influence anything. Still, they tried. They grabbed at cigarettes in a bar, fought over drinks they couldn't lift, apologized over and over to hurt loved ones, and spewed advice to deaf ears. They were suspended in misery. Ritchie reflected, "An eternity like that—the thought sent a chill shuddering through me—surely would be a form of hell. I had always thought of hell, when I had thought of it at all, as a fiery place beneath the earth where evil men like Hitler would burn forever. But what if one level of hell existed right here on the surface—unseen and unsuspected by the living people occupying the same space? What if it meant remaining on earth but never but never again able to make contact with it?"

Ritchie calls this realm "astral." An important insight from his first book is that certain conditions, like passing out in a drunken stupor, can crack open that protective aura, leaving an opportunity for a lingering ghost to actually enter that body and share its space and experiences. The original soul must then share the body with a completely different soul that can influence the mood and thoughts of the person affected.

The second realm he called "Astral, Purgatory? Terrestrial?" It was deeper into the astral dimension and was not mentioned in the first book. It was like a city imposed over the earthly city, but it wasn't actually of earth. Dr. Ritchie wasn't sure what to call it. It was a city like any other, but it was totally inhabited by astral beings. "We were still in the same area where the large city had been visible, but all I could now see were dwelling places where the astral beings lived, which were definitely of a less dense, or more ethereal material than our dwellings. I had the impression they were more of a product of these beings' thoughts than are dwellings in our human realm."

In this realm people of like thinking congregated together. When souls arrived, as many did due to the war, they lingered in a trance-like state until angels helped them to awaken and realize that they are still alive in an eternal sense. There was no "soul sleep." In spite of what Ritchie referred to uncertainly as angels, there were places in this realm where a soul might feel uncomfortable or threatened. In his uncertainty, he writes, "Maybe this is the realm Jesus referred to as paradise when he spoke to the thief on the cross. As you can see by the various titles that I have placed upon it, I do not know what to call it."

The third realm was not difficult to name—**"Hell,"** but perhaps only a layer of hell. Here were suicides who killed themselves out of revenge, hatred, bitterness, jealousy, and a disdain for themselves and others. "We were in another location of this plane. We were standing on a high porch in front of this huge building. What I saw horrified me more than anything I have ever seen in life. Since you could tell what the beings in this place thought, you knew they were filled with hate, deceit, lies, self-righteousness bordering on megalomania, and lewd sexual aggressiveness that were causing them to carry out all kinds of abominable acts on one another . . . Here was a place totally devoid of love."

My own question as I read these pages: did these souls receive a life review? Dr. Ritchie wrote of his impression that it was still possible for these unhappy beings to continue spiritual growth if and when they choose. Whether he was given to understand this or assumed it due to his own caring nature I cannot say. Christian doctrine says hell is final and eternal.

Frankly, I hope Ritchie is right. In other sources, NDEers have described being thrown into fiery caves or even total darkness. Robert Monroe's weird OBE world was full of creepy, lewd, and dangerous entities that had to be avoided very carefully.[6]

The fourth realm, "Knowledge, Paradise? Terrestrial?" It is this realm which removes forever the concept that we stop learning or progressing in knowledge when we die. I could call this the realm of research, or the mental realm, or the realm of intellectual, scientific, and religious knowledge. All would be correct. In his first book, Ritchie called this the Temple of Wisdom. In the second he describes a musical observatory from whence came glorious music. There seemed to be "centers of learning" similar to our universities and research facilities. There was a building with at least four floor levels connected by escalator-like stairs.

"I picked up an intensity of concentration, dedication and loyalty to their fellow workers that showed a high sense of integrity." So these were not the evil scientists who falsified data or plagiarized another's work. Some of the instruments that Ritchie saw there in 1943 appeared years later in a 1952 Life Magazine article about the second US atomic submarine. That particular experience put Ritchie in the company of remote viewers. Remote viewing as a spying technique did not develop until the 1970's.

Next they moved to the largest building that Ritchie had ever seen. All of the holy books of the universe were stored there. The researchers in this library wore brown robes like monks as they studied the various approaches to God in the universe. Jesus communicated an interesting, if not contradictory thought to Ritchie, "You are right, for if I, Love, be lifted up, I shall draw all men unto me. If you come to know the Father, you will come to know me. If you come to know Me, you will know that Love includes all beings regardless of their race, creeds, or color."

In the Bible, Jesus said that if you come to know Him, you will know the Father. Here he turns that statement around for those seeking God with no reference to Christ. So jihad, in which we kill the infidel, does not wash in this realm of existence. (Jesus seems to be implying that somewhere in time, or timelessness, these souls will find their way to both God the Father and thereby to Himself. This is consistent with universal love, but Jesus is still the ultimate gateway to the Kingdom of God.)

---

6. The late Robert Monroe founded the Monroe Institute for the purpose of teaching people how to leave their bodies and travel in the astral realm. He never saw Jesus, angels, or heaven on those journeys. He did encounter lost souls and many lewd and dangerous entities. I once knew a former CIA medical consultant who tried Monroe's method. He told me that he came face to face with a thoroughly ugly, demonic entity that scared him half to death. He never tried that method again. Monroe wrote four books about his adventures in this sinister world.

The fifth realm was also easy to name because it was a glimpse of "Heaven." To see it, he and Jesus had to leave the planet. Unlike beings from the other realms, two beings from the emerging holy city were able to see Ritchie and Christ, and like Him, they glowed with brilliant light and love. But before Ritchie could interact with these joyful entities, Jesus and Ritchie started the trip back. The Lord had one more revelation for the young soldier.

Just before losing consciousness Ritchie was shown two timelines. In the first, natural disasters such as hurricanes and volcanoes became stronger and more destructive. People became more selfish; governments fell apart as people thought only of themselves. There were explosions all over the planet and armies marched on the US from the south. In the second timeline, love increased. We took better care of the planet and of each other. Rather than extinction, mankind began to thrive. Jesus stated that He came to earth to show us by the life He led how to love. We must pay attention to that life and choose which fate will prevail on the earth. My own feeling is that, if Ritchie's experience is real, then both of those timelines are happening at once. There is arguably more love than ever, but plenty of hatred on the earth today, more concern for the environment, and more greedy poachers with AK-47s.

There is a lot that is missing in Ritchie's messianic revelation. There were no demons, and no mention of Christ's redeeming grace in the sense of a Christian theology. I would say that God's forgiveness and grace was shown in the lack of judgment and anger in Christ's demeanor. Scoundrels were cast into lower kinds of existence because they were not ready for anything better when they died. God's children received the reward promised them in the Bible, but it wasn't that God hated the one and loved the other. He loved them all.

Is There a Real Hell?

Unfortunately, one chapter isn't sufficient to cover the subject of NDE's. On the subject of hell, we can find plenty of material in books by Annie Fennimore,[7] Moody's various publications,[8] Richard Eby's two minutes there,[9] Osis and Haraldsson,[10] Jeffrey Long[11] and so many more.

---

7. Fenimore, *Beyond the Darkness*.
8. Moody, *Glimpses, Life after Life*, and *Reflections*.
9. Eby, *Caught Up*, 229–30.
10. Osis and Haraldsson, *Hour of Death*.
11. Long, *Evidence*.

Several Christians claim that Jesus showed them hell so that they would warn others. Almost any book on afterlife will have a few, if not several, descriptions of a real, unpleasant hell with ugly creatures, putrid smells, and anguished sounds. If there is any truth to these narratives, there is literally weeping and wailing and gnashing of teeth there. Many found themselves on the edge of a lake of fire, or saw a ring of fire at the gateway. Some described pitch darkness, others a void. In most cases there was heat.

One of my motives to research this topic was that I found the whole concept of a human soul languishing in such a place for eternity horrifying. I hoped to find evidence that a soul could work its way out of hell. If there is such a way, I didn't find much evidence of it, nor do I see it in the Bible. Space limits what I can say on the topic, so I want to simply recommend three more books that deal with the topic in an iconic and thorough manner. Maurice Rawlings was a cardiologist who had little interest in the depths of his churchy Christianity until the day when a patient dropped dead in his office in 1977. Charlie McKaig was a forty-eight year-old mail carrier who was taking a stress test on a treadmill in Rawlings's clinic office. He had a heart attack, dropped to the floor, and "died." During the resuscitation process, which had to be repeated several times, he pleaded for the doctor to pray for him or tell him how to stay out of hell. He was clearly panicked by what he claimed he saw on the other side. Rawlings had to reach into his Sunday School past to come up with some kind of prayer wherein the McKaig called on Jesus Christ and promised that if he lived he would be "on the hook" from then on. Two conversions occurred that day because the event alarmed Rawlings to the point where he began to read his Bible and research the issue of life after death. He began to interview patients as soon as they were resuscitated, and he asked other physicians to do the same and relate to any such experiences they may have had along the same lines. What he discovered was that patients needed to be interviewed immediately after coming to because if they had a negative experience, they may have no memory of it two days later.

As he studied the works of other medical researchers who became famous due to their earlier research, he realized that they avoided mentioning negative experiences. By publishing the happy ones where people see a glowing city with golden streets and happy people, they gave the impression that everyone goes to a good place when they die. Rawlings was so alarmed at what he was discovering that he offered to share his research with some of the other authors. All refused the offer, so he wrote two books mainly on the topic of negative afterlife experiences because as time went on he was more and more convinced that the world needed to be warned.[12] Between the two books, he shares many past and contemporary stories, both positive and negative, from his reading, his communication with colleagues, and his own interviews with patients.

Dr. Chauncey Crandall was another physician who had to resuscitate a patient who died as he checked himself in to the hospital. In this case Crandall was an active Christian. His faith had been warmed anew by the suffering of his beloved son with Leukemia. By the time Crandall answered the call to finalize the resuscitation attempts on Jeff Markin, all the classic signs of death had manifested: cyanotic lips and finger tips, flat-line on the heart and brain. Crandall pronounced Markin dead and was leaving the room as the nurse began preparing him for the morgue. When he got to the door, he felt the Holy Spirit command him to turn around and pray for the man. He brushed it off, but it came again, so he went back and prayed that Markin would arise from the dead. At that moment, the ER doctor entered the room, so Dr. Crandall requested that he shock the man one more time. The ER doctor protested, but Crandall persisted. One more hit with the heart paddles brought Markin back to life with a strong heartbeat.

In this case, Markin remembered what he experienced and was able to describe it two days later. He said he lay in his coffin for eternity and no one came to visit. He was so disappointed and lonely. Then some people came and took him out of his coffin and threw his corpse onto a trash heap. Dr. Crandall thought of Gehenna when he heard that, Gehenna being the place of burning trash in Jerusalem in the days of Christ's ministry on earth. Markin is now a devout Christian.

Reprising Genesis 1-3

For me, there is no horror story that can compare with the thought of an eternity in hell, no matter what configuration it takes. I have often wondered how God could create a universe where a human soul could suffer such anguish with no chance of escape or rehabilitation. I still hope we are wrong about that. The material earth is full of danger and violence. Both heaven and hell begin here with us. The non-material universe is similar to our earthly realm in that it isn't all peace and singing flowers over there. Humans who were malicious here will also be over there, and that negative energy simply cannot pass the gates of heaven to pollute God's eternal kingdom with hatred and greed. In Genesis 1-4 we see who we are. We are special, but we have the capacity for great good or great evil. The Bible

---

12. Rawlings, *Death's Door* and *To Hell and Back*.

between Genesis and Revelations is about how we are to live to come full circle and make those right choices. In the words of a song by Bob Dylan, we're gonna serve somebody. We'll serve the devil or we'll serve God. We would do well to come to terms with the dangers of that realm—the deception, the malignancy, the seriousness of its effect on us here—in order to know how to defeat the destruction that it poses to our existence. The ones who should be leading us in this understanding are pastors, but even scientists could have the courage to be open-minded about unseen worlds. Furthermore if Christian leaders and scientists could join forces, the battle against the dark forces that threaten us would be so much easier.

We are special, all of us. We are fearsome creatures, aspiring to wondrous deeds, reaching for the stars, and accountable to our Creator for good or for ill. The author of Psalm 49 warns us—and encourages us. Do what is right, love your neighbor, and connect with God. Rest easy, both here and in the grave, because God is the God of life and he will never forsake those who trust in him.

Appendix

Brain Twisting Genealogies

As we said, nothing goes uncontested in the Bible, so scholars propose various Korahs in the Scriptures as being the Korah of the Psalms. Keeping these clans separate is important because if the reader thinks they are all the same, which sometimes happens in scholarship, he or she could conclude that the Bible genealogies are contradictory and fictional. This is a difficult knot to untie for academics, let alone general readers! One Korahite clan that is not the center of our story was descended from the son of Esau, Jacob's brother (Gen 36:5, 14, 18; 1 Chr 1:35). In Gen 36:16 the name Korah appears in a list of "the chiefs among Esau's descendants, the sons of Eliphaz the firstborn of Esau." These Edomite Korahites would have pre-dated the Exodus by many years and would have settled in Transjordan and the southern Negev, ruling them out as a candidate for the Korah of the Exodus.

Another Korah of interest is listed in 1 Chr 2:43, the son of the Judahite named Hebron. This Korah is important because the confusion caused by these verses has influenced how scholars view King David, the author of so many psalms. This Judean Korah was related to a man named Caleb, the son of Hezron, the brother of Jerahmeel (also called Chelubai in 1 Chr 2:9). This Caleb had several concubines, including one called Ephah or Ephrathah, or Ephrath (1 Chr 2:19, 46, 51). These clans may have settled around Bethlehem in what is called Caleb-ephratah (1 Chr 2:24). Bethlehem was the name of the grandson or great-grandson of Caleb's concubine Ephrathah (1 Chr 2:51; 4:4), the result being that the regional names "Bethlehem" and "Ephrathah" became synonymous. Baruch Halpern noted that one source describes David as "an Ephratite" who was born in Bethlehem. Halpern casts doubt on David's connection to the Judeans of 1 Chr 2, even suggesting that in the tenth century BCE the tribe of Judah didn't exist. His reasoning is that there is also a Caleb whose clan settled in Hebron, the location of David's first crowning as King over Judah. Both Calebs had daughters named Achsah. Halpern suggests that they are the same, although their lineages don't match. Halpern concludes that David was never a Judean but an Ephramite (of the clan), and fictionalized a Judean lineage to impress the Hebronites, many of whom are actually descended from a different Caleb.[1] Halpern's theory does not stand up to scrutiny. The Caleb whose lineage is so carefully laid out in 1 Chr 2 was not the Caleb who inherited Hebron. That region was taken by Caleb the son of Jephunneh (1 Chr 4:15; 6:55). He seems to be descended from Kenaz, but his exact lineage is not clearly explained. He is the father of Iru, Ilah, and Naam, and had a daughter named Achsah. In Num 13, he represents the tribe of Judah as one of twelve spies sent out by Moses, but was he actually a Judean? We can't be sure. The record of Joshua giving him the region of Kiriath-arba/Hebron is recorded in Josh 15:13–19. Although Joshua is not mentioned in Judg 1:9–13, the record is clearly a duplicate. In spite of daughters with the same name, there is no reason for David to try to attach himself to Caleb-of-Hebron's line of descendants. His second wife Abigail was associated with the Calebites of Hebron, which undoubtedly helped him achieve status there. As a genuine Judahite, he fulfilled earlier prophecy that the scepter of God's people (the monarchy) would ultimately abide with the tribe of Judah (Gen 49:10).

Amongst scholars, there is much disagreement about the genealogies of Korah and Caleb. J. M. Miller sees all of the divergent Korahite groups, the Edomite, Calebite, Benjamite (his designation based on the usual misunderstanding of the genealogies), and Levitical, as emanating from the same tribal group that migrated from the south and settled in the region of Hebron.[2] He points to a sanctuary at the border fortress of Arad, where he worked for a season, to support his thesis. An ostracon was found there on which was written "sons of Korah."[3] However, the ostracon could be referring to Judahite-Calebite (son of Hezron) Korahites.

Martin Buss thought that the Korahites could not come from the northern regions of Israel because of the obvious loyalty to the Temple in Jerusalem,[4] but loyalty to the Temple is not at all incompatible with Levites living in distant locations. They would willingly make the pilgrimage to the royal capital to perform their priestly duties.

---

1. Levenson and Halpern, "Political Import," 508–10 and Halpern, *David's Secret Demons*, 271–72, in which Halpern claims that 1 Chr 2 is David's alternate lineage and that when he was born, the tribe of Judah did not exist.

2. Miller, "Korahites of Southern Judah," 64.

3. Ibid., 32. Cf. Aharoni's report of all five seasons, "Arad," 11.

4. Buss, "Psalms of Asaph and Korah," 387.

Another source of confusion in the genealogies is the meaning of the word *ephrati*. Ephraim can refer to the region allocated to the tribe of Ephraim by Joshua, which is located in the central hill country of Israel. *Ephrati* can refer to a person from the tribe of Ephraim or to a person from any other tribe who is living in the region. Or, it can refer to a person from the tribe of Judah living in the region of Bethelem-Ephrata in Judah (Gen 35:16, 19; 48:7; Ruth 1:2; 4:11; Mic 5:2).

A familiar Korahite who is described as an *ephrati* is Elkanah, the husband of Hannah and the father of the prophet Samuel. His genealogy is found in 1 Chr 6:16–27 and 6:33–38, where Zophai/Zuph, a descendant of Levi, lies embedded in the list. In 6:33–38 the line stretches from Heman, the grandson of the prophet Samuel back to the Patriarch Levi. In 1 Sam 1:1 Elkanah is said to have been both "a Zuphite from the hill country of Ephraim" and an *ephrati,* so he is a Levitical Zuphite living in the central hills, not a man from the tribe of Ephraim or a Judahite descendant of Caleb-Ephrata. This is important because to be leaders in worship before the Tabernacle of Solomon, the Korahites need to be from the Tribe of Levi (see also Judg 12:5; 1 Kgs 11:26).

As stated, references to Ephrathah are clearly equated with the town of Bethlehem (Gen 35:16, 19; 48:7; Ruth 1:2; 4:11; Mic 5:2). The double name shows that both designations were still current at the time of the writing of these texts. First Sam 17:12 reads, "Now David was the son of an Ephratite of Bethlehem in Judah, named Jesse..." M. D. Goulder erroneously assumes that Jesse (David's father) was therefore an Ephraimite located in Benjamin.[5]

---

5. Goulder, "Asaph's History of Israel," 73.

Bibliography

Achtemeier, Elizabeth. *Minor Prophets I.* In *New International Biblical Commentary.* Vol. 17. Peabody: Hendrickson, 2002. First published in 1996.
Alexander, T. Desmond. "The Old Testament View of Life after Death." *Themelios* 11.2 (1986) 41–46.
———. "The Psalms and the Afterlife." *Irish Biblical Studies* 9 (1987) 2–17.
Allen, Leslie, C. "Psalm 73: An Analysis." *Tyndale Bulletin* 33 (1982) 93–119.
Appiah, Kwame Anthony. *Cosmopolitanism: Ethics in a World of Strangers.* New York: W. W. Norton, 2007.
Avner, Uzi. "Sacred Stones in the Desert." *Biblical Archaeology Review* 27.3 (2001) 31–41.
Baumgartner, Walter. "Zur Etymologie Von Sch^e'ōl." *Theologische Zeitschrift* 2.3 (1946) 233–35.
Bean, William. *Dark Force: The Terrifying and Tragic Story of the Bean Family.* Green Valley, AZ: Journeymakers, 2009.
Beaulieu, Paul-Alain. "The Setting of Babylonian Wisdom Literature." In *Wisdom Literature in Mesopotamia and Israel,* edited by Richard J. Clifford, 3–19. Atlanta: Society of Biblical Literature, 2007.
Bennett, Robert A. "Wisdom Motifs in Psalm 14 = 53: nābāl and 'ēṣāh." *Bulletin of the American Schools of Oriental Research* 220 (1975) 15–21. http://links.jstor.org.
Berger, Peter L. *The Sacred Canopy: Elements of a Sociological Theory of Religion.* Garden City, NY: Anchor, 1969.
Bertman, Stephan. *Handbook to Life in Ancient Mesopotamia.* Oxford: Oxford University Press, 2003.
Birkeland, Harris. "Belief in the Resurrection of the Dead in the Old Testament." *Studia Theologica* 3 (1950) 60–78.
Braun, Joachim. *Life in Biblical Israel: Archaeological, Written, and Comparative Sources.* Translated by Douglas Stott. Grand Rapids: Eerdmans, 2002.
Brueggemann, Walter. *The Psalms & the Life of Faith.* Edited by Patrick D. Miller. Minneapolis: Fortress Press, 1995.
Brueggemann, Walter and Patrick D. Miller. "Psalm 73 as a Canonical Marker." *Journal for the Study of the Old Testament* 72.1 (1996) 45–56. Online: http://search.atlaonline.com.

Burnett, Joel S. "Forty-Two Songs for Elohim: An Ancient Near Eastern Organizing Principle in the Shaping of the Elohistic Psalter." *Journal for the Study of the Old Testament* 31.1 (2006) 81–101. Online: http://search.atlaonline.com.

Buss, Martin. "The Psalms of Asaph and Korah." *Journal of Biblical Literature* 82.4 (1963) 382–92. Online: http://search.atlaonline.com.

Campbell, Antony F. "Psalm 78: A Contribution to the Theology of Tenth Century Israel." *The Catholic Biblical Quarterly* 71 (1971) 51–79.

Charlesworth, James H., ed. *The Old Testament Pseudepigrapha*. Vol. 1. New York: Doubleday, 1983.

Clifford, Richard J. "Introduction." In *Wisdom Literature in Mesopotamia and Israel*. Edited by Richard J. Clifford. Atlanta: Society of Biblical Literature, 2007.

Collins, John C. "'Death Will Be Their Shepherd' or 'Death Will Feed on Them?' *mā*[insert macron over the a]*vet yirʾē*[insert aleph before the e, insert macron over the e]*m* in Psalm 49.15 (EVV v 14)." *Bible Translator (Ja Jl Technical Papers)* 46.3 (1995) 320–26.

Cox, Dermot. "'As Water Spilt on the Ground' (Death in the Old Testament)." *Studia Missionaria* 31 (1982) 1–17.

Craigie, Peter C. *Psalms 1–50*. In *Word Biblical Commentary*. Vol. 19. Waco, TX: Word Books, 1983.

Crandall, Chauncey W., IV. *Raising the Dead: A Doctor Encounters the Miraculous*. New York: Faith Words, 2010.

Dahood, Mitchell. *Psalms 1*. In *Anchor Bible Commentary*. Vol. 16. Garden City, NY: Doubleday, 1966.

Day, John. "Asherah in the Hebrew Bible and Northwest Semitic Literature." *Journal of Biblical Literature* 105.3 (1986) 385–408.

———. *Yahweh and the Gods and Goddesses of Canaan*. JSOTSup 265. Edited by David J. A. Clines and Philip R. Davies. New York: Sheffield Academic Press, 2002.

David, Rosalie. *Handbook of Life in Ancient Egypt*. Oxford: Oxford University Press, 1998.

Dell, Katharine. "'I Will Solve My Riddle to the Music of the Lyre' (Psalm XLIX 4 [5]) A Cultic Setting for Wisdom Psalms?" *Vetus Testamentum* 54.4 (2004) 445–58. Online: http://search.atlaonline.com.

Dolansky, Shawna. "A Goddess in the Garden? The Fall of Eve." In *Milk and Honey: Essays on Ancient Israel and the Bible in Appreciation of the Judaic Studies Program at the University of California, San Diego*. Edited by Sarah Malena and David Miano. Winona Lake, IN: Eisenbrauns, 2007.

Eaton, John H. *Kingship and the Psalms*. 2nd ed. In *Biblical Seminar 3*. Sheffield: JSOT, 1986.

———. *The Psalms: A Historical and Spiritual Commentary with an Introduction and New Translation*. London: T&T Clark, 2005.

Eby, Richard E. *Caught Up into Paradise*. Grand Rapids: Spire, 1996.

Fenimore, Angie. *Beyond the Darkness: My Near-Death Journey to the Edge of Hell*. New York: Bantam, 1995.

Flint, Peter W. "The Book of Psalms in the Light of the Dead Sea Scrolls." *Vetus Testamentum* (1998) 453–72.

Gerstenberger, Erhard S. "Chapter Five: Psalms." In *Old Testament Form Criticism*. Trinity University Monograph Series in Religion. Edited by J. H. Hayes. San Antonio: Trinity, 1974.

Goldingay, John. *Psalms 42–89.* Vol. 2. Grand Rapids: Baker Academic, 2007.
Goulder, Michael D. "Asaph's History of Israel: (Elohist Press, Bethel, 725 BCE)." *Journal for the Study of the Old Testament* 65 (1995) 71–81.
———. *The Psalms of the Sons of Korah.* JSOTSup 20. Edited by David J. A. Clines, et al. Sheffield: JSOT, 1982.
Hadley, Judith M. "Some Drawings and Inscriptions on Two Pithoi from Kuntillet 'Ajrud." *Vetus Testamentum* 37.2 (1987) 180–213. Online: http://web.ebscohost.com.naomi.fuller.edu.
Hallo, William W. *Context of Scripture.* 3 vols. Leiden: Brill, 2003.
———. "Sumerian Literature: Background to the Bible." *Bible Review* 4.3 (1988) 28–38.
Halpern, Baruch. *David's Secret Demons: Messiah, Murderer, Traitor, King.* Grand Rapids: Eerdmans, 2001.
Hestrin, Ruth. "The Lachish Ewer and the '[set ayin in front of the A]Asherah.'" *Israel Exploration Journal* 37 (1988) 212–23.
———. "Understanding Asherah—Exploring Semitic Iconography." *Biblical Archaeology Review* 17.5 (1991) 50–59.
Hippolytus. *Refutation of All Heresies*, 10.5. In *Ante-Nicene Fathers.* Vol. 5. Peabody, MA: Hendrickson, 1994.
Hooke, Samuel H. "Life after Death–V: Israel and the Afterlife." *Expository Times* 76 (1965) 236–39.
———. "Life after Death–VI: The Extra-Canonical Literature." *Expository Times* 76 (1965) 273–76.
Howard, David M. Jr. "Editorial Activity in the Psalter: A State-of-the-Field Survey." *Word & World* 9.3 (1989) 274–85. Online: http://search.atlaonline.com.
Hurvitz, Avi. "Linguistic Criteria for Dating Problematical Biblical Texts." *Hebrew Abstracts* 14 (1973) 74–79.
Irsigler, Hubert. "Quest for Justice as Reconciliation of the Poor and the Righteous in Psalms 37, 49, and 73." *Zeitschrift für Altorientalische und Biblische Rechtsgeschichte* 5 (1999) 258–76.
Joffe, Laura. "The Answer to the Meaning of Life: The Universe and the Elohistic Psalter." *Journal for the Study of the Old Testament* 27 (2002) 223–35. Online: http://web.ebscohost.com.naomi.fuller.edu.
———. "The Elohistic Psalter: What, How, and Why?" *Scandinavian Journal of the Old Testament* 15 (2001) 142–66. Online: http://content.ebscohost.com.library.capella.edu.
Johnston, Philip. *Shades of Sheol: Death and Afterlife in the Old Testament.* Leicester: Apollos, 2002.
Josephus, Flavius. *The Complete Works of Josephus.* Translated by William Whiston. Grand Rapids: Regel, 1981.
Jouon, P. "Glanes Palmyreniennes." *Syria* 19 (1938) 99–103.
Keel, Othmar. *The Symbolism of the Biblical World: Ancient Near Eastern Iconography and the Book of Psalms.* Winona Lake, IN: Eisenbrauns, 1997. Originally published in 1972. Translated from German by the author in 1978.
Keller, Edmund B. "Hebrew Thoughts on Immortality and Resurrection." *International Journal for Philosophy of Religion* 5.1 (1974) 16–44.
Keller, Werner. *The Bible as History.* 2nd rev. ed. New York: William Morrow, 1981.
Kelley, Curtis "Earthquake," with Diana Stone. *Bound to Lose, Destined to Win.* Cleveland, TN: CopperScroll, 2007.

Kikawada, Isaac M. "Two Notes on Eve." *Journal of Biblical Literature* 91 (1972) 33–37.
King, Philip J., and Lawrence E. Stager. *Life in Biblical Israel*. In *Library of Ancient Israel*. Edited by Douglas A. Knight. Louisville, KY: Westminster John Knox, 2001.
Kitchen, Kenneth A. "The Desert Tabernacle." *Bible Review* 16.6 (2000) 20–21.
Köhler, Ludwig. "Alttestamentliche Wortforschung: Sch^{e}ōl." *Theologische Zeitschrift* 2.1 (1946) 71–74.
Kramer, Samuel N. "Death and Nether World According to the Sumerian Literary Texts." *Iraq* 22 (1960).
———. *The Sumerians: Their History, Culture, and Character*. Chicago: University of Chicago Press, 1963.
Lattey, Cuthbert. "A Note on Psalm 49:15–16." *Expository Times* 63 (1952) 288.
Leick, Gwendolyn. *Mesopotamia: The Invention of the City*. London: Penguin, 2002.
Lemaire, André. "Who or What Was Yahweh's Asherah?" *Biblical Archaeology Review* 10.6 (1984) 42–51.
Levenson, Jon D., and Baruch Halpern. "The Political Import of David's Marriages." *Journal of Biblical Literature* 99.4 (1980) 507–18.
Levenson, Jon D. *Resurrection and the Restoration of Israel*. New Haven: Yale University Press, 2006.
———. "Resurrection in the Torah? A Reconsideration." CTI (Center of Theological Inquiry) *Reflections* 6 (2002) 2–29.
Levine, Baruch A., and Jean-Michel de Tarragon. "Dead Kings and Rephaim: The Patrons of the Ugaritic Dynasty." *Journal of the American Oriental Society* 104.4 (1984) 649–59.
Lichtheim, Miriam. *Ancient Egyptian Literature*. 3 vols. Berkeley: University of California Press, 1975, 1976, 1980.
Long, Perry, with Paul Perry. *Evidence of the Afterlife: The Science of Near-Death Experiences*. New York: HarperOne, 2010.
Maire, Thierry. "Dieu N'échappe Pas à La Réalité: La Réussite Des Impies: Un Défi Pour La Foi Du Psalmiste." *Études Théologiques et Religieuses* 69.2 (1994) 173–83.
Malz, Betty. *My Glimpse of Eternity*. Grand Rapids: Spire, 1977.
Marsden, George M. *The Outrageous Idea of Christian Scholarhip*. Oxford: Oxford University Press, 1998.
Metzger, Bruce M. "Important Early Translations of the Bible: Part 1 of 4 Parts." *Bibliotheca Sacra* 150.1 (1993) 35–49.
Meyers, Carol L. "Of Drums and Damsels: Women's Performance in Ancient Israel." *Biblical Archaeologist* 54 (1991) 16–27. Online: http://search.atlaonline.com.
Miller, J. Maxwell. "The Korahites of Southern Judah." *Catholic Biblical Quarterly* 32.1 (1970) 58–68. Online: http://search.atlaonline.com.
Mitchell, David C. "'God Will Redeem My Soul from Sheol': The Psalms of the Sons of Korah." *Journal for the Study of the Old Testament* 30.3 (2006) 365–84. Online: http://search.atlaonline.com.
———. *The Message of the Psalter: An Eschatological Programme in the Book of Psalms*. JSOTSup 252. Edited by David J. A. Clines and Philip R. Davies. Sheffield: Sheffield Academic, 1997.
Mitchell, T. C. *The Bible in the British Museum: Interpreting the Evidence*. Mahwah, NJ: Paulist, 2004.
Moody, Raymond A. Jr., with Paul Perry. *Glimpses of Eternity: Sharing a Loved One's Passage from this Life to the Next*. New York: Guideposts, 2010.

———. *Life after Life*. Harrisburg, PA: Stackpole, 1976.
———. *Reflections on Life after Life*. New York: Bantam, 1988.
Moran, William L. *The Amarna Letters*. Baltimore: Johns Hopkins University Press, 1992.
Mowinckel, Sigmund. *The Psalms in Israel's Worship*. Two volumes in one. Translated by D. R. Ap-Thomas. Grand Rapids: Eerdmans/Dove Booksellers, 2004. First published 1962 by Basil Blackwell.
———. "Psalm Criticism from 1900–1935." *Vetus Testamentum* 5.1 (1955) 13–33.
Na'aman, Nadav. "The Trowel vs. the Text: How the Amarna Letters Challenge Archaeology." *Biblical Archaeology Review* 35.1 (2009) 52–56, 70–71.
Oates, Joan. *Babylon*. London: Thames and Hudson, 1991. Originally published, 1979.
Olyan, Saul. "Zadok's Origins and the Tribal Politics of David." *Journal of Biblical Literature* 101.2 (1982) 177–93.
Ornan, Tallay. "Twins: A Dangerous Pregnancy." *Biblical Archaeology Review* 35.1 (2009) 57–60.
Osis, Karlis, and Erlendur Haraldsson. *At the Hour of Death*. New York: Avon, 1977.
Owens, John J. *Analytical Key to the Old Testament*. 4 vols. Grand Rapids: Baker Book House, 1995.
Pietersma, Albert, and Benjamin G. Wright, eds. *A New English Translation of the Septuagint*. New York: Oxford University Press, 2007.
Pitard, Wayne T. "The Ugaritic Funerary Text RS 34.126." *Bulletin of the American Oriental Society* 232 (1978) 65–75. Online: http://links.jstor.org.
Pleins, J. David. "Death and Endurance: Reassessing the Literary Structure and Theology of Psalm 49." *Journal for the Study of the Old Testament* 69.1 (1996) 19–27.
Pritchard, James B. *Ancient Near Eastern Texts Relating to the Old Testament*. Princeton: Princeton University Press, 1969.
Quintens, Werner. "La vie du roi dans le Psaume 21." *Biblica* 59 (1978) 516–41.
———. "Le chemin de la vie dans le Psaume XVI." *Ephemerides Theologicae Lovanienses* 55.4 (1979) 233–42.
Ramaroson, Léonard. "Immortalité et résurrection dans les Psaumes." *Science et Esprit* 36.3 (1984) 287–95.
Rawlings, Maurice S. *Beyond Death's Door*. Nashville, TN: Thomas Nelson, 1978.
———. *To Hell and Back: Life after Death—Startling New Evidence*. Nashville, TN: Thomas Nelson, 1993.
Redford, Donald B. *Egypt, Canaan, and Israel in Ancient Times*. Princeton, NJ: Princeton University Press, 1992.
Rendsburg, Gary A. *Linguistic Evidence for the Northern Origin of Selected Psalms*. The Society of Biblical Literature Monograph Series 43. Edited by Adela Yarbro Collins. Atlanta: Scholars Press, 1990.
Ritchie, George G. Jr. *My Life after Dying: How 9 Minutes in Heaven Taught Me How to Live on Earth*. Charlottesville, VA: Hampton Roads, 1998.
Ritchie, George G., with Elizabeth Sherrill. *Return from Tomorrow*. Grand Rapids: Fleming H. Revell, 1978.
Roberts, J. J. M. "The Davidic Origin of the Zion Tradition." *Journal of Biblical Literature* 92.3 (1973) 329–44. Retrieved on January 25, 2008 from the Academic Search Premiere Database.
Rosenberg, Roy A. "The God Sedeq." *Hebrew Union College Annual* 36.1 (1965) 161–77. Online: http://search.atlaonline.com.

Rothenburg, Beno. *Timna: Valley of the Copper Mines*. London: Thames & Hudson, 1973.
Rowley, H. H. "Zadok and Nehushtan." *Journal of Biblical Literature* 58.2 (1939) 113–41. Online: JSTOR II, http://links.jstor.org.
Rust, Eric C. "Destiny of the Individual in the Thought of the Old Testament." *Review & Expositor* 58.3 (1961) 296–311. Online: http://search.atlaonline.com.
Sandars, N. K. *The Epic of Gilgamesh*. Rev. ed. New York: Penguin, 1983.
Sarna, Nahum M. "Mythological Background of Job 18." *Journal of Biblical Literature* 82.3 (1963) 315–18. Online: http://search.atlaonline.com.
Sawyer, John F. "Hebrew Words for the Resurrection of the Dead." *Vetus Testamentum* 23.2 (1973) 218–34. Online: http://search.atlaonline.com.
Schmidt, Brian. "Afterlife Beliefs: Memory as Immortality." *Near Eastern Archaeology* 63 (2000) 236–39.
Shanks, Hershel. "A Fortified City from King David's Time: Answers and Questions at Khirbet Qeiyafa." *Biblical Archaeology Review* 35.1 (2009) 38–43.
Shedd, Charlie W. *What Children Tell Me about Angels*. Ann Arbor, MI: Servant, 1995.
Sherwin, Byron L. "Jews and the World to Come." *First Things* 164.1 (2006) 13–16. http://web.ebscohost.com.naomi.fuller.edu.
Smith, Mark S. "The Invocation of Deceased Ancestors in Psalm 49:12c." *Journal of Biblical Literature* 112.1 (1993) 105–07.
Smith, Mark S., and Elizabeth Bloch-Smith. "Death and Afterlife in Ugarit and Israel." *Journal of the American Oriental Society* 108 (1988) 277–84.
Sparks, Kenton L. *Ancient Texts for the Study of the Hebrew Bible*. Peabody, MS: Hendrickson, 2005.
Spangenberg, Izak J. J. "Constructing a Historical Context for Psalm 49." *Old Testament Essays* 20.1 (2007) 201–14.
Spawn, Kenneth L. "Sacred Song and God's Presence in 2 Chronicles 5: The Renewal Community of Judah and Beyond." *Journal of Pentecostal Theology* 16.2 (2008).
Spronk, Klaas. *Beatific Afterlife in Ancient Israel and the Ancient Near East*. In Alter Orient und Altes Testament 219. Kevelear: Butzon & Bercker; Neukirchen-Vluyn: Neukirchener-Verlag, 1986.
Stenzel, Meinrad. "Psalm 49:14–16a." *Theologische Zeitschrift* 10 (1954) 152–54.
Sumer: The Cities of Eden. Alexandria, VA: Time Life Books, 1993.
Tate, Marvin E. *Psalms 51–100*. In *Word Biblical Commentary*. Vol. 20. Edited by John D. W. Watts. Dallas: Word Books, 1990.
Trible, Phillis. "Bringing Miriam out of the Shadows." *Bible Review* 5.1 (1989) 14–25, 34.
Tromp, Nicholas J. *Primitive Conceptions of Death and the Netherworld in the Old Testament*. Rome: Pontifical Biblical Institute, 1969.
Trull, Gregory V. "An Exegesis of Psalm 16:10." *Bibliotheca Sacra* 161.3 (2004) 304–21. Online: http://search.atlaonline.com.
Van Buren, E. Douglas. "The God Ningizzida." *Iraq* 1.1 (1934) 60–89.
Watts, John D. W. *Isaiah 1–33*. In *Word Biblical Commentary*. Vol. 24. Edited by John D. W. Watts. Nashville: Thomas Nelson, 1985.
Wifall, Walter. "Son of Man—A Pre-Davidic Social Class." *Catholic Biblical Quarterly* 37.3 (1975) 331–40. Online: http://search.atlaonline.com.
Wilkinson, Richard H. *The Complete Gods and Goddesses of Egypt*. New York: Thames & Hudson, 2003.

Wilson, Gerald H. *The Editing of the Hebrew Psalter.* Society of Biblical Literature Dissertation Series 76. Edited by J. J. M. Roberts. Chico: Scholars Press, 1985.

———. "The Shape of the Book of Psalms." *Interpretation* 46.2 (1992) 129–42. Online: http://search.atlaonline.com.

Witte, Markus. "'Aber Gott Wird Meine Seele Erlösen'—Tod Und Leben Nach Psalm XLIX." *Vetus Testamentum* 50.4 (2000) 540–60. Online: http://search.atlaonline.com.

Wright, David P. "Music and Dance in 2 Samuel 6." *Journal of Biblical Literature* 121.2 (2002) 201–25.

Younger, K. Lawson Jr. "The Azatiwada Inscription." *Context of Scripture: Monumental Inscriptions from the Biblical World.* Vol. 2. Edited by William Hallo. Boston: Brill, 2003.

———. "The Bar-Rakib Inscription." *Context of Scripture: Monumental Inscriptions from the Biblical World.* Vol. 2. Edited by William Hallo. Boston: Brill, 2003.

———. "The Hadad Inscription." *Context of Scripture: Monumental Inscriptions from the Biblical World.* Vol. 2. Edited by William Hallo. Boston: Brill, 2003.

———. "The Kulamuwa Inscription." *Context of Scripture: Monumental Inscriptions from the Biblical World.* Vol. 2. Edited by William Hallo. Boston: Brill, 2003.

———. "The Panamuwa Inscription." *Context of Scripture: Monumental Inscriptions from the Biblical World.* Vol 2. Edited by William Hallo. Boston: Brill, 2003.

Zucker, David J. "The Riddle of Psalm 49." *Jewish Biblical Quarterly* 33.3 (2005) 143–52.

www.ingramcontent.com/pod-product-compliance
Lightning Source LLC
Chambersburg PA
CBHW071437150426
43191CB00008B/1162